Frederick Treves

Physical education

Being an article contributed to an encyclopedic work on hygiene

Frederick Treves

Physical education
Being an article contributed to an encyclopedic work on hygiene

ISBN/EAN: 9783337222604

Printed in Europe, USA, Canada, Australia, Japan

Cover: Foto ©Andreas Hilbeck / pixelio.de

More available books at **www.hansebooks.com**

PHYSICAL EDUCATION.

TREVES.

A Treatise on Hygiene.

In Two Volumes. 8vo.

EDITED BY

THOMAS STEVENSON, M.D., F.R.C.P.,

LECTURER ON CHEMISTRY AND ON MEDICAL JURISPRUDENCE AT GUY'S HOSPITAL;
OFFICIAL ANALYST TO THE HOME OFFICE;

AND

SHIRLEY F. MURPHY,

MEDICAL OFFICER OF HEALTH TO THE COUNTY OF LONDON.

Vol. I., about 1020pp., which will be published in May, contains:

Air. By J. LANE NOTTER, M.A., M.D., Professor of Military Hygiene at the Army Medical School, Netley.

Warming and Ventilation. By W. N. SHAW, F.R.S., Lecturer on Experimental Physics in the University of Cambridge. With 53 Illustrations.

Meteorology. By G. J. SYMONS, F.R.S., Secretary of the Royal Meteorological Society. With 27 Illustrations.

Influence of Climate on Health. By C. THEODORE WILLIAMS, M.A., M.D., F.R.C.P. With Two Illustrations.

Water. By THOMAS STEVENSON, M.D., F.R.C.P. With Three Illustrations.

The Influence of Soil on Health. By S. MONCKTON COPEMAN, M.A., M.D., D.P.H., Assistant Lecturer on Physiology at St. Thomas's Hospital. With Four Lithographic Plates.

Food. By SIDNEY MARTIN, M.D., F.R.C.P., Assistant Physician to University College Hospital. With 21 Illustrations.

The Inspection of Meat. By E. W. HOPE, M.D., D.Sc., Assistant Medical Officer of Health; Lecturer on Public Health, University College, Liverpool.

Clothing. By GEO. VIVIAN POORE, M.D., F.R.C.P., Physician to University College Hospital. With Lithographic Plate.

Physical Education By FREDERICK TREVES, F.R.C.S., Surgeon to the London Hospital.

Baths. By W. HALE WHITE, M.D., F.R.C.P., Physician to Guy's Hospital.

The Dwelling. By P. GORDON SMITH, F.R.I.B.A., and KEITH D. YOUNG, F.R.I.B.A. With 60 Illustrations.

Hospital Hygiene. By H. G. HOWSE, M.S., Surgeon to Guy's Hospital.

The Disposal of Refuse. By W. H. CORFIELD, M.A., M.D., and LOUIS C. PARKES, M.D., D.P.H. With 24 Illustrations.

Offensive Businesses. By T. W. HIME, M.D., Medical Officer of Health for Bradford.

Slaughterhouses. By E. W. HOPE, M.D., D.Sc., Assistant Medical Officer of Health, Liverpool.

The Writers in Vol. II., which will appear in the Summer, are:

DR. E. KLEIN, F.R.S.—THE PATHOLOGY AND ETIOLOGY OF INFECTIOUS DISEASES. With 42 Plates.

DR. T. W. THOMPSON.—THE NATURAL HISTORY AND PREVENTION OF INFECTIOUS DISEASES.

DR. McVAIL.—VACCINATION. Illustrated.

DR. H. E. ARMSTRONG.—SHIP HYGIENE. Illustrated.

DR. J. L. NOTTER.—MILITARY HYGIENE. Illustrated.

SIR T. SPENCER WELLS, BART.—DISPOSAL OF THE DEAD.

DR. ARTHUR RANSOME.—VITAL STATISTICS. Illustrated.

DR. ALFRED ASHBY.—DUTIES OF THE MEDICAL OFFICER OF HEALTH.

MR. C. N. DALTON.—SANITARY LAW.

Philadelphia: P. BLAKISTON, SON & CO., 1012 Walnut Street.

BEING

AN ARTICLE CONTRIBUTED

TO AN

ENCYCLOPEDIC WORK ON HYGIENE

BY

FREDERICK TREVES, F.R.C.S.,

SURGEON TO AND LECTURER ON ANATOMY AT THE LONDON HOSPITAL; MEMBER OF THE
BOARD OF EXAMINERS OF THE ROYAL COLLEGE OF SURGEONS.

---

*Printed from the advance sheets of "A Treatise on Hygiene," by various authors.
See opposite page.*

PHILADELPHIA:

P. BLAKISTON, SON & CO.,
1012 WALNUT STREET
1892.

PUBLISHER'S PREFACE.

THE subject of Physical Education as a Hygienic measure has recently attracted so much attention from School Boards, the Medical Profession, and Sanitarians generally, that it now ranks in importance with the various branches of study pursued in our public schools and colleges. To the average city man or woman of sedentary occupation, physical exercise is of quite as much consequence as it is to school children and college students. It is however often taken up unwisely and to the lasting harm of those who in ignorance attempt methods that are unsuited to their physical condition.

It has therefore been thought advisable to publish from the advance sheets of "A Treatise on Hygiene" this paper by one of the best known medical writers of the day, that it might be within the reach of those who would not perhaps care to purchase the larger work in which it will be included.

(v)

CONTENTS.

INTRODUCTORY.

WRITERS are not yet weary of enlarging upon the marvels of civilization, upon the intellectual development of the human race, upon the triumphs of human ingenuity, and the might and magnificence of human culture. He has, indeed, much to marvel at who measures the gulf which separates the polished citizen of the world from the half-naked and quite savage barbarian. The inventive genius of the modern, the high development of each craft and industry which he has cultivated, the skill of the nineteenth-century artisan, the general intellectual condition of the masses in the great centres of civilization, are all features of attraction for those who are unceasing in the glorification of the race. The great elements in human progress afford, indeed, proper material for admiration. There is no one but would admit that the advantages of the civilized man over the savage are such as to make reasonable comparisons scarcely possible; but there follows upon this the question as to whether the so-called blessings of civilization represent an unmixed good. The intellectual victory has been great, but it has not been effected without cost. We have in our midst the inventor, the man of genius, the handicraftsman, but we have also the weakling, the delicate, the misshapen, and that most modern product of all, the mannikin of the city. This pale, wizened, undersized creature represents no little sacrifice; he is a product of civilization, an unintentional manifestation, but a characteristic one.

If one watches the stream of men, boys and girls which pours out at the close of day from a great city factory, the question may well be asked: Are these superior to the savage in all things, and are there no points in which the barbarian could claim some advantage over his modern descendant?

The savage Norseman who first sailed the northern seas knew little of art and less of science, but he had great lungs and a stout heart and mighty muscles and exhaustless strength, and was a stranger—it might be assumed—to many of the aches and pains and petty illnesses which the modern town-dweller regards as a natural heritage.

In the face of a marvellous social, moral and intellectual development, we are apt to lose sight of the fact that man is an animal, that he cannot yet do

2

(2)

without a body, and that a strong receptacle for the mind is better than a frail one.

The higher type of savage was perfect in form, lithe in movement, keen of vision and strong of arm. He felt in his veins the glow of life, the joy of mere vigor thrilled his muscles, the instincts of mere health dignified his movements. If he pursued physical culture to an exclusive degree, it is possible that his civilized brother may carry intellectual finish to an equal extreme.

There is evidence to show that an exclusive development of what are quite properly termed the higher faculties of man is not of unmixed advantage. Progress is so rapid, and the movements of daily life are so exacting, that there is a tendency to overlook the fact that man cannot live by intellectual bread alone. The young lad is taught to read as soon as he can lisp, and to write as soon as he can grasp a pen. At school he is forced and fostered like a hot-house plant, and when he is old enough to take his place in the race in life he at once feels the fever of competition and the strain of incessant endeavor.

It is, however, becoming obvious that one great element of success in life is bodily strength ; and that he who has every mental requirement and the finest intellectual finish may find that he still lacks the one thing needed. Sound physical health enables a man to work with vigor and freshness, to pass unharmed through periods of unusual pressure, to withstand the evils of worry, to preserve a clearness and acuteness of mind when others are worn and fretful and uncertain, and to still press forward when others have fallen in the race.

He will do well who still retains in the midst of his city life some of the qualities of the men of the plain. He will find that muscular strength and good lungs are not without value, even though he be no longer dependent upon the hunter's skill for his daily meal. The attributes of the trapper and the seaman are attributes which cannot be without service, even in the murkiest life in the wilderness of a great city.

It is now more or less clearly recognized that no skill, no learning, no intellectual greatness, can carry with it its fullest influence without a certain element of physical capacity in the individual.

The unduly diligent student who burns the midnight oil, who cannot tear himself away from his books, who moves in a world in which the only sunshine is that of learning, and the only breeze is that which blows from the erudition of the past, is often a miserable object enough as a human being. His face is wan, his arms are feeble, his eyes are dim, he lives in an atmosphere of little ailments, and he has few pleasures other than the joys of the bookworm. Such a man would make no less progress in the present, and would effect no less influence in the future, if he would devote some leisure to the cultivation of his body. A clear eye, a wiry limb, and a ruddy cheek, are not inconsistent with the greatest intellectual development; while on the other hand there are many poor lads who have been crammed and cultivated until they are mere learned invalids. It may well be asked of their learning, ' What will they do with it?" Many a "city man" can have but little knowledge of living, however much he may know of "life." His hurried hours of work are followed by a period of dulled rest. He lives in the maze caused by the rush of passing events, he knows little of the joys of the world as the barbarian knows them, and his journey through life is but at a halting and creaking pace. He remains a partly developed creature who has never attained to the full stature of a man.

Montaigne well says, in speaking of a man as he should be, " I would have the disposition of his limbs formed at the same time with his mind. 'Tis not a soul, 'tis not a body we are training, but a man, and we must not divide him."

In certain directions the importance of simple physical health and strength cannot well be exaggerated. The part they have played in the history of the British race has been magnificent enough. The glories of English enterprise, the daring and hardihood of the British seaman, the unconquerable pluck of the English soldier, have taken no little share in forming the greatness of the British nation. The love of sport among the English, the delight in manly games and outdoor exercises, the contempt for what is effeminate and feeble, are outcomes of a vigorous health and a sturdy growth.

There is no need to modify the fact that the position of Great Britain among European nations is due in no small extent to qualifications which have been the glory of savage peoples. The explorer may have profound knowledge and a preternatural judgment, but they avail but little if he be not possessed of mere rude health and strength. The main pride of the early navigator was his reckless courage and his sturdy endurance. The greatest commander would have proved a man of straw had he not at his call men who shirked no hardship and who felt no fear.

It may not be a graceful acknowledgment, but it is none the less true that the power of the English people has depended in no little degree upon those very humble qualities which make "a good animal."

There is an instinct which impels the human being to seek health in muscular exercise and pleasure in physical exertion. The very restlessness of the child is an expression of this. It is often said of a child that he or she is never still. It is an excellent feature. It is as unreasonable to expect a young lad to keep quiet as to expect him not to cough when he has a cold. The infant jumps and kicks and crows; the child shows its natural promptings by incessant restlessness. The schoolboy, if he be vigorous and healthy, appears to have acquired the art of perpetual movement. The mad rush of a crowd of schoolboys from the schoolroom the moment they are free is characteristic enough and pleasant to witness. The limbs and muscles which have been so long still feel the need of movement as a half-suffocated man feels the need of air. The boy who is the first to reach the open air beyond the school-house door has probably not an evil future before him; he has at least made a good beginning. He, on the other hand, who crawls out last, who feels no irresistible impulse to jump and shout, is in some way abnormal; he is ill in health or imperfect in construction. He may prove an excellent scholar, but the terrible earnestness of the race of life is not best met by mere scholarship.

Throughout life there exists in all healthly bodies this natural craving for exercise, and a man may consider that he has reached an unfortunate period in his career when he has ceased to feel that impulse.

Muscles can grow only by exercise and by the simple expedient of using them. The disused muscle wastes, and becomes fatty and anæmic. Muscular tissue occupies nearly every part of the body, from so delicate a piece of mechanism as the eye to so simple a structure as the biceps humeri. Exercise implies not merely the development of the muscles of the limbs, it implies also the healthy use of the muscle of the heart, of the muscles of respiration, of the muscular tissue of the arteries, and of the muscular elements of all parts capable of movement. Such movement carries with it of necessity an activity in the nervous system, an activity in the secreting organs and in the organs of excretion.

Movement, indeed, within proper bounds, is essential to the full development and perfect maintenance of the health of the body. The body is a machine with the peculiar attribute that the more it is used, within reasonable limits, the stronger and more capable it becomes. It gathers strength by movement, and that strength is to be gauged, not by mere muscular force, but by the perfect functional condition of every part and of every organ.

Physical Education involves exercise and movement. We know of no other means of developing any portion of the organism, provided that the supply of food and of air be sufficient. Exercise means growth, functional vigor, and the maintenance of a high standard of organic life. Undue rest implies decay, feebleness, and a debased standard of functional value. Absolute rest is found only in death.

Of artificial means of attaining physical perfection there are none. Every structure and tissue must be duly and accurately exercised and kept in proper movement ; and this applies as well to the ciliary muscle of the eye as it does to the great flexors of the leg, as well to the peptic glands of the stomach as to the cells of the cortex of the brain. The body is like a busy town ; so long as there is activity within its walls, and so long as every nook and corner is alive with the best energies of those who dwell therein, things fare well ; but when one section flags, when inactivity falls upon this quarter or upon that, there comes some retrogression, some halting in a progress which had hitherto been even and energetic. If the intellect is to be cultivated, the brain must be exercised. He who wishes to acquire the far vision of the seaman must use his eyes like a seaman, and he who would develop the hunter's keenness of hearing and powers of endurance must lead the hunter's life.

To learn how to rightly exercise every part and organ of the body, and how to effect this without undue effort or injurious strain, is to discover the elixir of life and such a philosopher's stone as will render the short tenure of human life as free from bodily troubles as the art of man can make it.

It is no longer possible to say, as Herbert Spencer did some twenty years ago, that the inhabitants of this country take an interest in the rearing of the offspring of all creatures except themselves. Civilization has not yet greatly impaired the unconquerable love of sport and the passion for movement and violent exercise which appear to be the heritage of the British race. There is some evidence to show that, taking averages, we have not diminished either in height or in girth. There is evidence of deterioration among the poorer inhabitants of great cities, but among the more favored classes it would appear that no change has taken place which indicates a distinct downward tendency. Within recent years there has been a remarkable revival of interest in sports, games and athletic exercises of all kinds. It was not until 1875 that the English Channel was crossed by a swimmer. So far as it is known, it was not until the year 1877 that a human being had ever leapt from the ground, without artificial aid, to the height of 6 feet 2 inches. A man can now jump across a gap 23 feet in width, a mile has been run in less than 4½ minutes, and 600 miles have been walked in one week.

It is quite obvious that the term Physical Education must include the regulation of the functions and movements of the entire body. With such as concern the supply of suitable food and wholesome air, and the observation of what are known as simple hygienic conditions, the present paper has no concern.

It is necessary here to deal only with that most conspicuous factor in physical culture which concerns the due and proportionate exercise of the muscles of the body.

In the following article we shall first consider the general effects of exercise, including the subjects of fatigue, overwork, and want of exercise, and secondly the effects of specific exercises.

THE GENERAL EFFECTS OF EXERCISE.

1. THE EFFECT OF EXERCISE UPON THE DEVELOPMENT AND PROPORTIONS OF THE BODY.

Exercise, as here understood, may be represented by such natural, systematic, and well-regulated exercises as enter into the life of every healthy public schoolboy, together with such special gymnastics which may be considered to be necessary in particular cases. It must be understood that the object of exercise—as here intended—is not to develop athletes, acrobats, and phenomenally strong men, but to encourage and maintain the highest and most equable development of the body.

The secret of the size and proportions of the future man lies buried in the ovum from which the individual is developed. It may be said, indeed, that there are two proportions possible in every human body—first, that which is congenital, inherited, and predetermined ; and, secondly, such an increase or modification of these proportions as may be effected by proper exercise.

The child of short and stunted parents will probably also be short and stunted, and may remain so in spite of an elaborate physical training. An infant Bushman, transported suddenly to a cotter's home in Scotland, could never be expected to attain the proportions of the young Highlanders with whom his lot had been cast. In estimating the effect of exercise and in speculating upon its possible powers in this direction, a constant reference must be made to those inherited factors which are quite beyond control. Exercise cannot make a man a giant, nor can it with any certainty develop a modern Hercules. It can, however, influence the growth and structural perfection of the body in a manner which is definite and to some extent remarkable.

Exercise increases the size of a muscle, the proportions of its tendon, and the power it can command. After undue rest, a muscle becomes thin, soft, wasted, and feeble. The stronger the muscles, the finer and denser are the aponeuroses with which they are connected, and the stouter are the fasciæ which hold them in position. Muscles act upon articulations. The duly exercised joint has a good covering of cartilage, powerful ligaments, and well-developed bony parts. The joint which has long been kept at rest has wasted ligaments, a thinned cartilage, and bones of smaller proportions. It becomes, moreover, hyperæsthetic from disuse, and the tissues around are found to be flabby and anæmic. Within certain somewhat narrow limits, the mechanical possibilities of a joint can be much extended by exercise.

Muscular strength, moreover, influences the size of the bones upon which the muscles act. The skeleton of a feeble individual compares in a very marked manner with the skeleton of a muscular person of the same height and the same age. The bone of the muscular individual is stronger, firmer, and denser; it is actually larger, and the so-called muscular surfaces and ridges are more conspicuously marked.

Exercise induces a more vigorous respiration, and under increased breathing efforts the lung capacity is increased and the size of the thorax is augmented. Exercise, moreover, accelerates the blood circulation, and it is needless to point out the effect an increased blood supply has upon the size and development of the tissues concerned.

1. *The Development of the Body.*—Before considering the special effects of exercise upon the growth of the body, it is necessary to take note of what may be termed the average measurements of the human organism.

The principal facts with regard to the growth of the body, its weight and height at various periods of life, its comparative proportions in males and females, and other features concerned in anthropometry, are briefly set forth in the following tables.

The principal tables are derived from Mr. Charles Roberts' "Manual of Anthropometry," and to this admirable and classical work the reader is referred for more extensive details. Much use has been made also of the report of the Anthropometric Committee of the British Association, 1882-3. This report was drawn up by Mr. Roberts and Sir R. W. Rawson, and has been published as an appendix to Mr. Roberts' "Manual." These two works provide the most precise data upon anthropometry, so far as the English race is concerned, which we possess.

It may in the first place be well to tabulate the periods at which the various parts of the skeleton are completed, so far as the facts of osteology guide us.

The Spine . . . .⎫
The Pelvis . . . . ⎬ The 25th year.
The Shoulder Girdle . . . . ⎭
The Upper Limb . . . . The 20th year.
⎧ The Femur the 20th year.
The Lower Limb . . . . ⎨ The Tibia the 22d year.
⎩ The Fibula the 24th year.

TABLE I.—*Showing the average* stature (*without shoes*) *and the average* weight (*including clothes*) *at all ages of the general population of Great Britain.* (*All classes. Town and country.*) Number of observations on which the averages are founded. *Stature:* Males, 37,574. Females, 4,616. *Weight:* Males, 33,043. Females, 4,685. (From the Report of the Anthropometric Committee, 1883.)

	MALES.					FEMALES.			
Age last birthday.	Average height, inches.	Increase in inches.	Average weight, pounds.	Increase in pounds.	Age last birthday.	Average height, inches.	Increase in inches.	Average weight, pounds.	Increase in pounds.
Birth	19.52	—	7.1	—	Birth	19.31	—	6.9	—
0-1	27.00	—	—	—	0-1	24.83	5.52	—	—
1	33.50	—	—	—	1	27.50	2.67	20.1	—
2	33.70	—	32.5	—	2	32.33	4.83	25.3	5.2
3	36.82	—	34.0	1.5	3	36.23	3.90	31.6	6.3
4	38.46	1.64	37.3	3.3	4	38.26	2.03	36.1	4.5
5	41.03	2.57	39.9	2.6	5	40.55	2.29	39.2	3.1
6	44.00	2.97	44.4	4.5	6	42.88	2.33	41.7	2.5
7	45.97	1.97	49.7	5.3	7	44.45	1.57	47.5	5.8
8	47.05	1.08	54.9	5.2	8	46.60	2.15	52.1	4.6
9	49.70	2.65	60.4	5.5	9	48.73	2.13	55.5	3.4
10	51.84	2.14	67.5	7.1	10	51.05	2.32	62.0	6.5
11	53.50	1.66	72.0	4.5	11	53.10	2.05	68.1	6.1
12	54.99	1.49	76.7	4.7	12	55.66	2.56	76.4	8.3
13	56.91	1.92	82.6	5.9	13	57.77	2.11	87.2	10.8
14	59.33	2.42	92.0	9.4	14	59.80	2.03	96.7	9.5
15	62.24	2.91	102.7	10.7	15	60.93	1.13	106.3	9.6
16	64.31	2.07	119.0	16.3	16	61.75	.82	113.1	6.8
17	66.24	1.93	130.9	11.9	17	62.52	.77	115.5	2.4
18	66.96	.72	137.4	6.5	18	62.44	—	121.1	5.6
19	67.29	.33	139.6	2.2	19	62.75	.23	123.8	2.7
20	67.52	.23	143.3	3.7	20	62.98	.23	123.4	.6
21	67.63	.11	145.2	1.9	21	63.03	.05	121.8	—
22	67.68	.05	146.9	1.7	22	62.87	—	123.4	—
23	67.48	—	147.8	.9	23	63.01	—	124.1	.7
24	67.73	.05	148.0	.2	24	62.70	—	120.8	—
25-30	67.80	.07	152.3	4.3	25-30	62.02	—	120.0	—
30-35	68.00	.20	159.8	7.5	30-35	⎫	—	120.8	—
35-40	68.00	—	164.3	4.5	35-40	⎬ 61.15	—	120.8	—
40-50	67.96	—	163.3	—	40-50	⎬	—	118.0	—
50-60	67.92	—	166.1	1.8	50-60	⎬	—	104.0	—
60-70	67.41	—	158.1	2.0	60-70	⎭	—	—	—
70	69.22	1.22	182.1	—	70		—	106.0	—

The following comments upon the series of tables of which the above is an abstract are furnished by the Anthropometric Committee :—

1. Growth is most rapid during the first five years of life.

2. From birth to the age of five years the rate of growth is the same in both sexes, girls being a little shorter in stature and lighter in weight than boys.

3. From five to ten years boys grow a little more rapidly than girls, the difference being apparently due to a check in the growth of girls at these ages.

4. From ten to fifteen years girls grow more rapidly than boys, and at the ages of eleven and a half to fourteen and a half are actually taller, and from twelve and a half to fifteen and a half years actually heavier than boys. This difference appears to be due to a check in the growth of boys as well as an acceleration in the growth of girls incident on the accession of puberty.

5. From fifteen to twenty years boys again take the lead, and grow at first rapidly, then gradually slower, and complete their growth at about twenty-three years. After fifteen, girls grow very slowly, and attain their full stature about the twentieth year.

6. The tables show a slow but steady increase in stature up to the fiftieth year, and a more rapid increase in weight up to the sixtieth year in males, but the statistics of females are too few after the age of twenty-three to determine the stature and weight of that sex at the more advanced periods of life.

"It is probably due to the greater or less development of the body at the time of the accession of puberty," writes Mr. Roberts, "that the final difference in the height of individuals is chiefly to be attributed ; hence the influences which promote or retard growth at this period are most deserving of study. In boys puberty occurs later, and is less regular and decided, than in girls. The transition from boyhood to manhood extends over a period of three to four years, and is accompanied by increased physical development of the body ; but girls develop into women in a few months, and with the complete establishment of puberty, growth in height is much diminished, and often ceases altogether."

As a further contribution to the subject of the growth of boys, the following tables, compiled by MacLaren, may be added :—

TABLE II.—*Showing the State of Growth and Development between the ages of 10 and 18 years, being the* averages *of the actual measurements of 100 boys* at each age. *(Maclaren.)*

Age.	Height.	Weight.	Girth of Chest.	Forearm.	Upper Arm.
Years.	Ft. in.	St. lb.	Inches.	Inches.	Inches.
10	4 5½	4 9	25¼	7½	7¾
11	4 7	5 0	26¼	7¾	8
12	4 8¾	5 8¼	27½	8	8¼
13	4 10¼	6 0¼	28½	8¼	8½
14	5 0¾	6 9	29½	8½	9
15	5 3	7 5¼	30¾	9	9¼
16	5 5	8 4½	32½	9½	10¼
17	5 7	9 2½	34¼	10	11
18	5 8	9 11	35¼	10¼	11¼

TABLE III.—*Abstract of preceding Table showing average Annual Rate of Growth and Development from year to year. (Maclaren.)*

	Height.	Weight.	Girth of Chest.	Forearm.	Upper Arm.
	Inches.	Pounds.	Inches.	Inches.	Inches.
From 10 years to 11 years	1½	5	1	¼	¼
" 11 " 12 "	2	8¼	1¼	¼	¼
" 12 " 13 "	1¾	6	1	¼	¼
" 13 " 14 "	2¼	8¾	1	¼	½
" 14 " 15 "	2¼	10½	1¼	½	½
" 15 " 16 "	2	13	1¾	½	¾
" 16 " 17 "	2	12	1¾	½	¾
" 17 " 18 "	1	8½	1	¼	¼

Some children appear to grow by fits and starts. Children who have remained for many successive years under the average height may suddenly shoot up and attain more than the normal stature when they reach adult age. (See in connection with this matter Case 4, Table VII.)

The extremes in development are well illustrated by the following observations made by Maclaren. They give the result of the examination of 100 University men (freshmen) who were not especially selected.

	The greatest developments.	The smallest developments.
Height	6 ft. 6 in.	5 ft. 2 in.
Weight	12 st. 2 lb.	7 st.
Chest girth	39 in.	27¼ in.
Forearm	11¼ in.	8¼ in.
Upper arm	12¼ in.	8¾ in.

The effect of occupation and social and physical condition upon development is well demonstrated by the statistics prepared by Mr. Roberts and the Anthropometric Committee.

The following tables are derived (in abstract) from the report of the committee :—

TABLE IV.—*Relative Height of Boys at the age of 11 to 12 years under different social and physical conditions of life.*

	Average height.
Public schools (country)	54.98 inches.
Middle-class schools:	
Upper (towns)	53.85 "
Lower (towns)	53.70 "
Elementary schools:	
Agricultural laborers	53.01 "
Artisans (town)	52.60 "
Factory hands (country)	52.17 "
Factory hands (towns)	51.56 "
Military asylums	51.20 "
Industrial schools	50.02 "

TABLE V.—*Relative Height of Adults of the ages from 25 to 30 years under different social and physical conditions of life.*

	Average height.
Upper classes, professional classes	60.13 inches.
Commercial classes, clerks, shopkeepers, &c.	67.95 "
Agricultural laborers, miners, sailors, &c.	67.51 "
Artisan classes (towns)	66.64 "
Factory hands, workers at sedentary trades—e. g. tailors.	65.92 "

The question of the relation of weight to height will be found considered in Table I.

Table VI. gives the average chest-girth in males at different periods of life (see also Tables II. and III.) The chest-girth in males shows an increase at a rate similar to that of the weight up to the age of fifty years, but it appears to have no definite relation to stature.

TABLE VI.—*Average Chest-girth (empty) in inches in Males of all classes at different ages (Report of Anthropometric Committee).*

Age next birthday.	Chest-girth in inches.	Age next birthday.	Chest-girth in inches.	Age next birthday.	Chest-girth in inches.
10	26.10	16	31.53	22	35.33
11	26.53	17	33.64	23	35.62
12	27.36	18	34.15	24	35.82
13	28.03	19	34.49	25-29	36.18
14	28.46	20	34.98	30-35	37.08
15	29.74	21	35.25	30-36	37.58

The effect of systematized exercise upon the growth and development of boys and men may now be considered. In the Report of the Anthropometric Committee the measurements of eighty-nine professional and amateur athletes are given with the following result. " Their average stature exceeds that of the general population from which they are drawn by 0.68 inch, while their average weight falls short of that standard by 14.5 lb. The ratio of weight to stature is in the athletes 2.160 lb., and in the general population 2.323 lb. for each inch of stature. Thus a trained athlete whose stature is 5 feet 7 inches should weigh 10 stone, while an untrained man of the same height should weigh 11 stone."

TABLE VII.—*To show the Effects of Systematized Exercise upon growth and development.* (*Maclaren.*)

—			Measurements, etc.					Increase.					Remarks.
Case.	Date.	Years.	Height.	Weight.	Chest.	Fore-arm.	Upper-arm.	Height.	Weight.	Chest.	Fore-arm.	Upper-arm.	
			Ft. in.	St. lb.	In.	In.	In.	In.	Lb.	In.	In.	In.	
1	1861, June.	10	4 6¾	4 10	26	7¼	7½						Height *above* average. Other measurements average. From commencement, growth rapid and sustained, with regular and uniform development.
	1862, Sept.	11	4 9½	5 5	28½	8½	8½	2¾	9	2½	1¼	1	
	1863, Sept.	12	4 10¾	6 0	30½	8½	8⅞	1¼	9	2		⅜	
	1864, June.	13	5 2¼	7 2	32½	9⅜	9⅞	3½	16	2	⅞	1	
	1865, May.	14	5 5⅝	8 3	35½	9¾	10¼	3⅜	15	3	⅜	⅜	
	1866, May.	15	5 9	10 2	37½	11	12	3⅜	27	2	1¼	1¾	
	1867, Sept.	16	5 9½	10 13	38½	11⅛	12⅝	½	11	1	⅛	⅝	
	1868, Sept.	17	5 10¾	11 2	39½	11¼	13⅜	1¼	3	1	⅛	1	
							Total increase . .	16	90	13½	4½	5⅞	
2	1860, Jan.	12	4 1⅝	3 13	23½	6½	6						Height and all other measurements greatly *below* average. Whole frame stunted and dwarfish. Advancement at first slight and very irregular, afterwards rapid and comparatively regular.
	1860, July.	12	4 3¾	4 0	24	7	6¾	1⅝	1	½	½	¾	
	1860, Dec.	13	4 4½	4 1	24½	7	7	¾	1	½	—	¼	
	1861, Dec.	14	4 4½	4 7	25	7¼	7¼	—	6	½	¼	¼	
	1862, July.	14	4 5⅜	4 8	26	7½	7½	⅞	1	1	¼	¼	
	1863, Mar.	15	4 7¼	4 12	26½	7⅝	7⅝	1⅞	4	½	⅛	⅛	
	1864, July.	16	4 11¼	6 6	29½	8⅝	8¾	4	22	3	1	1⅛	
							Total increase . .	9⅝	35	6	2⅛	2¾	
3	1859, Dec.	14	4 5	6 1	26½	8	7¾						Height greatly below average; other measurements also considerably below average. Instant and extreme acceleration of growth with moderate increase in development.
	1860, Sept.	14	5 2	6 4	29	9	9½	11	3	2½	1	1¾	
	1861, July.	15	5 4½	7 7	30	9	9½	2½	17	1	—	—	
	1862, Sept.	15	5 7¼	8 12	34½	10	11¼	2¾	19	4½	1	1¾	
							Total increase . .	16¼	39	8	2	3½	
4	1859, Oct.	19	5 2⅝	8 0	30½	9	9½						Well proportioned. A remarkable feature is the renewal and steady continuation of the upward growth which had been prematurely arrested.
	1859, Dec.	—	5 3¼	8 1	33	9½	10¼	⅝	1	2½	½	¾	
			5 3⅝	8 1	33	9½	10¼	⅜	—	—	—	—	
	1860, Jan.	20	4¼								lost		
	— —	—	5 4	8 1	33½	9¼	10¼	½	—	½	¼	—	
	— June.	—	5 4½	8 3	34	9¼	10¼	½	2	½	—	—	
	— —	—	5 4⅝	8 5	34¼	9½	10½	—	2	¼	¼	¼	
							Total increase . .	2	5	3¾	½	1	
5	1859, Oct.	17	6 0	9 4	30½	8¼	9¼						Of delicate frame: chest flat and narrow, with sternum much depressed.
	1860, Jan.	17	6 0	9 9	32½	9¼	10	—	5	2	½	¾	
	1860, June.	18	6 0½	9 11½	34	9¾	10¼	½	2½	1½	½	¼	
	1860, June.	18	6 0½	9 13	34½	9¾	10½	—	1½	½	—	¼	
							Total increase . .	½	9	4	1	1¼	

This question of the effect of systematic exercise upon development has been fully dealt with by Mr. Maclaren.

His tables dealing with the subject are of great value, and should be consulted by all those who are interested in the matter. In the appended tables a selection from these statistics is given. The normal increase in height and weight, as given in Table I., must be taken into consideration.

TABLE VIII.—*Measurements of twelve Non-commissioned Officers (selected to be qualified as Military Gymnastic Instructors after eight months' training.) (Maclaren.)*

		Increase noted at end of period.			
Age.	Height.	Weight.	Girth of Chest.	Forearm.	Upper Arm.
Years.	In.	Lb.	In.	In.	In.
19	3/8	13	4½	1	1¾
21	¼	10	3¼	1	1½
23	3/8	9	3½	1	1½
23	1/8	9	1½	1¼	1
23	¼	10	1	½	1
23	1/8	9	2	¾	1
23	3/8	5	2½	¼	1
24	1/8	12	5	1	1½
26	5/8	6½	3	¼	1¼
26¾	3/8	9	1	—	1
28	½	13	3	1¼	1¼
28	1/8	16	3	1¼	1

In an examination of Tables VII. and VIII. the increase in weight under systematized exercise, after allowing for normal increase, is noteworthy.

In the matter of increase in growth, Case 4, Table VII., is interesting as showing the renewal of growth after premature arrest, the young man growing 2 inches after nineteen. Mr. Maclaren gives several other instances of this sudden growth after premature arrest. In Table VII. the increase in height of the older men in the list is of interest. In the majority it may be due to a greater erectness of the figure, to the lessening, therefore, of some of the curvature of the spine, and perhaps to some increase in the intravertebral substances.

In the case of the soldiers in Table VIII. the question of the improvement of the carriage can scarcely come into consideration, and the increase in height from ⅛th to ⅝ths of an inch in the last four men must be ascribed to changes in the tissues. In case 3, Table VII., the immediate effect of systematized exercise is apparently shown by a remarkable increase in height of no less than 11 inches in a period of nine months.

A further point in these tables must be noticed, and that is the remarkable increase in the circumference of the chest, which, it would appear, may be obtained by systematic exercise.

An increase of 3 to 4 inches in the girth of the thorax may no doubt be in great part ascribed to muscular development in the pectoral and scapular regions. It involves, however, an increased respiratory power, and a greater breathing capacity.

In a country where lung diseases are so common as they are in England, it is difficult to speak too strongly of the importance of obtaining a full development of the chest.

Physicians recognize the part played by a narrow thorax and a feeble breathing power in aiding the evolution of chronic lung disease and in promoting the progress of such processes as are acute.

Considering the definite and apparently assured results of physical training in this direction, it appears culpable to allow a child to grow up surrounded by the undoubted dangers which attend the possession of a constricted chest.

It will be observed from the above tables that a great increase in the circumference of the chest can take place as an almost solitary feature of development. Mr. Maclaren gives the case of a lad of nineteen whose height was not increased by systematic exercise, but who increased the girth of his chest by $4\frac{1}{2}$ inches in nine months.

It is well also to note that an improvement in the measurements of the chest can be effected many years after the period of youth has passed. Thus Maclaren cites the case of a gentleman aged thirty-five who at the end of two months' exercise at the Oxford Gymnasium had increased the circumference of his thorax by no less than $4\frac{1}{2}$ inches. His height was diminished by an eighth of an inch, due probably to an increase in the curvature of the thoracic part of the spine.

In considering the general question of increase in chest girth care must be taken not to ascribe this increase—as some appear inclined to do—entirely to an increase in the capacity of the thoracic cavity. This is probably in all cases of much less effect than muscular development. Those who practice excessively with gymnastic apparatus acquire a peculiar conformation of the chest, the main factor in which is certainly not an increase in the capacity of the thorax.

2. *The Proportions of the Body.*—A proper physical training does something more than merely increase the size of the limbs and possibly the height

of the body. It tends to render all parts of the body symmetrical and more perfectly proportioned.

A well-proportioned body has a grace which is independent of mere size, height, and strength. It is in women especially that the great lack of a perfect proportion is so often conspicuous. In one the hips are out of proportion to the shoulders; in another the width of the chest is totally out of keeping with the height of the body; in a third the length of the upper limbs is not in proportion to the dimensions of the trunk.

Those who have taken properly arranged exercise from their earliest youth may still need many graces, but they will probably possess the peculiar grace which belongs to a symmetrical body.

Of all animals man is the most subject to variations in proportion and in symmetry. It is certain that in some children the body develops unevenly: one side appears to be larger than the other; one limb may be longer than its fellow; one side of the thorax may be of greater circumference than the other. Such deviations—which in no sense constitute deformity—a well-directed system of physical training may correct.

It is common to meet a long, lanky lad with spider-like arms and legs, a meagre neck, and a narrow chest. It is probably said that he has "outgrown his strength." In reality his growth in height has been out of proportion to his growth in muscular power. With proper training such a lad ceases to be lanky; he becomes merely tall, his chest fills out, his arms acquire a greater girth, his neck becomes sinewy, and the "scarecrow" of the schoolroom becomes possibly a lithe, well-proportioned youth.

Another lad may be squat and "stumpy" and heavy looking. He has a big head and a wide chest and limbs which appear to be ridiculously out of proportion to his burly trunk. He begins to pursue every available form of exercise and outdoor recreation, and in a few years he has sprung up. His wide chest has stood him in good stead, and his limbs are now no longer out of keeping with his body.

The following account of the normal proportions of the body is founded upon that given by Mr. Roberts in his "Manual of Anthropometry."

The Head.—Of all parts of the body, the head varies least in its proportions during growth. In the average adult it is considered to form the seventh part of the whole height. From birth to the period of full development the head only doubles its height, while the whole body elongates three or four times its original dimensions. The most active growth of the head is during the first two years of life. The lower parts of the face grow at a greater rate than the upper, and all the horizontal measurements of the head develop less than those of height.

The Trunk.—The height of the neck increases irregularly. The most rapid growth is at puberty. The neck ultimately attains to double its original dimensions. The other parts of the body increase with greater energy, and growth is greater the further the parts are situated from the summit of the head. Thus, while the measurements of the head and neck are only doubled, those of the trunk are tripled, and those of the lower extremities are more than quadrupled. The transverse diameters of the trunk increase nearly in the same ratio as the height. They triple from birth to the period of full development. At the age of six or seven, this diameter is already doubled. The antero-posterior diameter of the thorax increases less rapidly and is not doubled until about puberty.

At the time of birth, when the child is about the sixth of the height it will ultimately attain to, the point which divides the total height into two equal parts is a little above the navel; at two years of age it is at the navel; at three years, when the child has attained half its total height, the central point is on a line with the upper borders of the iliac bones; at ten years of age, when the child has attained three-fourths of its total height, the central point is on a line with the trochanters; at thirteen years it is at the pubes, and in the adult man it is nearly half an inch lower. In the adult woman the central point is a little above the pubes.

The Upper Limbs.—The space covered by the arms extended horizontally is equal to the total height of the body from birth to puberty.

In the adult man the ratio of the height to the measurement of the extended arms is as 1 to 1.045; and in the adult woman as 1 to 1.015. The length of the arm—excluding the hand—is doubled at the age between four and five years, tripled between thirteen and fourteen, and quadrupled at the period of full development. The hand develops less rapidly. After the age of seven or eight the length of the hand has the ratio to the total height of one to nine, This applies to adults both male and female.

The Lower Limb.—The lower extremities in adults are five times the length they were at birth. They double their length before the third year, and at twelve they are four times their original length. The length of the thigh varies considerably, and has much to do with the differences in the total height of individuals. The foot at all ages of life and in both sexes forms from the 0.15 to 0.16 of the total height of the individual. It is only about the age of ten that the length of the foot is equal to the height of the head. Before that period the head is the longer, and after it the shorter.

The perfect Female Form.—The relative proportions of a perfect female form as deduced by modern sculptors from Greek statues have been given as follows. Her height will be five feet five inches. With the arms extended the measurement from finger-tip to finger-tip should be equal to her own height. The hand should be $\frac{1}{10}$th of this, the foot $\frac{1}{7}$th, and the chest diameter $\frac{1}{5}$th. From her perineum to the ground she should measure just what she measures from the perineum to the top of the head. The knee should be midway between the perineum and the heel.

The distance from the elbow to the middle finger should be the same as from the elbow to the middle of the chest. The head should be about the length of the foot. A woman of this height should measure 24 inches about the waist, 34 inches around the chest if measured under the arms, and 43 if measured over them. The upper arm should measure 13 inches and the wrist 6. The circumference of the thigh should be 25 inches, of the calf of the leg $14\frac{1}{2}$ inches, and of the ankle 8 inches.

In determining the rate of growth and development of the body the following system of measurements, advised by Mr. Maclaren and given in his well known work, may be followed out :

System of Measurements.

Height (without boots).—The position of attention, the heels together, the knees braced back, the chin raised, the head held steady, the shoulders square to the front, the heels, hips, shoulders, and head touching the pillar of the standard.

N. B.—This measurement, when repeated, should always be taken at the same time of the day, and after the same amount of bodily exertion.

Weight—In working costume, i. e., in light shoes, flannel trousers, flannel shirt or jersey.

N. B.—This measurement, when repeated, should always be taken at the same time of the day, and with reference to any circumstance which would affect its accuracy.

Chest—Over the jersey or naked breast. The position of attention, but with the arms horizontally extended, the palms of the hands held upwards and open, the finger straight. The tape should be passed around the chest in the line of the nipple.

N. B.—Care must be taken that the chest is not inflated beyond its usual expansion during ordinary breathing. Where a single measurement is taken the above line is the best, as gauging approximately at once the muscular and respiratory capacity; but when the latter quality is of primary importance (as in rowing) a second measurement should be taken lower down the chest, the tape being passed over the ninth rib.

In measuring recruits in the British army, the man stands erect, with the arms hanging loosely by the side. The lower edge of the tape should touch the nipple. The man is required to count ten slowly during the operation, to prevent him from keeping his lungs over-inflated.

Forearm (skin measurement).—The arm extended as in the preceding measurement, but with the hand tightly closed, the tape to be passed around the thickest part of the arm, and its girth at that point reckoned.

N. B.—With men who have taken little exercise this line will always be found near the elbow joint, but as the limb becomes developed, and the numerous muscles of the forearm acquire bulk and power from exercise, the greatest girth will be found from to 2 to 3 inches below it. Unless this circumstance be kept in view the actual increase will not be perceived.

Upper arm (skin measurement).—The hand closed, the arm bent at the elbow, and the hand brought down towards the shoulder. This should be slowly and gradually done, bending the joints of the fingers, clenching the fist, and bringing the forearm down upon the upper arm, the tape to be passed in a straight line around the thickest part of the arm.

N. B.—When the whole arm is fully developed, the difference in size between the fore and upper arm in an adult of medium stature will be about 2 inches, and it will almost invariably be found that when the upper arm is feeble the upper region of the chest will be feeble also. With a chest of 40 inches the arm would probably be 12 inches and 14 inches.

Calf (skin measurement).—The limb to be held stiff and straight, the heel raised from the ground, the toes pressed strongly down, and the knee braced back. The tape is to be passed around the thickest part of the calf; and as the position of this line will somewhat vary with different men, and with the same limb in different stages of development, one or two points should be tried, and that which shows the greatest girth selected.

Thigh (skin measurement).—The limb placed as in preceding measurement, the tape to be passed in a horizontal line around the thickest part of the limb, which will be at the highest point of the thigh admitting of horizontal measurement.

2. The Effect of Exercise upon the Muscular and Nervous Systems.

Of the exact changes which take place in active muscle, and of the circumstances attending muscular contraction, it is needless to deal at any length. The matter is fully considered in every text-book of physiology.

The following brief account of the metabolism in muscle may be given : In an active muscle the blood-vessels are dilated. The neutral or feebly alkaline reaction of the passive structure becomes an acid reaction when the muscle is contracting, owing, it is supposed, to the formation of paralactic acid. A considerable quantity of carbon dioxide is excreted from the active muscle, while a large proportion of oxygen is consumed. The amount of glycogen and grape sugar is diminished in an active muscle, the tissue of which contains less extractives soluble in water, but more extractives soluble in alcohol. During exercise the amount of water in muscular tissue increases, while that of the blood is diminished in proportion. Heat is formed in a muscle in a state of activity.

Turning to more general matters concerning the muscular system, it has been well said that " function makes structure," and it is certain that muscular exercise makes muscular tissue. Not only is the exercised muscle increased in size, both as a whole and as far as its individual parts are concerned, but there is eliminated from it such tissue as is other than muscular. The fat contained among its meshes is reduced to a minimum, the connective tissue is lessened in amount, the aponeurotic parts are strengthened, and the structure of the muscle is so amended that it is hampered by no material other than that concerned in actual movement. It is freed, moreover, of such nitrogenous substances as are capable of giving rise to superabundant waste products of combustion.

There is a limit, of course, to the growth of muscles, and muscles exercised to too great an extent will, after attaining a certain size, commence to waste. The contractile force of the muscle is increased, and an improvement takes place in those conditions which insure the speedy and complete contraction of its fibres. It has been pointed out that the muscles of an athlete when in training contract with extraordinary force under the electric current ; the muscular sense is developed to its utmost, and the circumstances involved in the performance of a reflex act are placed under improved conditions ; the power of co-ordination possessed by the individual is augmented ; he acquires the art of causing muscles, which may be said to have been hitherto estranged, to act in concert, so that movements which were complex and effected with difficulty are ultimately carried out with ease. In this way the nervous system is saved a great expenditure of force. Acts which were performed with effort and by conscious will become automatic, and there is a saving in the expenditure of active force in the spinal cord and in the cerebral cortex. Complicated movements become " organically registered in the brain " and cease to be difficult. One conspicuous feature in muscular training is the increase in the possibilities of automatism. As time goes on, and the individual practices more and more, he finds the work becomes easier and easier. This depends, not only upon an increase in the actual strength of the parts, but upon the greater ease with which the muscles concerned act in co-ordination and upon the muscular experience of the individual, which prevents him from misplacing his strength, and enables him to attain a desired end with the minimum amount of force.

He who is beginning to practice any muscular exercise, such as fencing,
bicycling, or rowing, will feel that he moves stiffly. The constant comment
of the instructor in physical exercises is, "Don't keep so stiff!" "Let your
arms go loose!" The beginner has not yet learnt how to balance one set of
muscles against their antagonists. His movements are at first very delibe-
rately planned, but in time the will ceases to concern itself. A memory is
developed in the spinal cord and in the muscular centres, and one great
element of fatigue is removed.

Nothing in physical training is more remarkable than the economy of force
which results from muscular education. The well-trained athlete, moreover,
acquires the art of using his respiratory muscles with the greatest economy.
He does not exhaust himself with needlessly vigorous breathing ; he learns to
precisely regulate his respiratory movements to his immediate needs, and he
brings the muscles of his thorax into co-ordination with the other muscles
which he employs.

Just as muscles increase with use and waste with disuse, so the whole nerve
apparatus concerned in movement is structurally improved by systematic exercise. The athletic man has better developed nerves, a more elaborate or-
ganization of his spinal cord and of certain parts of his brain, than has the
individual whose muscular system is imperfectly formed. Just as a certain
segment of the spinal cord and of the cerebral cortex wastes after the removal
of a limb, so it may be inferred that those parts become hypertrophied and
elaborated when the limb in question is unusually employed.

"The differences," writes Sir Crichton Browne, "which we notice between
man and man in deportment, gait and expression, are but the outward and
visible signs of individual variations in the development of the motor centres
of the brain, and the stammerings, grimacings, twitchings, and antics which
are so common and annoying, alike to those who suffer and who witness them,
are probably in many instances the effects of neglected education of some of
those centres, and might have been abolished by timely drill and discipline."

He who has been well trained physically possesses not only a complete but
an intelligent use of his muscles. His movements are powerful, are under
absolute control, are precise, and capable of the finest and most elaborate
adjustment.

The art of the athlete consists, not in employing the greatest amount of
power in effecting a movement, but in carrying out that movement with the
least possible expenditure of force. The tyro at cycling will use an amount

of muscular force in riding a mile which would probably carry an experienced rider some twenty miles.

3. The Effect of Exercise Upon the Tissues and Organs Generally.

It is needless in this place to deal with the subject of bodily heat, with the manner in which it is developed and employed, with the conditions which regulate it and attend its disposal. It is necessary only to say that in the body work and heat are always associated, and it is believed that the heat is the cause, and not the effect of the work. No muscular contraction can occur without the production of heat, but of the precise manner in which heat acts upon muscle and makes it contract, little is known.

Commenting upon this matter, Dr. Lagrange, in his work on "The Physiology of Bodily Exercise" (page 37), observes: "Heat causes in muscular fibres the first stage of contraction, or at least an aptitude for coming into action more quickly under the influence of the will. A heated muscle seems to have stored, in a sense, a latent force. It has been ascertained that the maximum aptitude for contraction is exhibited by human muscles at about 40° C. It follows that a man whose muscles are at this temperature is able to act more quickly, and at once can make use of all his force.

"A bodily exercise is performed with more vigor and ease when heat has raised the temperature of the muscles. This fact is so well known that there are characteristic phrases to express it in common speech. We say of a man beginning an exercise of strength or skill whose movements have not yet acquired all their force and precision, that he has not yet warmed to his work."

The author compares the preliminary canter before a race, the preliminary sparring before a fight, and the strange movements of an angry animal before an attack, to the heating up of a locomotive. It may be pointed out also that there is a greater aptitude for bodily exercises in summer than in winter, and that muscular action becomes temporarily paralyzed by great cold.

The heat produced in the body depends upon certain chemical changes in the tissues, certain combustions which are mostly, but not exclusively, oxidations. These products of combustion, or of dissimilation, examples of which are afforded by carbon dioxide, urea, uric acid, etc., are noxious to life and must be ejected from the body in one way or another through the agency of special organs. The effects produced by an excess or by a retention of these products are dealt with in discussing the subject of fatigue.

Muscular exercise tends, moreover, to remove any accumulation of fat which may exist in the tissues. Fat is the type of what are known as the reserve tissues. It serves the part of fuel for combustion ; it undergoes dissimilation with remarkable ease, and may therefore be regarded as fuel of a most combustible character. As fat forms no permanent structural part of the organism, its removal is, within limits, effected with no inconvenience. The fat man who takes exercise finds that he soon becomes breathless and fatigued. His unwonted muscular exertion involves a great series of combustion processes. Fat would appear to be of all substances the one which most readily lends itself as material for such changes. The result is that in the corpulent individual the products of dissimilation are produced in excess, and he becomes, in a certain sense, poisoned by the accumulation of these products (see chapter on FATIGUE). He is hampered also by the unnecessary weight of his body, by his feeble muscles, and possibly, to some extent, by the mechanical obstacles offered by collections of fat. A corpulent man in rowing finds that his large abdomen is an actual mechanical obstacle in the way of his movements.

A fat man when in training loses his fat. As he becomes thinner he becomes stronger, his muscles act better, he is less breathless on exertion, less fatigued after long-continued effort, and may in time reach that excellent state of health known as "good condition."

The fat disappears first from the limbs, especially from the limbs which are particularly employed. Last of all the internal accumulations disappear, and the last feature to go will probably be the large abdomen, which is so terrible a trial to would-be athletes of middle age.

It may here be said that the deposit of a certain amount of fat within the abdomen is a common accompaniment of advancing age, and that its formation can best be prevented by exercise, and especially by such exercise as involves the contraction of the abdominal muscles. It is exceedingly rare to see a waterman who keeps up a good style of rowing present an unduly prominent abdomen.

Exercise, moreover, tends to improve the condition of the tissues generally. The soft parts become firmer, more resistant, less easily bruised when damaged, and in all respects sounder. A man in training is said to be "hard," and it is well known that no moderate blow will raise a bruise upon the person of a prize-fighter when he is in perfect "condition." The general standard of the nutritive activity of the body is improved. The stout and flabby man becomes thinner, harder and firmer under training.

The thin and spare man, on the other hand, often becomes stouter under training. He feels better, eats better, and his powers of nutrition are so improved that he gains flesh and weight.

Thus training may cause one man to lose weight and another to gain it, and both to look healthier and better for the change.

As Dr. Lagrange well expresses it, " Exercise produces in the system two absolutely different effects : it increases the process of assimilation, thanks to which the body gains new tissues, and it accelerates the process of dissimilation, which leads to the destruction of certain materials." Its action in the former direction depends upon the increased amount of oxygen introduced into the system by the improved circulation and respiration, and by the healthy stimulation of the various active organs of the body.

The need for exercise is felt as much by thin people, who assimilate too little, as by fat people, who do not dissimilate enough. Exercise may therefore be regarded as a great regulator of nutrition.

As the action of the heart rapidly increases in force and frequency during exercise, the flow of blood through all parts of the body is increased. The amount of increase is from ten to thirty beats, but it may be more. The skin becomes red with the blood contained in the full capillaries, and perspiration is much increased. The amount of fluid which is lost by the skin is very considerable.

The digestive apparatus is stimulated and strengthened by exercise. The appetite improves, digestion is more complete, absorption more rapid, and the circulation through the liver is more vigorous and even.

Muscular exercises, especially such as employ the muscles of the abdomen, have a very beneficial effect upon the bowels, promoting peristaltic movements and relieving such constipation as depends upon the torpidity of the intestine.

One other conspicuous effect of exercise is the increased elimination of carbon. This is eliminated mainly by the lungs. The observations of Pettenkofer and Voit give the following results :—

TABLE IX.

	Absorption of oxygen in grammes.	Elimination in grammes of		
		Carbonic acid.	Water	Urea
Rest day	708.9	911.5	828.0	37.2
Work day . . .	954.5	1284.2	2042.1	37.0
Excess on work day (with exception of urea)	246.6	372.7	1214.1	− 0.2

It is demonstrated that a considerable formation of carbonic acid takes place in the muscles. As, moreover, exercise is clearly necessary for a sufficient elimination of carbon from the body, it is needful, in a condition of prolonged rest, that the amount of carbon in the food be lessened to avoid an accumulation of that element in the tissues.

With regard to the vexed question of the elimination of nitrogen from the body during exercise, Parkes concludes his careful examination of the subject in these words :—

"On the whole, if I have stated the facts correctly, the effect of exercise is certainly to influence the elimination of nitrogen by the kidneys, but within various limits, and the time of increase is in the period of rest succeeding the exercise ; while during the exercise period the evidence, though not certain, points rather to a lessening of the elimination of nitrogen.

"It would appear from these facts that well-fed persons taking exercise would require a little more nitrogen in the food, and it is certain, as a matter of experience, that persons undergoing laborious work do take more nitrogenous food. This is the case also with animals."

Dr. Parkes thus sums up the action of exercise upon the kidneys : "The water of the urine and the chloride of sodium often lessens in consequence of the increased passage from the skin. The urea is not much changed. The uric acid increases after great exertion, so also apparently the pigment ; the phosphoric acid is not augmented ; the sulphuric acid is moderately increased ; the free carbonic acid of the urine is increased ; the chlorides are lessened on account of the outflow by the skin ; the exact amount of the bases has not been determined, but a greater excess of soda and potash is eliminated than of lime or magnesia. Nothing certain is known as to hippuric acid, sugar, or other substances."

4. The Effect of Exercise upon Personal Comeliness and Comfort.

We have already noted the effect a systematic training may have upon the growth and development of the body, upon the size of the chest, and the proportions of the limbs. Such training, moreover, can give an upright and symmetrical figure and an easy and graceful carriage. There is a swing about the body and a bearing of the head and shoulders which mark those whose muscular system has been fully developed.

Under proper training the shuffling and shambling gait disappears, the loutish boy ceases to look loutish, and the gawky girl no longer excites comment; rounded shoulders become square, and bending backs are made straight.

The athlete, so far as his body and his personal equation are concerned, has reached the full and perfect stature of a man, and the girl whose physical education has been complete reaches her point of physical perfection as a woman. The beauty of the body depends upon a fully formed skeleton and perfectly developed muscles, and not upon deposits of fat. The arm of a plump but ill-developed woman is rounded and free from conspicuous prominences about the elbow, but the outline is as meaningless and as unnatural as the part is flabby and lifeless. The arm of a woman in perfect physical condition has, on the other hand, an exquisite outline. It presents the contour given it by the muscles that move the limb. The graceful configuration of these muscles has not been hidden beneath a monotonous layer of fat. The arm has an individuality, and has reached the perfection of its growth. The beauty of the right arm of many female violinists is a matter of common comment.

Unfortunately there is comparatively little fat about joints, and the most trying feature in the feebly developed woman is a bony elbow. There are masses of muscle about the elbow, and if these are wasted the details of the skeleton become unpleasantly conspicuous. If they are, on the contrary, well-developed, the contour of the elbow becomes even and graceful. The arm of an individual who is not only thin, but is also ill-developed, is an unpleasant spectacle — it is a burlesque of a human limb.

In the neck and the upper part of the chest the effects of a sound physical training are very conspicuous. The long turkey-like neck of the ill-developed lad and the scraggy neck of the ill-nurtured woman are familiar enough. They are both unnecessary disfigurements.

A perfectly-shaped thorax gives to the human figure its most striking feature, and such a chest cannot be met with among those whose physical education has been quite neglected. There is little excuse for an ill-formed thorax, and yet at the present day it is met with on all sides and in all classes of the community.

The back of the ill-developed is characteristic. The spinous processes of the vertebræ, instead of being sunk in a medium groove formed by the two great masses of the vertebral muscles, stand out in the form of an irregular nodulated ridge. The back looks feeble, lifeless, wasted, and there is an air of muscular pauperism about it. It looks poor, and yet it must be owned that it is the type of back very commonly met with among the favored classes, and especially among the women.

The tissues of the ill-developed are flabby, doughy, baggy. They lack elasticity and consistence. The cheek of the overworked shop assistant who gets no real exercise can be seen to shake as he walks along the street.

The purposeless-looking extremities of those who are physically uneducated are well known. They have the appearance of the limbs of individuals who are recovering from serious illness. They are, as a matter of fact, the extremities of persons who have never been well.

The tissues of the well-developed are firm, elastic, resisting, active, and full of evidence of living. There is given to every part of the surface of the body that rapid change in contour and that indescribable aspect of vigor and soundness which are features of a healthy and well-knit frame.

In the above comments I am alluding merely to the results of a systematic physical training, and not to such exceptional results of muscular exercise as produce professional gymnasts and acrobats.

Undue and unsymmetrical muscular development may deform the body ; a circumstance well illustrated by some acrobats, whose lower limbs are of normal or sub-normal development, while their arms are enormous, their shoulders mountainous and uncouth, their necks coarse and bullock-like, and the upper part of the back arched or bowed. This is especially noticeable in gymnasts who practice upon the trapeze, horizontal bar, and other apparatus, and who have exclusively developed the muscles of the upper half of the trunk.

The skin of those who have taken pains to bring their bodies to perfection often compares in a marked manner with the integument of the neglected and uneducated. It is firm, clear, and wholesome. It is not to be argued that exercise will keep the integument free from marks and blotches, and render a naturally coarse skin fine, but it will bring about such differences in appearance as serve to distinguish what is healthy from what is unsound. The delicate and sensitive complexion of a young woman whose physical training has been efficient is in conspicuous contrast with the dull, loose, lustreless integument of the abstainer from muscular pursuits. The skin of the recluse is grey, greasy, and unpleasant-looking. The complexion of the young man about town is almost distinctive. It is aggressively unwholesome, and forms a contrast with that of his companion who has just returned from a shooting expedition or a long boating tour. Exercise, of course, involves more living

in the open, a freer and deeper respiration, and the coursing of a more vigorous flow of blood through the integuments ; it leads actually to a sounder
state of the general health, and such improvement is at once evident upon
the skin.   There is a certain brightness and vivacity of the look, and a certain degree of self-assertion in the carriage, of those who are in sound physical condition.   They contrast with the wan, hopeless-looking creatures who
never "stir out of the house," and who crawl through life in a semi-apologetic
manner.

In the matter of personal comfort no greater sense of pure pleasure can
influence the human mind than that which results from perfect health.   There
is the glorious delight of movement and of vigorous activity, quite apart from
the excitement and mental enjoyment which attend so many recreations and
outdoor sports.   The lad who is in perfect physical condition wakes up in the
morning, fresh and rampant ; and if it be the summer time he probably feels
an irresistible impulse to dash out into the open air and fill his lungs and
quicken his pulse and move his muscles.   Even the fatigue that comes over a
man who is in good condition, and who has taken a long spell at exercise, is
pleasurable.   Such a one eats well and digests well ; the functions of his
body are carried on normally, and he experiences to its full the delight of
living.

The youth who takes no exercise, who is always poring over his books,
misses at least one-half of the enjoyments which are available to man during
a comparatively short life.   He is a dull creature, dyspeptic probably, the
subject of headaches, constipation, and many minor ills.   To him joy cometh
not in the morning, and in the place of an honest fatigue he has the "fidgets"
and his weariness is painful.   His appetite is feeble possibly, his circulation
is poor, and very often he sleeps badly, and can envy the easy and profound
sleep of a companion who has come home after a long run across country.
The simplest, the purest, and the pleasantest recollections in life usually go
back to certain physical enjoyments in the open air, to some walking tour or
cricket match, to some river expedition, or to some great day upon the
moors.

When sudden exercise is forced upon the undeveloped individual, he is
more or less unable to meet it : he becomes breathless, perspires violently, is
uncertain of himself, is clumsy and the subsequent victim of a painful degree
of fatigue.   Of such a person it cannot be said—

Yea, this in him was the peculiar grace,
That before living he learned how to live.

5. The Mental and Moral Effects of Exercise.

Moderate, regular, and systematic exercise by stimulating the circulation of the body improves also the circulation of the brain, and is therefore an aid to cerebral movements. It improves the health and the physical strength, and so increases the capability of the individual for mental work and for the physical strain incident upon mental concentration.

By organizing in the brain a series of muscular movements, by elaborating the powers of co-ordination, and by establishing automatism in a large and varied series of actions, it saves actual brain-work and renders a considerable number of movements independent of the direct action of the will.

It offers, too, an admirable change of employment. There is no better rest from severe mental work than well-selected bodily exercise. With many men to lie upon a beach and throw stones into the water is no rest. They would find a more complete repose in the pleasurable use of their muscles, in the pursuit of some congenial outdoor sport, and in rendering dormant the energies of one part of the nervous system by an engrossing employment of another part.

Such exercises as are indulged in when seeking rest from mental work must be simple, and so far as possible, such as are automatically performed.

" Prescribe fencing, gymnastics with apparatus, and lessons in a riding school," writes Dr. Lagrange, " to all those idle persons whose brain languishes for want of work. The effort of will and the work of co-ordination which these exercises demand will give a salutary stimulus to the torpid cerebral cells. But for a child overworked at school, for a person whose nerve-centres are congested owing to persistent mental effort in preparing for an examination, for such we must prescribe long walks, the easily learnt exercise of rowing, and failing, better the old game of leap-frog and prisoners' base, running games— anything, in fact, rather than difficult exercises and acrobatic gymnastics."

" Mr. Charles Paget, at one time M. P. for Nottingham, tried in the village school on his estate at Ruddington a very interesting experiment. He was not satisfied with the general progress made by the boys, and he provided for them a large garden. The school was then divided into two sections, one of which was kept to the ordinary school work for the ordinary hours, the other for half of these hours only, the rest of the school time being devoted to work in the garden. At the end of the term the half-time, or gardening boys, had excelled the others in every respect—in conduct, in diligence, and in the results of study." ("Health Exhibition Manuals," vol. xi., p. 327.)

There must be a proper distribution of mental and physical work. Just as "all work and no play makes Jack a dull boy," so all play and no work makes Jack a still duller boy.

An excessive and absorbing indulgence in physical exercises is undoubtedly bad. It tends to make the individual too much of an animal, and to afford neither time, opportunity, nor suitable conditions for the development of his brain. Under such circumstances even the body tends to become stunted if the practice be commenced early, and the lad develops not only an animal look, but some of the intellectual and emotional attributes of the animal.

Still, on the other hand, in these days of cramming and intense competition many a successful man has to thank Providence for the late recognized blessings of an idle youth.

The systematic and properly arranged pursuit of physical exercise tends to develop certain admirable qualities, and notably those which are so much prized among Englishmen, and which are well designated as "manly."

These qualities are brought out in those who are enthusiasts in outdoor sports and games. The football player has done more than merely develop, his muscles, the man who has rowed in his college eight has learnt something beyond the mysteries of the sliding seat, and the experienced "player" at almost any outdoor game has been improved by other means than those which the actual manoeuvres of the game demand. Such lads and men have learnt in a school where the principles of pluck, courage, endurance, and self-reliance are acquired. They have probably learnt to be ready, to be quick of eye and hand, and prompt in judgment. They may have appreciated the value of discipline and of self-control. They may have felt the inspiration of the chivalry of days gone by, and have experienced the influences of good fellowship and loyal comradeship. They may have learnt what it is to be patient, to be fair, to be unselfish, and to be true.

Many a man who in later life finds himself in a dangerous strait would wish for no one better by his side than the lad who pulled behind him in a racing eight. The cries and the cheers of the football field must have given heart to many a desperate soldier when hard pressed in the turmoil of actual war, and a sailor can say no more gracious thing of his mate than that he is "a man to stand by you in a gale."

There is a certain moral effect also which comes with a sound physical training. The schoolboy who is foremost in athletic exercises will probably be found to be more open, more straightforward, more simple, and more wholesome-minded than the lad who spends his time loafing at the pastry-cook's. Mr. Cathcart in his "Health Lectures" (Edinburgh, 1884,) brings this point well forward in the evidence he quotes from certain head-masters of large public schools in England. One head-master writes: "The worst boys intellectually, physically and morally, are the loafers," and another: "The boys who work hard and play hard do not ape the vices of men, and are free from the insidious evils that often fasten on unoccupied boyhood."

I think it may be safely said that that miserable creature, the juvenile sexual hypochondriac, is never to be found among those who are foremost at athletics and outdoor games.

FATIGUE.

This subject will be considered under the following heads: 1. Breathlessness; 2. Muscular Fatigue; 3. Muscular Stiffness; 4. General Fatigue.

1. BREATHLESSNESS.

The breathlessness which is a familiar attendant upon exercises of a certain character has received but little notice at the hands of physiologists. Dr. Lagrange has in his recent work, to which allusion has been already made, dealt very fully with the subject, and explains it by a theory which appears to be both sound and satisfactory. The phenomena of breathlessness are familiar enough. One has but to picture a man of middle age, who is out of training, and who has set himself the task of running a certain distance. He soon feels embarrassed in his breathing; he pants, his respiratory movements become jerky and irregular; he is aware of a terrible sense of oppression in his chest, a sense which increases with each step. His head throbs; he begins to find that his strength is failing him; he feels that he could run many more yards, so far as his legs are concerned, but the sense of suffocation arrests him. He staggers along, his steps become uncertain, his face haggard, his movements irregular, and he stops at last dead beat. As he rests he continues for many minutes to breathe in the same troubled way. The man is said to be "blown," to have "lost his wind." He has used his legs, but his legs have not given way. It is his chest which has failed him. This constitutes the remarkable feature of the phenomenon. The same man can exercise his arms with dumb-bells for three times the time occupied by the run, yet he is not "out of breath." He can row for ten miles without being inconvenienced, but he cannot run up two flights of steep stairs without being rendered quite breathless. The more athletic the man, the better condition of training he is in, the more practice he has had, the less breathless he becomes; but the most perfect athlete, even when in his prime, can soon "pump himself out" if he tries.

Dr. Lagrange offers the following explanation of the phenomenon:

Breathlessness is a form of dyspnœa due to an excess of carbon dioxide in the blood. The excess of this gas leads to an increase of the respiratory need. The condition may be spoken of as auto-intoxication of the body by one of its own products of dissimilation—carbon dioxide.

This excess of carbonic acid is produced by muscular work. It is a conspicuous product of such work, and it must be remembered that the muscles form at least half the weight of the entire body. The larger the muscles employed, and the more vigorous their action, the greater is the amount of the gas produced. The intensity of breathlessness during exercise is in direct proportion to the expenditure of force demanded in a given time. Running involves rapid contractions of the great mass of muscles forming the lower extremities. It induces breathlessness quicker than does moderate rowing, where the muscular expenditure in a given time is much less. "The quantity of carbonic acid," writes Dr. Lagrange, "produced by a group of muscles in a given time is in proportion to the amount of work they do. Further, the work which a group of muscles is able to do without fatigue is in direct ratio to the power, that is, to the number and size of the muscles forming this group. If, then, an exercise is localized in a very small group of muscles, fatigue will ensue before a large quantity of work has been done, and before a large dose of carbonic acid has been poured into the blood. The eliminating power of the lungs will exceed the power for work of the active muscles; muscular fatigue will precede breathlessness. If, on the other hand, the muscles put in action are very numerous and very powerful, they will be able before being fatigued to perform a large quantity of work, and consequently to produce a very large dose of carbonic acid. Their power for work will exceed the eliminating power of the lungs. Breathlessness will this time precede fatigue."

It is said that a horse "trots with its legs and gallops with its lungs." The gallop of a horse may be slowed down until the animal falls behind another horse which is trotting. Nevertheless, however slow the gallop may be, it will more quickly "pump" a horse than an equally rapid trot. Swiftness of movement does not suffice to produce breathlessness unless combined with intensity of muscular effort.

In breathlessness it is not inspiration which is difficult, but expiration. In running, inspiration is free, easy, deep, three times as long as expiration. The latter, on the other hand, is short, insufficient, and painful.

It is stated that in man there is discharged in a given time by respiration :

0.35 gramme of carbonic acid during sleep.
1.60   "   "   " while sitting.
1.65   "   "   " while running.

As accessory causes of breathlessness are certain disturbances in the circulation of the blood and some engorgement of the lungs resulting therefrom. These changes are discussed by Dr. Lagrange in the following words :—

"The first result of violent exercise is the quickening of the blood current and a consequent active congestion of the lungs. In these exercises the lungs are very quickly engorged with blood, and there is great need for their disembarrasment by increasing the activity of the blood current. The movement of inspiration increases the velocity of the current by a force of aspiration which tends to empty the over-filled capillaries. This aspiration lasts as long as the enlargement of the thorax continues ; hence this movement is an assistance to the breathless man ; on the other hand, as the thorax is diminishing in size during the expiratory movement, the blood current becomes slower and the lungs more engorged. Hence the discomfort and the irresistible impulse to a prompt repetition of the inspiratory movement."

"We may say that the lungs of the breathless man are placed between two different needs. On the one hand, they have to drive out carbonic acid and the other products of dissimilation, and for this a long expiration would be necessary ; but, on the other hand, they have to free themselves from vascular engorgement, and therefore expiration is cut short to return to inspiration, which helps the circulation through the lungs."

Dr. Lagrange divides breathlessness into three stages, and as he is the only writer who has fully dealt with this subject, the matter cannot be better discussed than in his own words :—

"In the *first stage* the respiratory movements are increased in frequency and in extent. The production of carbonic acid is increased, but the respiratory energy being greater, there is an equilibrium between the needs of the organism, which demands a more active elimination of this gas, and the working of the lungs, which is powerful enough to satisfy these needs. During a time which varies much with the individual, with his constitution, with his resistance to fatigue, and, above all, with his power of directing his respiration, gained from his respiratory education, these are only symptoms of greater vital activity, and there are as yet no signs of functional disturbance, no sensation which rises to the degree of discomfort. The man has a general sensation of warmth, some throbbing of the temples, and has an animated appearance, flushed, his eyes sparkling, and a general aspect of cheerfulness, due to the greater activity of the circulation and the resulting active congestions. In a word, it is the stage in which exercise causes a greater intensity of life without reaching the degree of discomfort or of danger.

"Here we have the really salutary dose of exercise, the limits within which we must keep in order that work may cause us no inconvenience. But nothing varies more with the individual than the duration of this inoffensive period, which is, in a sense, the preface of breathlessness. In some persons it is as long as an hour, in others the stage in which discomfort begins is reached in a few seconds.

"If violent exercise be prolonged, the equilibrium is soon broken between the production of carbonic acid, which becomes more and more abundant, and the eliminating power of the lungs, which is insufficient to free the organism from it. Respiratory distress occurs.

"In the *second period* the effects of insufficient respiration begin to show themselves, a vague discomfort is experienced, which is most accentuated in the præcordial region, but which is rapidly generalized throughout the body, and notably affects the head. In the chest there is a feeling as if it were oppressed by a weight, or bound down by a girdle of insufficient air. In the head there are clouds obscuring sight, sparks before the eyes, then murmurs and ringing in the ears, and finally a certain bluntness of sensation, a certain confusion in impressions and in ideas. All these disturbances are due to the action upon the nerve-centres of an excess of carbonic acid. They indicate the beginning of intoxication.

"In the face remarkable changes are to be noticed, which are the consequences of the respiratory distress, and of the efforts made to draw a greater quantity of air into the chest. The nostrils are dilated, the mouth and eyes widely opened. They all seem to be widely opened to favor the entrance of the air which the lungs so greatly need.

"The color of a breathless man shows very striking modifications. At the beginning of exercise we have said that there is animation, more color in the face, due to active congestion. But in the second period the picture has changed. To the lively red color has succeeded a pale and wan tint. There

4

is something peculiar about this pallor—it is not uniform. Certain parts of the face, such as the lips and the cheeks, have a violet blackish appearance ; the rest of the face is white and colorless.

"From the two colors, one darker and the other lighter, there results a gray, leaden, livid appearance. The violet tint is due to the retention of blood in the capillaries, which are losing their elasticity, and in which the circulation is failing. This blood, overcharged with carbonic acid, has lost its bright red color, hence in the lips and other more transparent parts of the face we see no longer the ordinary red color ; they have the blackish color characteristic of venous blood.

"As for the pallor, this is due to a transient anæmia, to the emptying of the arterioles. The heart, the energy of which diminishes in proportion to the increase of the breathlessness, does not send forward a sufficient quantity of blood, and it is easy to understand that a part receiving less blood is less deeply colored than usual.

"The leaden hue of the face in a breathless man indicates an already profound disturbance of the system. In no case should exercise be continued after it comes on, for it indicates the beginning of asphyxia.

"It is at this stage of breathlessness that we observe the very characteristic change in the rhythm of respiration which has been already described. The ordinary rhythm is lost, and the two periods of respiration become unequal. The first period increases and the second diminishes ; inspiration becomes three times as long as expiration. This change in the rhythm of respiration is an indication of blood stasis in the capillaries of the lungs. As soon as it occurs we can see that the organism, its force exhausted, can no longer fight to good purpose against the poisonous substance which permeates it. The congested lungs eliminate less carbonic acid than is formed by the muscles at work. Intoxication is imminent.

"If exercise be continued, the gravity of the condition rapidly increases. We may call the asphyxial stage the third phase of breathlessness into which the organism passes under the influence of forced exercise.

"This *third stage* is as follows : To the respiratory distress succeeds a sensation of anguish generalized throughout the organism. The head feels as if bound by an iron band. Vertigo is very distressing. All sensations become more vague ; the brain is overcome by a kind of drunkenness. The subject begins to become unconscious of what is passing, his muscles continue to work mechanically for a time, then they stop, and the man falls in a faint.

" At this time respiration is of a different type to that of the last stage ; the two periods are both short, jerky, occasionally interrupted : with them are mingled swallowing movements and hiccough. The heart-beat is feeble and intermittent. The pulse is small, irregular, and imperceptible. When exercise is continued to these extreme limits it is almost always stopped by grave syncope, and unless prompt help be given the syncope may be fatal."

An athletic man soon develops the art of regulating his breathing so as to reduce the degree of breathlessness as far as is possible. He is aware that it is at first that the trouble is intense, and that in time he can adjust the difficulty a little. The runner speaks of getting "his second wind." He has passed through a period of breathlessness in which excitement, sudden movement, and unnecessary extreme muscular contractions possibly have played some part ; he then settles down to his work, he uses his forces more economically and breathes more easily ; and it is common to hear a man out of condition explain the loss of a race by the fact that he never got his "second wind."

In sprint running the art of controlling breathlessness reaches its highest point, and to some extent sprint running is a test of the respiratory capacity in this direction.

2. MUSCULAR FATIGUE.

If a man in sound health hold out his arm at right angles to his body he experiences, in a time which varies according to his physical condition, so much inconvenience in the muscles involved that he is at last compelled to drop the limb. If he exercise his will to the utmost he may prolong the period of extension, but a time soon comes when by no possible effort can he continue to hold out the extremity.

The muscles in question are said to be fatigued.

The fatigue is termed relative because, if a proper electric current be applied to the muscles as soon as the limb is dropped as helpless, the muscles again contract, and the hand is once more lifted.

If the muscles of an animal be subjected to an electric current, they contract ; on repeating the application they contract again and again. The contractions, however, become feebler, and are in time ultimately abolished. The parts are in the condition of relative fatigue.

If now a stronger current be employed, the muscles again contract, and again in time lose their power. The experiment can be continued with a stronger current until finally the muscles cannot be made to contract by any current or any stimulus of any kind.

They have reached the state of absolute fatigue.

Local fatigue of muscle is explained by the following conditions :

1. The actual power or function of the muscle is exhausted. This condition has been termed "dynamic exhaustion," and is parallel to the exhaustion which is noticed in certain reflex acts when they are indefinitely excited, and to the exhaustion of the retina to certain rays when one color is contemplated for too long a time.

The functional power of a muscle is placed within definite limits, and in fatigue that limit is reached. This exhaustion is modified by the strength of the muscle, by its local condition, by the practice it has been subjected to, and by the nerve condition of the individual.

2. In fatigue, nerve exhaustion is largely concerned. This especially applies to complicated acts, the repetition of which involves a special and definite effort of the will.

The comparative absence of exhaustion in the incessant movements in chorea is explained by the circumstance that in these movements a voluntary nerve mechanism is not concerned. Dr. Lagrange lays down the axiom that, "the muscular work being equal, the sensation of fatigue is the more intense the more active the intervention of the cerebral faculties demanded by the exercise."

3. Some local effect may be exercised upon the muscle by the products of combustion or dissimilation which are developed within its tissues, and which, not being got rid of in time enough, accumulate in excess.

"If," writes Dr. Langrange, "we submit the muscles of a frog to the action of a powerful electric stimulus, and prolong this action until fatigue is complete, that is, till the limbs of the animal remain motionless under the most powerful stimulation, we shall have in the fatigued muscles the elements necessary for a most curious experiment. Their substance rubbed in a mortar and made into a fine soup contains a principle capable of producing in healthy muscle at rest the fatigue which had exhausted the first muscles. If we inject into a second frog this extract of fatigued muscles, we bring about in this animal all the phenomena of fatigue, and its limbs will fail to respond to electric stimuli."

The possible character of this local effect is thus dealt with by Landois in his well known "Text-book of Physiology" (translated by Stirling). The cause of local muscular fatigue "is probably partly due to the accumulation of decomposition products—'fatigue stuffs'—in the muscular tissues, these products being formed within the muscle itself during its activity. They are phosphoric acid, either free or in the form of acid phosphates, acid potassium phosphate, glycerin-phosphoric acid(?), and carbonic acid. If these substances be removed from a muscle by passing through its blood-vessels an indifferent solution of common salt . . . the muscle again becomes capable of energizing."

Dr. Lagrange gives a more detailed account of these tissue changes, and in adding his account it is necessary to say that his statements are not entirely in accord with the teaching of most physiologists.

"Muscles which have worked to excess have undergone a change in their chemical composition. Alkaline in a state of repose, they have become acid ; they contain lactic acid, which was not present before work ; they contain less oxygen and more carbonic acid than when at rest. Numerous nitrogenous materials resulting from the combustion of muscular tissues are considerably increased. These substances, of which the last stage of combustion is urea, form a series of bodies only differing in containing more or less oxygen, and being consequently at a different degree of oxidation or combustion. All authors enumerate amongst them kreatin, hypoxanthin, inosite, etc., and finally the best known one, and the most interesting because of the part it plays in the production of gout, uric acid."

4. It is possible also that some actual lesion, such as that attending the compression of nerves, may occur in a fatigued muscle, and may serve to partly explain the tenderness of the over-used structure and to establish a condition akin to that produced by the violent and irregular contractions of cramp.

5. MUSCULAR STIFFNESS.

Another feature associated with local fatigue, with the over-use of muscle, is stiffness. This is a common but not a necessary accompaniment of the overwork.

A rowing man who is entirely out of condition, and who has taken no exercise for months, is asked to fill up a place in a racing four for a short "practice." He finds the exertion a terrible strain ; he soon becomes breathless, his limbs ache, his head throbs, every limb seems out of condition, and he is soon exhausted. He does his best through the short spin, but next day he aches all over ; he is stiff ; he feels as if he had been beaten ; he cannot move without some pain, nor can he grasp any part of his body without discovering some tenderness.

In a day or so the unpleasant condition passes off. This very man may have rowed many races without experiencing a trace of stiffness. He may have gone through three times the amount of exertion without any but momentary inconvenience. The difference has been simply this: at one time he was in practice and in condition, at the other time he was both out of practice and out of condition.

The intensity of the stiffness is not always proportionate to the immediate fatigue, nor is the extent of the exercise a measure of the stiffness which may result.

Stiffness depends rather upon the condition of the individual than upon the character or amount of the muscular work done. Muscles may be fatigued without afterwards becoming stiff.

The local symptoms of stiffness probably depend upon an exaggeration of those conditions in the muscles which are supposed to underlie local fatigue, and notably to the retention in the tissues of the products of combustion.

These local changes have already been described.

4. GENERAL FATIGUE.

The general disturbances which may accompany muscular exhaustion and which are present in some degree in such fatigue as is attended by stiffness are of very varying character.

The individual may be left simply exhausted, "tired out," listless, and to some extent prostrate.

In more advanced degrees he complains of heaviness in the head, of utter feebleness, of inability to take food, and of painful weariness and restlessness, followed by want of sleep.

In other and still more pronounced cases he may exhibit febrile phenomena, and present the condition described as the "fever of over-exertion." This fever may be attended with such malaise and with such nerve disturbances as to be mistaken for the early period of an infective fever.

This condition has been elaborately considered by Dr. Knott, of Dublin, in his excellent monograph on "The Fever of Over-exertion" (Dublin, 1888). He takes the case of a greatly overworked farm laborer. The symptoms may or may not commence with a rigor. The patient's temperature runs up rapidly, even to 103° F. or 104° F. within a few hours, and this change is accompanied by the general symptoms of malaise, congested face, thirst, loss of appetite, etc. He sometimes takes a day or two of rest, when, feeling a little better, he makes a desperate effort to go back to work, although still suffering from the same symptoms in a slighter degree. His efforts are now necessarily less vigorous, but he does enough to feed the slow fire of febrile combustion which has been already kindled in his muscles.

The temperature maintains a standard of about 101° or so; the pulse is permanently quickened; thirst, constipation, loss of appetite, and loaded urine continue.

In such cases, when the pernicious attempts at manual exertion are continued for a number of days, the unhappy individual afterwards fails to recover. Gradual wasting goes on; the pulse maintains its frequency and becomes weaker, the strength by degrees fails, the patient is obliged to take to bed; the fever tends, after some months, to assume a hectic type. Increasing emaciation is marked, and the patient not very rarely falls a victim to some intercurrent disease.

Dr. Knott ascribes the phenomena to the throwing into the circulation of a greatly disproportionate quantity of the products of muscular waste. These, he maintains, lead to an overthrow of the governing powers of the thermotoxic nerve centre, or, in other words, are the substantial cause of the fever. He considers that urea and uric acid represent the most important of these products.

Dr. Lagrange supports the same view, and contends that the marked constitutional disturbances which may follow upon severe muscular exercise are all due to the accumulation in the circulation of a large excess of the chemical products of muscular waste, to a species of self-infection by the excess of combustion products developed in the muscles. He also considers that these products are mainly represented by urea and allied compounds.

It is noteworthy that a degree of fatigue leading to muscular stiffness, but not necessarily to the constitutional symptoms named, will be attended by a deposit of urates in the urine. This may be quite independent of any fever.

Those who pursue athletic exercises are well aware of the association of a deposit in the urine with the appearance of stiffness. In a man out of condition the tissue waste induced during unwonted exercise is very considerable. The tissues afford abundant reserve material for the necessary combustions. The nutritive condition of his muscles is comparatively low. In an athlete in training, on the other hand, the material available for combustion is not in excess. The tissues have long been rid of all superfluous matter. The nutritive state of the muscles is in the best possible condition, and the circumstances which favor the development of a great deposit of urates is not forthcoming.

EFFECTS OF EXCESSIVE OR UNSUITABLE EXERCISE.

It is unnecessary to deal in a separate section with the ill-effects of an absence of physical exercise upon the body. The matter has been considered in such of the foregoing paragraphs as are concerned in the general effect of muscular exercise.

In estimating the actual value of the work done in any physical pursuit, or in attempting to express what is meant by "excessive" or "unsuitable" in relation with muscular labor, I have been unable to make any use of the physiological method of measuring work by "foot-tons." This mode of measurement is no doubt of value to the physiologist, but to those concerned in physical education it is practically useless. Many of the results do not accord with what would be inferred from practical experience, nor can they be put to any practical use. The amount of muscular expenditure incurred in rowing one mile at racing speed is said to be represented by 18.56 foot-tons. But walking a mile at an ordinary pace causes an expenditure of 17.67 foot-tons, from which it must be inferred that there is very little difference between these two forms of exercise, so far as the use of the muscles is concerned. Those who are interested in athletic matters would not be able to recognize the correctness nor the value of these estimates, especially when they are compared with one another. Even when every allowance is made for the quickness of the stroke and the breathlessness induced by rowing at a racing pace, yet still it would be urged that the actual output of muscular force would be represented by a different figure when such exercise is compared with the walking of one mile.

Rowing six miles at racing speed would, upon the same estimate, be represented by 111.36 foot-tons, while walking the same distance would be expressed by 106.02 foot-tons—a result which makes the comparison still more marked.

So far as the present purpose of this paper is concerned, the terms "excessive exercise" and "unsuitable exercise" must be considered relatively, and with reference rather to the individual than to the actual physiological amount of muscular work expended.

What may be excessive or unsuitable exercise to one man may be moderate and quite excellent exercise to another.

In considering the phenomena of fatigue and the effects of any given exertion, the estimate must be based upon the condition of the individual rather than upon the actual character of the work carried out. In this matter the age and bodily development of the man, the state of his general health, and the scope and extent of his muscular education, play prominent and essential parts.

The effects which may follow upon excessive or unsuitable exercise, or upon exercise which, from the point of view of him who practices it, may be termed violent on the one hand and rash on the other, are very varied.

We have seen in the sections on breathlessness and on general fatigue what results may follow after severe exertion, so far especially as the respiratory functions and the general state of the body are concerned.

A sprint runner may fall senseless upon the path, succumbing to the results of his breathlessness.

A boy may remain completely "knocked up" for several days after a paper-chase, and may be really ill and exhibit the febrile phenomena which have been already described.

There is no doubt that in not a few instances the pursuit of violent and extreme exercise has led to results which have had a permanent effect upon the health of the individual. In some cases an actual organic lesion has been produced; in others the body has been placed in a condition favorable for the development of disease; in a third series of instances there supervenes merely a feebler state of health.

The children of tubercular parents have acquired a spinal caries, or a diseased joint, as a result of injuries received through improper gymnastic exercises.

Children with a weak muscular system have acquired a lateral curvature of the spine through the pursuit of unsuitable exercises, which, so far as their spinal muscles are concerned, have been excessive and unequal.

It may be true, as is often asserted, that phthisis has appeared in those who are phthisically inclined, as a result of the strain and the exposure incident to severe exercises of endurance in the open air.

Many serious troubles may certainly be ascribed to acts of indiscretion and to exposure to cold and wet under trying circumstances during the pursuit of physical exercise; but such ills can scarcely be laid at the door of muscular training. The attack of acute rheumatism, which may have followed a long boating tour in the late autumn, may more justly be ascribed to camping out in the wet than to the effect of mere rowing.

Quite apart from any obvious lesion or disease, not a few individuals appear to suffer permanently in health as the result of some specific excess in the matter of exercise. A lad may "knock up" after winning a three-mile race, and never be fit for much in the matter of athletics after that. A man of about middle age may, with probable reason, date a distinct and persistent decline in health to some one holiday in Switzerland, when he did more than his age and his condition justified.

Many inferences of this character may be unsound, but a few appear to be undoubted.

On the whole, however, it must be allowed that the injury which may follow, and no doubt has now and then followed, upon severe physical exertion represents but a small fraction when compared with the undoubted benefits which accrue from moderate and reasonable exercise.

Dr. John E. Morgan, of Manchester, in a work entitled "University Oars : a Critical Inquiry into the Health of the Men who Rowed in the Oxford and Cambridge Boatrace, from 1829 to 1869," has dealt with the effect of violent exercise, as illustrated by racing in boats, upon the general health.

His evidence shows that such exercise is, in the great majority of instances, no other than beneficial ; that it is not a cause of disease or of premature death ; and that, out of the large number of individuals dealt with, in only the insignificant proportion of 6 per cent. could any permanent ill effect be claimed to have followed the pursuits of earlier years. In most of these cases even the evidence that rowing was to blame was indefinite or doubtful.

Mr. Walter Rye, the well-known authority on cross-country running, writes thus : "We can speak from an experience now covering nearly twenty years, and can positively say that we know of no man of the hundreds with whom we have been acquainted who has been injured by distance-running, and the rate of mortality among running men is singularly small."

Similar evidence has been given by others with regard to forms of athletic exercise which may be considered to be violent.

Certain specific effects which may follow upon excessive or unsuitable exercise will now be considered.

The Heart and Blood-vessels.

The heart has been ruptured during very violent exertion, as in attempting to lift or support an immense weight. This has happened to men of great muscular strength, but more often to the feeble, the ill-conditioned or the aged.

Excessive exercise may lead also to hypertrophy of the heart, to dilatation of its cavities, and to valvular disease. The cases of hypertrophy appear to be most usual in the athletic, and in those whose employments involve constant severe labor—e. g., blacksmiths, miners, etc. In the matter of dilatation of the heart, Dr. W. Osler writes (Pepper's "Medicine," vol. iii. p. 631) : "Overtraining and heart-strain are closely connected with the question of excessive dilatation during severe muscular effort. Both mean the same thing in many cases. A man, perhaps not in very good condition, calls upon his heart for much extra work during a race or the ascent of a very steep mountain, and is seized with cardiac pain and a feeling of distension in the epigastrium, and the rapid breathing continues an unusual time, but the symptoms pass off after a night's quiet. An attempt to repeat the exercise is followed by another attack, and, indeed, an attack of cardiac dyspnœa may come on while he is at rest. For months such a man may be unfitted for severe exertion or may be permanently incapacitated. He has overstrained his heart and has become broken-winded."

Hæmorrhages of various kinds have resulted from, or have been ascribed to, violent exertion, and have been met with in almost all parts of the body. Cases of cerebral and of spinal apoplexy have occurred during extreme exertion, and Lagrange mentions an instance in which the spinal veins underwent rupture and led to paraplegia.

ANEURYSM.

The part played by exercise in the production of aneurysm is definite, but at the same time not necessarily predominating. In addition to violent movement come the factors of actual injury to the vessel, constitutional diseases, especially syphilis, and the conditions which lead to chronic arteritis. The author once saw a popliteal aneurysm in an acrobat of twenty-eight, who was in perfect health, and who considered it had been developed by the practice of hanging by the knees from one trapeze while he caught his companion, who was swinging from another. In this case great and well-localized pressure was exerted upon the ham. The form of exercise which appears to be most effective in the production of aneurysm is violent intermittent exercise, or sudden exercise when out of condition, or such actions as involve extreme movements of certain articulations.

Aneurysm is much more common in men than in women, and in the laboring than in the favored classes. It is noteworthy that in the etiology

of aneurysm age plays a conspicuous part. Aneurysm is *not* most common
at the age when violent physical exercises are most usually indulged in, but it
is most frequent in individuals who have reached or have passed middle life.
The occurrence of aneurysm under these circumstances affords another argument against the folly of violent and extreme exertion in men who are over
thirty, especially when they are out of condition.

VARICOSE VEINS.

The frequently repeated statement that varicose veins in the lower limbs
are produced and maintained by exercise is based upon very questionable
foundations. It is said upon equally questionable grounds that those who
indulge in running, bicycling, riding or exercise involving long standing, are
in great risk of developing varicose veins. It is quite true that dilated veins
are met with among athletes, runners and bicyclists; but it has not been
shown that the condition is more common among them than it is with other
individuals, and on the other hand, it is easy to produce any number of professional runners, athletes, gymnasts, and others who are constantly practicing
the very exercises which are said to produce varicose veins, and yet have not
an enlarged vein in either of their lower limbs.

It is remarkable, moreover, that varicose veins are so much more common
among women than among men, and that they are very often met with in
women who take little or no exercise. There is, in fact, evidence to show
that exercise has little if anything to do with the production of the disease;
that the trouble is due to certain congenital defects in the vessels themselves, and that when such defect does exist, muscular exertion may tend to
increase the abnormal condition. This view is very strongly insisted upon
by Mr. Bennett in his elaborate monograph upon "Varicose Veins" (London,
1889). He shows that there is a distinct hereditary history in more than
50 per cent. of the cases. His cases prove that the trouble occurs in the
active and the sedentary, in the weak and the strong, in the short and the
tall. In females pregnancy and constipation play a conspicuous part in the
etiology. Bennett is unable to connect the occupation of the patient in any
definite degree with the actual production of the disease. While exercise
probably has nothing to do with originating varices, it certainly tends to
increase the trouble when it exists. Running, walking, jumping, cycling,
and forms of exercise and recreation involving long standing, are noteworthy
in their ill effects upon varicose veins. Indulgence in these exercises would

be unwise for those who are the actual subjects of the disease, but the fear of enlarged veins should never be an obstacle in the way of a free pursuit of the sports mentioned, nor can the possibility of varicose veins be legitimately urged as an argument against these sports.

THE LUNGS.

Hæmoptysis and emphysema are stated to have been produced by violent exertion, and many chronic lung troubles have no doubt followed upon exposure and neglect during and after such exertion. Dr. Parkes states that congestion of the lungs may follow upon excessive or badly arranged exercise.

BONES AND MUSCLES.

Bones have been fractured by pure muscular violence, notably the clavicle and humerus, but in the majority of such instances the bone has proved to have been diseased at the seat of fracture.

Violent exercise may lead to all kinds of lesions of the muscles. Muscles may be ruptured in whole or in part, tendons may be rent across or torn away from the bone, or may be displaced from the grooves in which they lie. In many instances the subject of these lesions is out of condition, or is in feeble health or aged, or is suffering from definite disease.

The Hon. E. Lyttleton well says (" Health Exhibition Manuals," vol. x. p. 121) : "To an athlete the first premonition of coming old age is to sprain himself somewhere."

Muscles which are over-exercised for a considerable time waste and become soft. The legs of professional runners are occasionally quite atrophied from over-use of the muscles of the parts.

The abuse of certain movements and the excessive repetition of the same may lead to some permanent contraction of the muscles concerned. Thus in professional gymnasts who use the flexors of the arm to excess, the elbow may be found to be a little flexed and full extension of the joint to be impossible. Sailors on sailing vessels who are constantly holding or hauling ropes not infrequently develop a condition of the hand which prevents full extension of the fingers.

The finer muscles when unreasonably employed may become the subject of such nervous changes as are illustrated by writer's cramp and other forms of spasm incident to certain employments.

Joints may be injured by violent exertion. Synovitis may follow upon

over-use of an articulation, and one very common accident among the athletic
is a displaced semi-lunar cartilage in the knee-joint.

Certain deformities of the body may follow restricted and often repeated
exercises and the excessive employment of certain muscles. Gymnasts who
have developed to an extreme degree the muscles of the upper limbs and
upper half of the trunk have a rounded back in addition to their unwieldy
shoulders.

Fencing tends to produce a lateral curvature of the spine, with (in right-
handed fencers) the concavity of the curve to the right. The author has
observed a permanent degree of lordosis in an acrobat who produced extraordinary results by his power of bending the body backwards at the lumbar
region.

HERNIA.

The influence of muscular exertion in the etiology of hernia is so fully dealt
with in the ordinary text-books of surgery that it need not be considered at
length in this place.

In cases of congenital hernia and in such other forms as depend upon defects in the vaginal process of the peritoneum, and in those instances of hernia
generally which are met with in young children, the rupture is made manifest
by some expulsive effort as a rule, and not by any movements that can be
considered as constituting exercise.

Acquired herniæ are beyond doubt produced by forces tending to cause
the intestines to protrude.

Violent effort is a recognized factor in the production of these ruptures. It
is very rarely indeed, however, the sole factor. Certain anatomical conditions
are present which render a hernia possible in one man and almost impossible
in another.

It is noteworthy that the main safeguard against hernia is a perfect and
vigorous muscular development. The greater number of examples of acquired
hernia are met with, not only in men of imperfect muscular development,
but in individuals who are out of condition. Such herniæ are commoner in
those who return to laborious work after an illness or when in feebler health,
in men who undertake heavy work without any preliminary training, in persons who by reason of their age or their habits are losing muscular tone, are
becoming coarse, soft and flabby, are developing fat within the abdomen, and
who exhibit the phenomena of relaxed tissue. Gymnasts and acrobats, in
spite of the immense muscular effort they put forth, are seldom the subjects

of hernia. If they become ruptured, the hernia will appear late in their career, at a time when they are falling off and losing tone, or at any period when they are out of condition and out of training.

Carefully selected, systematic and well-graduated exercise is the best protection against hernia, and the objections against athletics founded upon the production of hernia are unjust and unsound. An acquired umbilical hernia is unknown in muscular men with firm abdominal walls. It is common in those who have large, flabby and pendulous bellies and who take no exercise at all. So far as acquired hernia is concerned, it would be more accurate to state that rupture is due to want of excercise rather than to excessive indulgence in the same.

TRAINING.

With " training " in the sense of preparing the body for athletic competitions and great feats of endurance the present article has no concern. The subject may be considered only in so far as it throws light upon the mode of living which may be observed by those who are anxious to get themselves into condition and to take a considerable amount of moderate exercise.

Upon this subject a number of books, pamphlets, and articles have been written, and, it must be confessed, a great deal of nonsense promulgated.

Strange elements of superstition and gross ignorance have entered into the older methods of training, and there are still professional athletes who keep the details of their training secret, or who ascribe their success to some article of food or some particular rite or observance.

The old system of training was quite remarkable. The unfortunate man had his weight reduced by profuse sweating, especially by walking and running in thick and heavy clothes. He was purged every day, he was almost starved in the matter of water, and took sparingly of old ale, spirits, and port. He lived mainly upon half-cooked beefsteaks and bread, and was encouraged to gorge himself upon this monotonous diet.

Matters are now entirely changed, so far, at least, as amateur athletes are concerned, and without entering into detail as to the exact methods practiced by one modern system or another, the general features of a reasonable mode of training may be briefly discussed.

In the first place time must be considered. "A man of twenty-five and upwards," writes Mr. Woodgate, "who has been lying by for months, or it may be for a year or two, can do with three months of training. The first half should be less severe than the last. He can get into 'hunting' condition in the first six weeks, and progress to 'racing' condition in the succeeding six. University crews train from five to six weeks. College crews cannot give much more than three weeks to train for the summer bumping races."

During training a man's life must be as regular as a clock; his meals must be taken to the minute; his exercises must be systematized and so adjusted as to be progressive and well-timed. He should retire to bed early and rise early, should sleep in a well-ventilated room, should bathe night and morning, should be particular as to the kind of clothing worn, and take every precaution to avoid cold. In all things he should be moderate and methodical. His meals are best represented by a substantial breakfast, a light lunch, a still lighter tea, and a substantial dinner in the evening when his day's work is over. He should take plenty of sleep. He should rest after each meal. Smoking should be absolutely forbidden, and no form of alcohol should be allowed. There is overwhelming evidence to support the practice of training upon water. In the matter of diet a man should be moderate, should not gorge himself, and should, within certain limits, consult his own taste in the selection of food.

He will do best with the most easily digested foods, and may take beef, mutton, chicken, fish, and game, while he should avoid pork and veal and lobster, and other well-accredited producers of dyspepsia. He should under no circumstances be debarred from eating fat and butter. A man in training needs a good supply of carbon in his food.

It is well to avoid much sloppy food, such as soups and broths, to be very moderate in the consumption of starchy foods and of sugar, to avoid coarse vegetables and large quantities of potatoes. Some green vegetables and some fruit should be taken every day. It is needless to say that he should avoid pastry and sweets, and the confused and uncertain forms of food known as entrées. Cheese may well be omitted from his dietary, and salad take a constant place. Meat will be eaten at breakfast, lunch, and dinner.

In the matter of liquids, he should not drink for the sake of drinking. He should take as much only as is needed to quench his thirst, and he should not consider the time of his drinking. The custom of allowing men to drink only a certain quantity of water at certain fixed times of the day is obviously silly. A man should drink when he is thirsty, and should not be compelled to suffer with a parched mouth simply because the drinking hour has not come. Men differ immensely in the quantity of fluid they need.

The matter cannot be settled by rule. It may be taken as certain that the least quantity is consumed when taken in small amounts and often, and not when the individual has been tortured with thirst and swallows a quart or more when his time for drinking comes.

Under a reasonable and liberal system of training, no man should break down or become, as the expression goes, "stale."

The old system of training was rather a test of strength than a means of developing it, and those who train in modern times should make themselves familiar with the follies of those who trained in days gone by.

SPECIFIC EXERCISES.

WALKING

Is the most usual, the most simple, the most easy, and one of the most valuable modes of taking exercise. It is suited for individuals of all ages and of all states of development. It is the main exercise of the quite young child, a prominent feature in the training of the athlete, and usually the only form of exercise indulged in by the aged.

It is a mode of exercise which requires neither apparatus nor special locality, and there can be few so engaged in the pursuit of living as to find a legitimate excuse for not indulging in this simple means of keeping the body in health.

While walking exercises mainly the muscles of the legs, it brings into play also the muscles of the loin and of the back and abdomen. Not only has the individual to move, he has also to keep erect. The circulation and respiratory movements are increased, and the general beneficial effects of exercise are brought about.

The actual mechanics of walking and the precise nature and extent of the movements involved are admirably illustrated by the photographs published by Mr. Eadweard Muybridge, of Philadelphia. Certain of these are reproduced with a very lucid explanation in Keating's "Cyclopædia of the Diseases of Children" (Vol. iv., 1891)

Walking is distinct from marching, in which a less easy attitude of the body is maintained. Other things being equal, slow walking is more tiring than walking at a moderate pace.

It is important that the style of walking be cultivated, that the spine be kept straight, the head erect, and the shoulders well back. An easy and perfectly graceful mode of walking is not common among civilized people. The countryman rolls along walking from his hips, the over-dressed lady steps stiffly and gingerly like an automaton, the untrained lad slouches in a manner well termed slovenly.

A purposeless walk, such as is the common exercise and often the only exercise in ladies' schools, where the pupils walk in procession, side by side, over a stated distance, is somewhat depressing and does not develop the exercise to its fullest. Walking with an object represents the best and most pleasant form of this element in physical training. Shooting involves, not only the delights and excitement of sport, and the use of the hands and arms, but also a long walk over often irregular and difficult ground. The admirable game of golf, which is said to date from the time of Edward III., represents one of the very best forms of walking with an object. This game has a fascination both for the young and the old, and is one of the most perfect, and in every way the most admirable form of exercise for men who are past middle life or have reached old age.

Walking races are contests more or less of endurance, and test rather the staying powers than the skill or the muscular strength of the competitor. Many professional walkers walk vilely. In walking for a race, " it is absolutely necessary," writes a great authority (Mr. Shearman), "to have the muscles so hard all over the body that ' knocking off' for any space of time becomes fatal to all chances of success."

In walking competitions the mile has been covered in 6 minutes 23 seconds, three miles in 20 minutes 21½ seconds, twenty miles in less than 3 hours, and fifty miles in less than 8 hours.

RUNNING

Is the exercise for children and young people. It employs the muscles of nearly the whole of the body, and, by increasing the rate and depth of the respirations, is an admirable element in developing the chest. Children appear to be the subjects of an irresistible impulse to run, an impulse that should never be checked.

Running has been described as a succession of leaps. It undoubtedly has a most beneficial effect upon the circulation of the viscera, strengthens the heart, when indulged in in moderation brings out the individual's powers of endurance as well as his strength and his capacity for rapid movement.

Muybridge's photographs show the mechanical details of the act of running very clearly. A reproduction of two of these photographs in Keating's "Cyclopædia" (*loc. cit.*) may be advantageously consulted.

Running, to any extent, as an exercise, is not advisable after the age of thirty, nor in those who have not kept themselves in practice and in sound condition. In the aged it may be ranked often as actually dangerous. The best ages for running are between eighteen and twenty five, and upon few forms of athletic exercise does age tell more certainly and accurately than in this.

So far as athletic excellence is concerned, it may be said that a runner is born, not made. There are many who would never attain a first position as runners, in spite of unlimited practice. Sprint running or sprinting is the term applied to running a short distance at top speed without a break. Three hundred yards is considered to represent the limit of sprinting distance. "In sprinting," writes Mr. Shearman, "the front muscles of the thigh which bring the leg forward are the most important factors for speed, as it is on the rapid repetition of the stride that the main result depends; in the running of longer distances the back muscles of the thigh, which effect the propulsion, bear the chief strain. Both sets of muscles are, of course, used in every race, but the longer the distance the less important the front muscles become." The sprinter, however, runs rather with his lungs and heart than with his legs. Breathlessness is *the* difficulty with which he has to contend. Thus it happens that the sprinter may be tall or short, may be a feather weight or scale at 13 stone, may have limbs like a deer or calves which would cause the envy of a footman.

Long-distance running is a matter, not only of strength, but also of endurance and lung power. Some of the best long-distance runners have been short men, very strong, light of weight, and with large and deep chests.

Hare and hounds and the paper-chase form most exciting and admirable forms of running. The sport, however, is only open to those who are young, who are in perfect condition, and who have increased the distances they have run from time to time by gradual steps.

For children a hoop forms one of the most popular means of giving a purpose to running and of infusing interest into what in the abstract is a somewhat monotonous form of exercise.

On the racing track 100 yards have been covered in 10 sec., and 300 yards in 30 sec. A mile has been completed in 4 min., 12¾ sec., three miles in 14 min., 29 sec., twenty miles in a few minutes short of two hours, and fifty miles in a little short of six hours.

JUMPING,

Like running, has certain very definite age limits. Jumping in competitions is limited to individuals under thirty or more usually under twenty-five. Twenty may be taken as the best age. In jumping, the muscles of the lower limb are of course mainly employed, but in addition to these it will be noticed that nearly every muscle in the body is in action as the leap is taken. The details of the movement are well shown in Muybridge's photographs (*see* Keatings "Cyclopedia," vol. iv., photo. v.).

A jumper of any excellence is, like a runner, born, not made. Celebrated jumpers, especially long jumpers, have been of almost any size and weight. W. B. Page, who cleared a height of 6 ft. 3 ¼ in., was only 5 ft. 6 in. in height.

Jumping as an element of physical education has some especial points of value. It encourages very vigorous, instantaneous and well co-ordinated muscular contractions, and cultivates that form of muscle intelligence which is called spring.

I am of opinion that jumping is not quite the exercise for women, or for young girls who have passed the period of puberty. Certain uterine troubles have with some show of reason been ascribed to an indulgence in this exercise. For flabby people and young subjects who are disposed to be stout, and for any who are not in very sound condition, the exercise is not without risk. It may well be left to lads and to youths in the prime of athletic life.

In the high jump 6 ft. 3 ¼ in. have been cleared, and in the long jump the remarkable distance of 23 ft. 2 in.

Allied to jumping must be considered the exercise of skipping. A more admirable and more perfect form of exercise, considering its simplicity, could not be practiced. It employs the muscles, not only of the legs and loins, but also of the back, abdomen, and neck, and even the muscles of the arms; it especially tends to strengthen the ankles and knees and the arches of the foot; it is admirable for children with weak backs; it increases the respiratory movements to a marked extent; and if practiced upon grass and in the open air it is one of the most perfect forms of exercise for young girls that could be devised.

Those who consider skipping too simple and too trivial to form a serious element in a physical education may be surprised to know that many athletes and gymnasts, and notably, it must be owned, prize fighters, take a very large part of the exercise prescribed during training by means of the skipping-rope.

It would be well if those parents who consider that nothing in the way of physical training can be done without a gymnasium or a drill-sergeant would invest in a hoop and a skipping-rope and take note of the effect produced by these simple means.

A skipping competition upon a lawn or in a field is, when kept within limits, one of the most perfect forms of recreation a girl can indulge in. It should be carried out in slippers or light shoes, and if it were a little more popular, the feeble ankles and flat feet which are so common among girls and women would certainly be less often met with.

SKATING

Is another admirable exercise, especially valuable from the fact that it can be practiced at a time when few forms of outdoor recreation are possible, and when girls and women are apt to sit at home and huddle over a fire or weary themselves by dancing, until the small hours of the morning, in a heated ball-room.

Skating is a form of modified walking, but it calls into play a greater variety of muscles. The balance has to be maintained and the muscles of the abdomen, back and loins have much to do. It is exhilarating, it is admirably adapted for persons of almost all ages, and is as well suited for females as for males ; it comes at a time when the want of exercise in the open air is probably telling upon the health and spirits, it tends to give an easy and graceful carriage to the body ; it strengthens the ankles, and is a fine antidote for the flimsier form of nervousness. No mode of progression upon the feet is more delightful, easy or invigorating. In a country house, when every form of indoor amusement has been exhausted, when the roads are too dirty for walking and the ground too heavy for pleasant riding, a hard black frost comes as a boon, and the manner in which the young and the old, the strong and the frail, turn out and hurry to the ice, gives the impression that the instinct for exercise in human beings is as strong as the impulse which leads the duckling to the water.

In racing, the following distances have been covered in the times named : 100 yards in 10 sec., one mile in 3 min., 26 sec. ; three miles in 10 min., 33 sec. ; twenty miles in 1 hr., 14 min ; fifty miles in 4 hrs., 13 min.

RIDING

Is a mode of taking exercise and fresh air which is not open to all, and is within certain narrow limits denied to the inhabitants of cities.

The muscles exercised in riding are those mainly of the adductor segment of the thigh and of the back. The movement undoubtedly improves the visceral circulation and affords a remedy for hepatic congestion and constipation ; it promotes a deeper respiration and a more active pulse ; it combines in a remarkable manner both active and passive movement and is a specific for the dyspepsia and other ills which attend a sedentary life ; it provides a means of strengthening the spine, and it should be remembered that a good "seat" implies rather the power of keeping the trunk well balanced than the power of gripping the saddle with strong adductor musles.

It is a pursuit that can be indulged in from childhood to old age, and it is one of the most popular forms of exercise among Englishwomen.

Children should learn young and should be well taught. The exercise is not good for girls with commencing lateral curvature, nor should it be taken up by children who have "outgrown their strength," and are tall, weedy, and of feeble muscular development, until the muscles have been strengthened by other methods. Overgrown girls who indulge in no other exercise but riding are apt to become round-shouldered and round-backed and to acquire a very ungraceful seat. Lateral curvature of the spine is certainly often induced and fostered by riding.

In any instance a young girl should be taught to ride upon either side of the saddle, and this precaution should be especially observed in the case of those who are supposed to have weak backs. After a very long ride a man feels most tired in the lower part of his spine, and is very disposed to loll in the saddle. In a young girl the most important muscular strain comes upon the back, and is concerned in keeping the body erect.

It is not uncommon to see girls, who have been badly taught, riding with the body much bent to one side, or with the spine "all in a heap," and in the attitude of cyphosis. Riding is not the best kind of exercise for the round-shouldered and for such girls as have unequally developed chests.

Horse exercise, so far as ladies are concerned, is a little hampered by the fashion which demands that a riding habit should fit like a glove, and that, as a consequence, the waist should be compressed so as to reach fashionable proportions. The long skirt of the riding habit adds not a little to the danger of horse exercise for women.

Riding forms an admirable exercise for men who have reached or have passed middle life, and the saddle is very often the last thing that an old sporting man relinquishes as infirmity creeps on.

Professional horsemen (grooms, postilions, jockeys, etc.) are apt to develop a certain deformity of the lower limbs and back. The legs tend to become concave or bowed, and seem often to have been stunted in growth. The back—especially in jockeys—tends to become arched and rounded, and the shoulders high. An old ostler and an old jockey have often a quite characteristic figure and attitude.

The deformity, such as it is, is evidently the result of style in riding, as it is not observed in artillerymen and other cavalry soldiers.

SWIMMING

Should be taught as a matter of routine to every child, and it is a disgrace to this country that this very simple accomplishment is so rare. Swimming is easily learned at any age, and when once mastered is never forgotten. It is acquired nearly as quickly by girls as by boys, and the first lessons may be given between the ages of eight and ten.

Swimming calls into use a new set of muscles, or rather a new combination of muscles. In the early struggles of the learner an immense amount of force is expended in carrying out the unaccustomed movements. As proficiency is attained the movement becomes easier and easier, until it is as simple as walking, and the limits of the swimmer's powers are restrained rather by the temperature of the water than by his muscles.

Few modes of exercise are more enjoyable, especially when practiced in a broad river or the open sea.

The muscles of both the upper and lower extremities are concerned, and to a lesser degree the muscles of the back and abdomen. The scapular muscles, the deltoid, the pectorals, and, above all, the latissimus dorsi, are especially employed in swimming. The arms tire before the legs, and the sense of exhaustion is always experienced most about the shoulder.

Work in a gymnasium is an excellent means of developing the swimming muscles, and, so far as long distances are concerned, the chief factors are strong arms and a good chest.

Swimming increases the respiratory movements and straightens the back. The movements of the limbs are very free, and afford a striking contrast to most of the other forms of exercise which concern the lower limbs.

Swimming should be well taught. Considering the facilities afforded in this country for acquiring the art, it is astounding that among those who do swim a fine and easy style of swimming is so rare.

Probably some 70 per cent. of those who can swim can just "swim a little," and can not do more than keep themselves afloat by extravagant movements for fifty or a hundred yards.

I do not think that the practicing of the swimming movements on land is of much value, although it forms a great feature in the gymnastic course in France.

The most remarkable swimming feat was that of Matthew Webb, who swam from Dover to Calais in 21 hours 45 minutes. In a race 100 yards has been covered in 1 minute 6 seconds.

FENCING

In the Badminton Library volume on fencing, the history of this art is detailed, together with the circumstances and manner of its development, and to the account is appended a quite remarkable bibliography of the subject.

Fencing, as it is at present practiced, is an extremely scientific, precise, and highly elaborated art. It is no mere slashing with a protected foil. Every move has been systematized ; every method of attack and defence has its individual name. The movements are as complex, and yet as well defined, as the movements of the men upon a chess-board. No mode of exercise has reached a more elaborate degree of finish. Fencing is pre-eminently an exercise of skill. Considerable employment is given to all the muscles of the body, to the lower limbs, and to the back, but principally, it is needless to say, to the right or sword arm. The beginner will, after his first few lessons, ache from head to foot. He will believe that he has been fencing with every muscle he possessed, a belief which will be well founded. As, however, he becomes more proficient, he will feel that the strain falls to a great extent upon the right upper extremity.

Fencing is as much an exercise of the brain as of the muscles. He who has acquired some proficiency in the art will find that he becomes tired in his brain and cord rather than in his limbs. The bout induces rather a nerve than a muscle fatigue.

Fencing develops certain faculties in an admirable manner. It requires quickness of eye, extreme readiness of action, accurate muscular sense, great precision and fineness of movement, and perfect powers of ready co-ordination. It involves the practice of a quick decision, a rapid judgment, and a good memory. A fool could never become a good fencer, even if he were endowed with the most excellent physical qualifications.

Fencing has become more popular of late years, and is an excellent exercise for busy men. It is to be regretted that the practice often takes place in somewhat ill-ventilated rooms. Fencing for elder children and for ladies forms, as it is usually practised, but a somewhat imperfect development of the proper art. It is not the exercise which would be recommended to excitable, nervous, or overworked children. It is better adapted for those who appear to be apathetic or dull. A dull boy will find a fencing lesson an infinitely greater "fag" than whole pages of irregular verbs.

It should never form for children, or indeed for adults, an exclusive or even predominant form of exercise, on account of the unequal muscular development it encourages. It is well suited to encourage in lads and in elder girls a good carriage, free movements, a lissom and graceful attitude of the body, great agility, and both muscular and mental quickness. If it is possible to make an individual "sharp," fencing may be considered as capable of doing it.

The exercise must be recommended with great care. It would be injurious to those who have a disposition to lateral curvature, and to any who are the subjects of unequal muscular development.

In the physical education of the young it can occupy but a small space. It is a perfect exercise for adults, especially for men who lead sedentary and monotonous lives. Dr. Lagrange asserts that "every one who has fenced *much* shows, in a more or less pronounced degree, a lateral curvature of the spine." In right-handed fencers the concavity of the curvature is to the right, in the left-handed to the left. The shoulder of the arm which holds the foil is lowered. Dr. Lagrange founds his conclusions upon the examination of twenty experienced fencers. The tendencies to deformity are very unequally marked. In some the deviations are quite trivial, in others they are pronounced. This evidence is of considerable importance in forming an estimate of the value of fencing as a muscular exercise, especially to those who are under twenty or twenty-five years of age.

BOXING,

If carried out under proper conditions, and especially if practiced in the open air, is an admirable exercise for lads and young men. Unfortunately, the surroundings of a boxing saloon are not always the best adapted for the education of youth, and the so-called "professors" of the art are not usually the best associates for plastic minded lads.

The exercise itself, however, is admirable. It brings into play practically all the muscles of the body. A vigorous blow is struck as much from the leg and trunk as from the arm. It has been well said that a good and powerful blow starts from the foot. Mitchell, in the monograph upon boxing, in the Badminton Library series, says: "It may seem paradoxical and provoke a smile to say that the first necessity for using the fists properly is to understand the use of the feet." The boxer needs to be agile, to be able to use his legs, to be quick with the movements of his head and his trunk. Boxing, moreover, gives excellent use to the left arm, which is apt to be neglected in many other forms of exercise. It calls for rapidity of movement, ready decision, good judgment, and a control of the temper. It promotes the circulation, and in a vigorous round the boxer is very soon rendered breathless.

The atmosphere in a boxing saloon is not always so well supplied with fresh air as it might be.

BOATING.

It may perhaps be said, without fear of contradiction, that boating presents one of the most complete, uniform and delectable forms of exercise. It is an exercise which is especially associated with the English, and it is in England that the sport is the most highly elaborated and the most widely practised. Boats of one form or another appear among the environment of such primitive peoples as have lived by the sea or about the banks of navigable rivers; but the development of boating as a fine art, the perfecting of this picturesque and enjoyable mode of locomotion, rests with the sturdy and water-loving sons of England. Surrounded on all sides by the sea, and living in a land permeated by many rivers, it is not unnatural that an English lad should take to the water like a duck, and should feel that enthusiastic love for the sea which appears to be almost an hereditary taste, and which is possibly not a little influenced by the great naval records of the country.

For every professional rowing man in our midst there will be hundreds of amateurs who are by no means a discredit to the sport. At all public schools situated within reach of water, rowing is a prominent feature of school life. At the two great universities of Oxford and Cambridge, boating occupies a position which the less robust section of the public are apt to consider a little too conspicuous. The whole length of the Thames, from Oxford to London, during the few months of the English summer, is alive with boats, and is animated by rowers of all classes and all ages. Among this busy, sun-browned, and white-flanneled community, may be seen old men and maidens, as well as young men and children.

The sheer delight given by the mere circumstances of boating requires little comment. It needs merely the conception of a stretch of fair water, the early morning of a day in the English summer, a light outrigger and a pair of sculls, to every point of which the sculler has fitted his muscles. There is the crisp grasp of the water, the swish of the blades, the shooting of the tiny craft across the polished river, the whistling of the wind about the rower's head, and the rippling of the water as the prow runs through the magic lights and shadows which are thrown from the bank.

Boating offers, moreover, one of the most charming forms of touring. A man may spend many summer holidays in a boat or in a canoe before he has exhausted the beauties of the rivers of Great Britain.

Across the Channel, the system of canals on the continent offers an unparalleled opportunity for a journey such as has been described—as no other pen could have described it—by R. Louis Stevenson in his "Inland Voyage."

It is greatly to the credit of England that her waterways are more densely peopled with boating folk than are the waters of any other country of like population.

With regard to boats, it is only necessary to say that for racing the keelless boat is employed. Its bottom is round and smooth. Such a boat is extremely unsteady, and requires all the skill of a novice to "sit it." The beginner may find no difficulty in propelling such a boat, but he will experience considerable difficulty in keeping in it. The sculler in a racing boat has, like the bicyclist, first to balance himself and then to move.

The outrigger was introduced in 1842 by Clasper.

This very simple improvement enables a greatly increased length and greater advantage in leverage to be given to the oars, while at the same time it allows the dimensions of the racing craft, and especially of the beam, to be much reduced. The ordinary length of an unrigged pair-oared pleasure boat or gig is 22 ft., and the beam 3 ft. 9 in. The length of a racing sculling boat will be about 31 ft., and the beam about 11 inches.

Another noteworthy improvement—the invention of an American—was the sliding seat, which was first used in England in a race in 1871. The general features of the sliding seat will be sufficiently familiar. Its precise mechanical value has been very ably described by the Rev. E. Warre, of Eton, in the following words :—

"Mechanically speaking, in rowing the water is the fulcrum, the boat is the weight to be moved, the oar is the lever, and the man applies the power. The leverage is most powerful when applied at right angles to the weight; but in the problem to be solved, owing to the motion of the oar itself through the water and the motion of the boat through the water, the moment at which this can be the case is extremely transient. Could any satisfactory mechanism be devised by which the weight—that is, the thowl against which he rows—could be moved forward during the stroke, while the oarsman was still in the position to exert his full power against it, we might expect a great increase of speed. This, however, is a structural problem not yet solved. But the sliding seat in some measure answers the purpose by enabling the oarsman or sculler to continue his physical effort by the straightening of his legs in such a way that his power and his weight, which are most available at the beginning of the stroke, are operating in the water for a longer period during each stroke than could be if he were on a fixed seat. The gain is much less than that of a moving rowlock would be, because, owing to the rising of the knees when the slider is forward, a man cannot obtain a much greater reach forward than he could on a fixed seat. It is when the body has moved up towards the perpendicular, and the water has already been got hold of, that the advantage of the sliding seat begins. As the slider moves back, the uncoiling of the human spring, which is imbedded in the stretcher, can go on with undiminished force for the distance of the slide, when the pressure of the legs ceases and the weight of the body is again entirely thrown on the seat. The mechanical advantage is here mostly after the rowlock, and that is the least valuable part of the stroke, especially in a light boat. Still the gain is considerable, as it enables more weight and more strength to be applied to the oar for a longer portion of the stroke.

" Further, there has been for grown men a physical gain in that the increased length of stroke enables the same pace to be attained with fewer strokes per minute. The pace of the inferior or mediocre crews accordingly has been improved. Moreover, the effort of springing the body forward to its fullest reach, which on the fixed seat was necessary, is now greatly reduced by the mechanism of the slide, and consequently the exertion to heart and lungs is much less. This is a gain to those who, by reason of age and figure, are not so lithe and active as in boyhood, but it has been a loss to public school crews, who could make up formerly by pace of stroke and agility for their inferiority in strength to men."[*]

Health Exhibition Handbooks, vol. x.

The sliding seat is estimated to give a gain of about 18 in. in the length of the stroke upon a 9 in. slide.

"The sliding seat," writes Mr. Woodgate, in the Badminton Library volume on Boating, "decidedly relieves the abdominal muscles and respiratory organs during the recovery. The point wherein a tiring oarsman first gives way is in his recovery, because of the relative weakness of the muscles which conduct that portion of the action of the stroke. It therefore is obvious that any contrivance which can enable a man to recover with less exertion to himself will enable him to do more work in the stroke over the whole course, and still more so if the very contrivance which aids recovery also gives extra power to the stroke."

The increase in speed has not been so great as might have been imagined.

Rowing and Sculling.

Rowing, it is needless to say, involves the pulling of one oar with both hands, and sculling the pulling of a pair of sculls, employing, of course, one hand to each.

The details of the stroke in rowing should be well understood in order that the muscular features of the act might be recognized and the qualities of a good stroke appreciated. The following description of the rowing stroke by the Rev. E. Warre is precise and lucid, and can hardly be improved upon :—

"The moment the oar touches the body, drop the hands smartly straight down, then turn the wrists sharply and at once shoot out the hands in a straight line to the front, inclining the body forward from the thigh joints and simultaneously bring up the slider, regulating the time by the swing forward of the body according to the stroke. Let the chest and stomach come well forward, the shoulders be kept back, the inside arm be straightened, the inside wrist a little raised, the oar grasped in the hands, but not pressed upon more than is necessary to maintain the blade in its proper straight line as it goes back, the head kept up, the eyes fixed on the outside shoulder of the man before you. As the body and arms come forward to their full extent, the wrists having been quickly turned, the hands must be raised sharply, and the blade of the oar brought to its full depth at once. At that moment, without the loss of a thousandth part of a second, the whole weight of the body must be thrown on to the oar and the stretcher by the body springing back, so that the oar may catch hold of the water sharply and be driven through it by a force unwavering and uniform. As soon as the oar has got hold of the water, and the beginning of the stroke has been effected as described, flatten the knees. and so, using the muscles of the legs, keep up the pressure of the beginning uniform through the backward motion of the body. Let the arms be rigid at the beginning of the stroke. When the body reaches the perpendicular, let the elbows be bent and dropped close past the sides to the rear—the shoulders dropping and disclosing the chest to the front, the back, if anything, curved inwards rather than outwards, but not strained in any way. The body, in fact, should assume a natural upright sitting posture, with the shoulders well thrown back. In this position the oar should come to it and the feather commence."

Among the particulars to be noted in the stroke are the following. The back should be set stiff and must not yield as the stroke is pulled. It should be straight while the chest comes well forward. The whole trunk should swing as a rigid column from the hips, moving forwards and backwards. The main pull of the arms is from the shoulders. The biceps should not do the work and the elbows must be kept well to the side. If this latter point be insisted upon the stroke can scarcely be rowed home by the arm muscles. When an oarsman is becoming "pumped," it is in the recovery that he feels the strain. He fails to shoot the hands forward from the chest the moment after they touch that point, and he becomes sluggish in reaching forward to take a fresh hold of the water.

Sculling is in all essential particulars identical with rowing, so far as the muscular movements are concerned. It involves, however, more precision, more skill, more practice. The sculler has to acquire the art of balancing himself, and a failure to ever do this well leads often to a fixed bad style, which no practice appears to remove.

The remarks already made apply to rowing and to sculling in its highest developments, but in all essentials they apply to the ordinary pleasure boat. In such a boat there is no need of great speed, there is no sliding seat to embarrass an already complex movement. The boat is steady enough. and the oarsman can devote all his energies to the pulling.

It is much to be regretted that many boating men and women are content simply to pull the boat along. They care nothing about the order of their going, they are perfectly indifferent as to style, and are content for the rest of their days to row badly. To row correctly is to row with ease. The better the style, the easier the movement and the better the pace. The better the style, moreover, the more complete and perfect is the exercise. Bad rowing is often bad exercise, and to row in the atrocious manner with which some holiday-makers have made us familiar is to indulge in a pursuit of very doubtful utility.

As an exercise, sculling may be considered to be better than rowing. To all ordinary individuals boating should imply a knowledge of sculling, and no person should be content with the capacity to pull one oar.

Sculling involves a more even employment of all the muscles of the body ; one side of the body is not more extensively employed than is the other ; there is no disposition to rotate or "screw" the back, or to pull, as it were, from one side. In sculling, the muscles of the two sides of the body are equally employed, and the exercise has the great merit of being perfectly symmetrical.

The Muscles Involved.

Let us imagine a man sculling in an ordinary gig with a fixed seat. He takes a good grasp of the sculls, using fully the muscles of the hand and of the flexor side of the forearm. He throws the hands forwards to take the stroke, using the extensor muscles of the arm, the pectorals, the serratus magnus and such scapular muscles as draw the upper limb forwards. The body is at the same time thrown forwards by the contraction of the abdominal muscles, the psoas and iliacus, and some of the anterior femoral muscles. The whole back is kept stiff, and the trunk swings forwards from the hip joints only. The sculls are now drawn through the water, the muscles of the upper arm contract, together with the posterior scapular muscles and the latissimus dorsi. The main agent, however, in effecting the stroke is provided by the great mass of the extensor muscles of the back and by the powerful glutei muscles. The man rows with his back, not with his arms. In pulling, he presses the feet against the stretcher, contracting nearly all the muscles of the lower limb. In feathering, he calls into action the extensors of the forearm.

Inasmuch as the head is kept erect and the chest well thrown forward, it will be seen that sculling and rowing do actually engage all the main muscles of the body.

If a sliding seat be employed, then the exercise is still more complete and uniform, for the muscles of the lower limb are used to a still greater extent in drawing the body forward and in shooting it back. Still the main strain in rowing and sculling falls upon the muscles of the back and hip.

The mechanics of sculling can be readily studied in Muybridge's ingenious photographs, and reference may be made to the description in Keating's "Cyclopædia" (vol. iv., photo. iv.).

The idea, often expressed, that boating involves the use of the arms only, is even more ridiculous than the equally common assertion that bicycling involves the use of the legs only. A muscular man going into hard training for rowing will find that his biceps muscles will actually diminish in size.

The bad oarsman rows or sculls with his biceps. Such an individual is often to be seen in the London parks. He sits with his back limp and arched, and very probably with his legs tucked away under the thwart. He leans forwards to take the stroke, grasps the water, and pulls the sculls through simply by the action of the muscles of the upper limb and mainly by the biceps. He does not extend the trunk beyond the perpendicular, and the manner in which he projects his elbows has been caricatured often enough. The movements he executes are not those of the oarsman, and, although the half-hour's pull may be better than no exercise at all, it tends to make the individual round-shouldered and clumsy, and to develop the muscles of his arms to the sacrifice of all the others.

The Adaptabilities of Boating.

Boating properly carried out must remain one of the most perfect forms of muscular exercise we possess. The degree of muscular effort involved can be regulated to any degree, and a girl of eleven may scull with as much style as an athlete of twenty.

Boating is an exercise which does not cause breathlessness. An elderly man can pull a boat day after day on a long river tour without difficulty, provided the pace be moderate, when he would be utterly out of breath on ascending a hill or even a great flight of stairs. It can be indulged in by individuals with weak hearts and weak lungs, provided, of course, that the pace is strictly moderate.

Boating is not suited for the subjects of hernia nor for those with a disposition to hernia. The posture assumed in leaning forwards to take the stroke and the contraction of the abdominal muscles at the same time favor a hernial protrusion.

Boating, however, tends to develop and to strengthen the abdominal muscles, and to lessen the size and improve the tone of the pendulous abdomen not uncommon after middle life.

Rowing and sculling are admirable exercises for girls and women. Ladies should row without corsets, or with corsets of the slenderest possible make. Perhaps no exercise is better suited to remedy the muscular defects which are conspicuous in the gentler sex. It expands the chest, strengthens the back, and gives tone to the muscles of the abdomen.

Boating should be recommended with certain precautions, and of course in properly selected cases to the subjects of lateral curvature of the spine, especially to those who exhibit the deformity in its early condition.

Such individuals should scull, not row. All those who take to boating should first learn to swim. Boys may begin to learn to row at six, and girls at eight. It is a matter of the utmost importance that the learner be well taught.

It is well to begin in a light half-outrigged boat which will seat two, the teacher and the pupil. The water should be smooth. The pupil should be-gin by pulling one scull only, rowing for equal periods upon the right and the left side. He will in this way learn the rough details of the stroke and the rhythm of the movement. He should from the first be made to keep time.

The exercise with one scull should be brief, and the sooner the pupil takes to both sculls the better. There is usually much difficulty with the left hand.

As soon as the pupil can scull moderately well he should row behind a good oarsman, and in this way he will pick up the swing of the movement and the proper points of the stroke.

Sea Rowing is inferior to river rowing as an exercise : the boat is heavy, the gunwale is high out of the water, the stroke is short, and the movement is not susceptible of the finish possible in a river boat.

Those who have rowed much on the sea will probably never row well on the river. The exercise involves more muscular exertion, which is, however, of a rougher, more clumsy and unfinished kind. To row a sea boat the in-dividual must be strong. Sea rowing is not well adapted for children or for those who are muscularly feeble ; and, while as an exercise it has admirable points, it should be borne in mind that on fresh water alone is the pursuit of boating capable of assuming its most perfect form.

Canoeing.

For the purpose of the present paper canoes may be considered to belong to two classes—the Rob Roy canoe and the Canadian.

6

In the former the canoeist sits amidships with his lower limbs extended straight upon the floor of the craft. The paddle is of considerable length, and has a blade at either end. The canoeist holds it about breast high, and drives first one blade through the water and then the other. His back is supported by a rest.

In this form of canoeing the muscular exertion involved is limited to the muscles of the arms and shoulders, including the pectorals, trapezius, serratus magnus, and latissimus dorsi. The muscles of the neck and upper part of the back are concerned, but the body below the thorax is practically motionless. The exercise, therefore, is one of limited muscular applicability.

The exercise is good for those who wish to develop the arms or who from some deformity or defect are unable to use the lower limbs. It is not an exercise to be recommended to those who aim at developing the whole muscular system, or who are the subjects of any spinal weakness.

In the Canadian canoe as adopted for use in England the canoeist sits at the extreme stern, either on the floor or upon a seat nearly flush with the gunwale, and with his feet on a stretcher. He has a short paddle with a single blade. He paddles upon one side of the craft only, and steers by manipulating the blade at the completion of each stroke. In all but the smallest form of Canadian canoe a second seat is provided close to the prow for a second paddle. The fore paddle may be shorter, and is worked at a diminished advantage, and the steering of the craft must still remain with the paddle in the stern.

The Canadian canoe involves a much more complete form of exercise than does the Rob Roy canoe. The canoeist has no support for his back. He must keep himself erect by muscular effort. In effecting the stroke he employs, not only the muscles of the upper limb, but also the muscles of the trunk. The whole body undergoes some rotation in the vertical axis at each stroke. After long paddling, a sense of exhaustion is felt in the back and about the loins, but not in the arms. The canoeist has also to balance himself, and as the Canadian canoe is carvel-built and keelless, this involves some extra muscular expenditure. The after-paddler can make considerable use of his legs, moreover; a help which is, to a great extent, denied to the paddler in the bow of the canoe. The canoeist should change his side from time to time—in other words, should not paddle for too long a time at a stretch upon one side. Paddling upon one side tends to produce much lateral bending of the vertebral column.

This exercise is not well adapted for the weakly, nor for those who have weak backs and a disposition to lateral curvature. For the robust it is admirable, and forms a very pleasant variation to rowing or sculling.

A voyage in a canoe usually involves exercise of the most varied kind: there are hard paddling against a stream, nervous steering down a rapid, the dragging of the craft over shallows and past milldams, and the very arduous task of making a way through thick rushes and weeds.

CYCLING.

The history of athletic sports provides probably no more remarkable feature than is afforded by the introduction and development of cycling. Twenty years ago the bicycle was unknown in this country. Even fifteen years ago riders upon bicycles were regarded as little other than acrobats and mountebanks. Within so short a period this form of athletic exercise has developed with almost incredible rapidity and with phenomenal vigor. Cyclists are now to be counted in tens of thousands; the sport has been taken up by individuals of all ages and in all stations of life, and has been enthusiastically patronized by women as well as by men.

The history of cycling is very admirably given by Mr. G. Lacy Hillier— himself a well-known rider—in the Badminton volume on "Cycling."

The general features of the cycles now in use must be familiar enough. There are two forms of bicycle, the "Ordinary" and the "Safety." The Ordinary represents the earlier pattern. In this machine the wheel is driven by the direct action of the pedals. The size of the wheel depends upon the height or "the reach" of the individual rider. A diameter of 50 inches will represent an average size. With this wheel the rider steers, and upon it he balances himself. In propelling this machine there is no waste of muscular force. The rider is placed directly **over** his work," or, as it would be expressed with reference to other exercises, "close to his work." No power is lost upon cog-wheels and chains, and **the weight** of the body can be admirably utilized in aiding progression.

The Safety **bicycle represents** the machine of the immediate future. The varieties of this cycle are legion, but the form most commonly used is founded upon what is known as "the Rover" pattern.

The Safety bicycle is represented by a machine with the following characters. **The two wheels** are comparatively small, and are either of equal size **or** are nearly so. The diameter of each will be about 28 or 30 inches. The front wheel is the steering-wheel, and with it the handles are connected : its movement, so far as the act of steering is concerned, is effected through a nearly horizontal joint, " the head." The hinder wheel is the driving wheel. It is not propelled by the direct action of the pedals. The pedals act upon a small cogged or toothed wheel carrying a chain, and through this chain the movement is communicated to the rear wheel. The rider sits directly over the chain-wheel to which the pedals and their cranks are attached, and is therefore placed between the two running wheels of the bicycle. The machine is said to be " geared." If the two pulley-wheels with which the chain is connected are of equal size the machine is said to be " level-geared." In such case one complete revolution of the pedal involves one complete revolution of the driving-wheel. If the pulley wheels with which the chain is connected are of unequal size, and if the wheel connected with the pedal is the larger, the machine is said to be " geared-up." In such case the pedal revolutions are fewer than the revolutions of the driving-wheel. The Safety bicycle is usually " geared up to 54 ; " that is to say, the relation between the wheel moving the chain and the wheel moved by it is such that the driving-wheel, which has an actual diameter of 28 inches, revolves at each complete turn of the pedal through a range of movement equal to that made by one complete revolution of a wheel with a diameter of 54 inches.

Some tricycles are " geared down," by which term is implied the fact that the hinder of the two pulley-wheels is the smaller, and therefore more than one revolution of the pedal is required to produce one revolution of the driving-wheel.

In this question of gearing it must be remembered that one factor of the equation, viz., the strength of the rider, is a fixed quantity, and that either speed or power must be sacrificed when the other conditions of the problem are varied. If the machine be geared up, the rider can make fewer revolutions of the pedal than would be required if the gearing were level, but he must employ more force. On the other hand, if the machine be geared down, an increased number of movements of the foot is required ; but the amount of force involved is much less. A young man of light weight or an individual of feeble muscular power may prefer to use his legs with greater activity, provided he can employ a lesser degree of muscular effort. Such an individual may prefer a cycle geared low. A man of more advanced years, of more than average weight, and of considerable muscular strength, would probably be glad to expend an undue amount of force on each stroke of the foot rather than to feel the necessity of moving his pedals rapidly. Such a rider would select a machine with a higher gearing.

While a roadster Safety will usually be geared to 54, a racer Safety of the same type may be geared to 63.

The Humber Roadster tricycle ("gents' light cripper") is geared to 57 in the maker's catalogue, the ladies' tricycle of the same pattern to 54, the corresponding racer cripper to 63.

The weight of a racing Safety may be reduced to 20 lb. complete. The weight of a racing tricycle (Humber Cripper) is given as 30 lb. A roadster Safety weighs from about 36 to 42 lb. A Roadster tricycle may scale from 45 to 56 lb.

The tricycle is well represented by the excellent machine known as the Humber Cripper. In this tricycle the front or steering wheel has a diameter of 24 in., the two driving wheels of 30 in. A single chain is employed. The saddle is placed well over the pedals, and the machine in all general features is based upon the mechanical lines of a Safety bicycle. The introduction of the ingenious ball-bearing joint to cycles of all kinds has reduced the amount of friction in running to a minimum.

The Safety bicycle if taken against any obstacle sufficient to stop the front wheel merely falls over on its side. The rider's feet are so close to the ground that it needs no very great inclination of the machine to enable him to bring one foot to the ground, and so prevent a fall.

The term "Safety" is well merited. An accident, when it occurs, is probably the fault of the rider alone, and is inexcusable. There are many who have ridden these machines for years over some thousands of miles of road, and who have yet never met with what may be termed an accident, or even a nasty fall.

One disadvantage which has been urged against all cycles is that of vibration. There is no doubt that long-continued vibration communicated to the body is injurious. It is unpleasant, it induces fatigue, and leads to earlier exhaustion of the muscles.

The effects of vibration are less felt in the young, and upon the bodies of lads under eighteen, who still possess many epiphyseal cartilages, a long-continued vibration may tell but little. But in older individuals, in those whose bodies have become more rigid in the process of development, and especially in persons with a sensitive nervous system, vibration has certainly an unfavorable effect. They return from a long ride over rough roads with an undue sense of fatigue—they feel "shaken," the back aches, the arm muscles are a little tremulous, and there often follow a headache and a sleepless night.

Vibration has been to a large extent overcome by the use of "cushion" or "pneumatic" tires, or by means of a suspending spring, such as has been introduced, with the greatest success, in what is known as the "Whippet" bicycle. The Whippet machine may be said to bear the same relation to the usual Safety bicycle which a cart with springs bears to one without springs.

The following records will give an idea of the possible speed which can be attained on a cycle :—

	Bicycle.			Tricycle.		
	h.	m.	s.	h.	m.	s.
Half-mile.		1	8		1	17
One mile		2	20		2	37
Three miles		7	40		8	6
Ten miles		26	40		28	13
Twenty miles		55	0		56	40
Fifty miles	2	25	26	2	38	44
Hundred miles	5	50	5	6	9	26

Cycling as an Exercise.

Bicycling.—A ride upon a bicycle involves not only an admirable muscular exercise, but it involves of necessity exertion in the open air. The exercise is continuous and not intermittent ; it can be regulated to any degree, and can be indulged in equally by the athlete and the weakling.

He who owns a bicycle has at his command one of the most admirable and certainly one of the least expensive means of traveling. He is dependent solely upon himself, and can without difficulty travel fifty miles a day. No horse could compete in endurance and in long distances with the bicycle rider.

Cycling has undoubtedly done more than has any other form of physical exercise to improve the bodily condition of the city clerk and the shop assistant. The lad who is pent up in a close office all day has now no difficulty in finding a means for well occupying the summer evening or the few hours at his disposal before the work of the day begins. He has merely to mount his bicycle, and in an hour he is ten miles away from the din of city life, and is breathing a clearer and brisker air. He who is an early riser can in the summer months well manage a twenty-mile ride before breakfast.

Unlike the player of cricket or football or the rowing man, the cyclist is dependent upon no one but himself. His means of exercise is always at hand, and he can occupy a spare half-hour or the entire afternoon with the same amount of preparation.

The specific features of the exercise of bicycling may best be reviewed by discussing the objections which have been urged against the sport.

1. It is said to be dangerous. This objection without doubt applied to the high wheel bicycle, but it can scarcely be said to be just as regards the more modern machine—the Safety. The rider rides with his feet but a few inches from the ground. If he is falling he has simply to step off. The machine cannot turn "head over heels;" it can merely fall upon its side. The brakes now applied to these machines are so strong that they can bring the bicycle to a standstill in a moment.

The most serious accidents have occurred in riding through crowded streets ; and unless a rider is perfect at his work, and is as quick as a hare, he is merely foolhardy if he attemps to ride through a very busy thoroughfare.

Bicycling may be said to be less dangerous than riding on horseback, especially when the distances travelled are taken into account, and to be certainly less risky than skating.

2. A second objection to the bicycle is that it is a very partial exercise, and that it involves the use of the muscles of the legs only. It may be said at once that the first difficulty of bicycle riding is not the propelling of the machine, but the maintenance of a proper balance. The learner after his half-hour exercise will not complain of aching in his legs, but of aching in his arms, and to a lesser degree, in his back. The beginner is apt to believe that the whole strain of the exercise comes upon the forearms. In other words, the grip of the steering wheel and the easy, immediate, and complete control of that part of the machine are the first principles in bicycle riding. To preserve the upright position many muscular movements are required, and in these practically all the muscles of the trunk are concerned.

In course of time balancing becomes not only easy but quite automatic ; and while it is true that the upright posture is finally retained with a very modified amount of muscular exertion, still an extensive series of muscles are involved even if the power exerted be slight.

To sit upright for some hours without any support for the back is not a quite insignificant exercise, and after a long ride the bicyclist finds that he has been doing more with his back than he thought.

So far as the movements of the legs are concerned, an opinion of bicycling as a muscular exercise should not be formed by observing the riders one often sees in the streets of a great city on Sunday or on the suburban roads on a bank holiday.

The ill-taught or inexperienced rider rides from his hips ; he moves his lower limbs like pistons ; his action is extreme ; his ankle is fixed ; his foot and leg move as one.

Pedalling is, to a great extent, a matter of the ankle-joint. The more the ankle-joint is employed the more is muscular power economized, and the more graceful is the rider's movement.

While bicycling does certainly involve in the main the muscles of the lower extremities, it at the same time gives excellent employment to the muscles of the upper limb (especially of the forearm) and to the muscles of the trunk.

Cycling does not tend to develop the chest or exercise the great muscles passing from the trunk to the upper limb, and herein lies the defect of the sport as an exercise. It cannot be recommended as a predominating mode of exercise to a tall, lanky lad with a narrow chest and a stooping back. Such an individual should take to rowing and leave the wheel alone.

3. In the third place it is said that bicycle riding induces a very pernicious posture of the body—a posture which has been well caricatured by Du Maurier in the pages of " Punch." The posture complained of can be seen any day among those who hire a bicycle now and then for an hour and tear wildly through the streets thereon. The rider is leaning so far forwards as to have his body nearly horizontal. His back is bowed and arched, his elbows stick out like the limbs of a startled cat, his chest is almost upon the handle bar, and his chin is thrust well ahead.

This attitude is, to some extent, a necessity upon the racing track, and there is no doubt that it is practically essential in riding at the highest possible speed.

For riding upon the road it is ridiculous, and as out of place as the posture of a jockey at the finish of a horserace would be in an individual taking a canter in Rotten Row.

This absurd attitude when assumed by riders on the road may be put down in part to sheer ignorance, in part to bad teaching, and in part to a foolish imitation of the racing man. It is unnecessary, inelegant, and distinctly injurious.

The rider should sit quite upright, with his back straight and with the upper part of the body as still as possible. The head should be erect, the shoulders well thrown back, and the elbows at the sides. He should sit, moreover, well to the back of his saddle, and, as one writer expresses it, " push out in front, using the saddle to push from." The handles of the machines are now made so as to render a perfectly erect position possible ; and in ordering a machine it is important that this matter of the handles should be attended to.

There is no doubt that some riders who have been utterly careless of their attitude have to thank the bicycle for rounded shoulders and a stooping back.

4. It is said that in cycling injurious pressure is brought to bear upon the perinæum, and that perinæal abscess, urinary fistula, and other troubles have resulted therefrom. The writer has not been able to find any evidence to support this assertion.

It is possible that cycling may lead to mishief if practiced by a patient with an inflamed urethra ; it is conceivable that it may act injuriously in the subjects of urethral stricture and enlarged prostate. For even this last-named possibility there is very little scientific support. Among tricycle riders the writer is acquainted with more than one subject of prostatic, hypertrophy, and by such individuals he has been assured that cycling causes no aggravation of such symptoms as they present. In the advanced stages of prostatic trouble in elderly men, when vesical symptoms are present, cycling could scarcely be practiced.

In perfectly healthy individuals it may be stated that cycling does not produce an injurious degree of pressure upon the perinæum.

In the modern saddle a suspended slip of leather is the only part which comes in actual contact with the perinæum. No metal-work can cause direct pressure upon that part.

Any discomfort about the perinæum in riding is probably due either to a form of saddle ill-adapted to the individual rider, or to a bad attitude assumed in riding.

The habit of stooping forwards, which has been already condemned, brings the perinæum unduly upon the saddle, and for this reason, if for no other, the attitude is to be strongly opposed.

In riding, the weight of the body rests upon the tuberosities of the ischia. These points alone should bear the pressure.

Many bicyclists wear suspensory bandages, on the ground that the testes are occasionally pressed between the body and the saddle. Such a precaution is unnecessary if the rider will make up his mind to sit his machine properly.

It is needless to say that long-continued pressure upon the tuber ischii may lead to some pain along the long scrotal nerve, and may induce an enlargement of the bursa over that process of bone.

The circumstance is, however, very rare, and is no more likely to occur after cycling than it is after daily riding in a third-class railway carriage.

5. Cycling is accused of producing varicose veins in the leg, and hernia. The case of the first-named affection is considered elsewhere, and need not be again dealt with.

With regard to hernia there is little to add to what has been already said, except to point out one fact. It is true that in easy riding the abdominal muscles are but little used, and that, therefore, little pressure is brought to bear upon the abdominal viscera.

Indeed, in ordinary riding the abdominal muscles have singularly little to do. This circumstance may appear to render bicycling a suitable exercise for those who are disposed to hernia. It must, however, be noted on the other side, that the attitude of the rider tends to so relax the tissues about the hernial orifices as to render the circumstances favourable for the descent of a hernia. When the rider "puts on pace" in racing or in avoiding an obstacle, he leans forwards, throws his abdominal muscles into action, and places himself in a condition certainly favourable for the formation of a rupture. In "mounting" also a sudden and pronounced contraction of the belly muscles is called for, and that, too, while the individual's body is flexed.

It may be said, therefore, that bicycle riding should be avoided by those who have weak inguinal regions or a disposition to hernia, and that it should not be practised by the actually ruptured.

Bicycling is well suited for the young, nimble, and active; it is, however, not ill-adapted to the middle-aged and to those who have lost the elasticity of youth. A man of forty, weighing 13 or even 14 stone, may take to bicycling as an exercise, may attain considerable proficiency as a rider, and may derive unmixed benefit from the pursuit. He needs be nimble enough to mount and to dismount quickly, but this involves little more agility than is required to enter or to leave an omnibus while in motion. Bicycling is not adapted for men past middle iife, and there are very few riders who may be classed as old men.

The exercise is admirable for all who require development in the lower extremities and who complain of being "weak in the loins." Those who are disposed to phthisis, or who desire to develop their lung capacity, should take up some other exercise than bicycling. It is not perhaps quite the exercise for the timid and nervous, and it should not be adopted by the subjects of urethral or prostatic disease, of hernia, of varicose veins, or of varicocele.

The exercise appears to have a very beneficial effect in relieving chronic constipation, and is adopted with advantage by those who are the subjects of dyspepsia, hæmorrhoids, and functional disorders of the liver.

As in other forms of exercise, racing and the breaking of records should be left to the young, well-trained, strong, and athletic, and the acquiring of tricks in riding to the acrobat, who has to live by his eccentricities. The ordinary rider when touring should satisfy himself with a pace of not more than ten miles an hour, and a distance not exceeding fifty miles in the day. The bicyclist should be well equipped, should wear well-cut, or better still, well-woven breeches, should be clad entirely in wool, and should burden himself with as little luggage as possible. He should avoid tight-fitting shoes, stiff collars, braided uniforms, gauntlets, rubber-soled shoes, and waterproof suits. The only waterproof worn should take the form of a loose cape. The best shoes are thin leather walking shoes.

Tricycling.—In tricycling the muscles of the lower extremities are almost the only ones involved. No balance has to be maintained, and the steering is accomplished with a very small amount of muscular exertion. The rider has to maintain the body erect, and must thus employ the muscles of the trunk. As an exercise, tricycling is undoubtedly inferior to bicycling. The machine is, moreover, comparatively large and cumbrous, and in a small London house is perhaps with difficulty disposed of. It cannot be so well conveyed from place to place, and when on a tour the rider must always seek a shelter for his machine. The small size of the bicycle and the convenient manner in which it can be disposed of are among its greatest advantages.

The tricycle rider must keep to main or principal roads. The bicyclist can take advantage of a footpath. The machine makes three tracks, and upon an uneven or frozen road with sharp ruts the tricycle has very decided disadvantages over the bicycle.

While in touring the bicyclist can make ten miles an hour, the tricycle rider will have to content himself with eight. On the other hand, the advantages of the tricycle are the following: The machine is very easy to ride, and can be ridden at once and without any teaching. No balancing is required. The machine can be driven with less muscular exertion, and by altering the gearing a machine can be adapted to almost every grade of muscular capacity. The tricycle can be ridden by the old, the nervous, the moderately feeble, the lame. It can be ridden by ladies and young girls. At the same time, with an athletic rider a great speed can be attained on the machine and enormous distances covered.

Three great and very decided advantages of the tricycle are these: the rider can stop the machine, and can rest and enjoy the scenery without dismounting; he can ride without taking very minute note of the road; he can carry a considerable quantity of luggage.

Tricycling is a most admirable exercise for those past middle life. They can take their exercise without fear and without trouble, and can moderate their exertions to any degree. It can be made a violent exercise or a very gentle one. It throws no great strain upon the heart or lungs. It appears to have a good effect upon dyspeptics and the subjects of chronic constipation. It can be indulged in within limits by the subjects of hernia. It involves all the advantages attending exercise in the open.

Cycling for Ladies and Girls.

Tricycling is extensively and enthusiastically adopted by many ladies and young girls. Many have attained considerable proficiency at the sport. The luxury of a tandem ride appears to be keenly appreciated: the freedom the lady tricyclist enjoys, and the wide tracks of country she can cover in company with her brother, husband, or other friend, are strong attractions for the vigorously inclined.

It is doubtful if tricycling can be declared to be a good or suitable exercise for young women and young girls.

It is not a severe exercise, it is true; and, indeed, the amount of muscular exertion demanded can be very precisely regulated. Many ladies are emphatic in their advocacy of the claims of tricycling to be considered a very suitable, very beneficial, and quite harmless exercise for females.

It must be remembered, however, that what applies to one woman may not apply to another, and that arguments applicable to the middle-aged may not be equally suited to the young.

The precise evidence which is required to decide the question of the value of tricycling for women and girls is a little difficult to obtain and to formulate.

These points may be drawn attention to.

It is a question whether an exercise involving extensive use of the lower limbs and of the muscles about the pelvis is an unmixed good during the years of active uterine life.

During the menstrual period it may be assumed that the exercise would, for many reasons, be regarded as most undesirable ; and there may possibly be some truth in the loose assertion that menstrual irregularities have been developed by tricycling. There is a real difficulty in the matter of the saddle. The modern ladies' saddle is a great improvement upon the older pattern, but the writer knows of no saddle which can be assumed to entirely do away with the possibility of pressure upon the pudendum.

Individuals have complained of much chafing in the pudendal region as a result of riding, and, without entering into further details, the question may be asked whether in young girls or in young women an exercise is good which may involve considerable pressure and friction in the pudendal region. The very detailed objections which have been allowed to apply to the use of treadle sewing machines by factory girls would appear to apply to the riding of a tricycle.

My personal opinion would take the form of suggesting that there are better exercises for the gentler sex than tricycling provides, that the exercise should not be undertaken by young girls and young women, but that it may be open to those who are married or middle-aged. I am aware of one or two instances in which ladies have abandoned tricycling after a few months' enthusiastic pursuit of the exercise, without affording a more definite excuse than that "it did not agree with them." That tricycling is not the exercise best suited for a girl about puberty or a young unmarried woman, I am convinced ; and one cannot help noticing that the most enthusiastic, most successful, and most persistent lady riders are no longer young.

Bicycle riding for ladies and girls may be condemned for the same reasons which have been mentioned in connection with tricycling. Very ingenious Safety Bicycles for ladies have been designed, but it is evident that—with the present shape of saddle at least—they cannot be ridden without producing pressure and friction in the pudendal region. The mounting and dismounting is difficult ; although it can be performed with perfect decency, the learning to ride involves greater pains, and the dress distinctly adds to whatever dangers may attend the machine.

There are many very admirable, harmless, and delightful exercises open to the tender sex, but among these cycling, and more especially bicycling, need not be included.

GYMNASTICS AND CALISTHENICS.

These terms have been, and are, employed in so many senses that they scarcely admit of any precise definition, and certainly of no definition which would meet with general acceptance.

The term "gymnastics" is usually considered to apply to a series of exercises of a somewhat severe or advanced character, and especially to such as involve the use of apparatus. The term "calisthenics" is usually associated with a milder form of systematic exercises, with "free movements," with exercises which involve no apparatus, with the simpler forms of drilling, and the like. The definitions of the words given in the "Century Dictionary" are convenient ones. "*Calisthenics :* The art or practice of exercising the muscles for the purpose of gaining health, strength, or grace of form and movement; a kind of light gymnastics." "*Gymnastics :* The art of performing athletic exercises."

The first expression which presents itself in the consideration of gymnastic exercises or the teaching of calisthenics is the unfortunate term "system." The question asked of any instructor is "what system does he teach?" and of any scheme of exercises, "what system does it follow?" Considerable discussions have ensued upon the question as to which system of gymnastics is the best : and while at one centre of physical education faith is fixed upon one system, an opposition belief holds sway at another.

When the details of opposed systems are considered, and the claims of rival schools are weighed, no little confusion arises. The impartial observer feels that he must seek for some great fundamental characteristics whereby to separate one method from another. He finds that original systems have been modified, reconstructed, added to, and even blended with methods from other sources. He observes that the conception one instructor of gymnastics has formed of a system of training differs materially from the interpretation another teacher has adopted of the very same system. Several of the more modern works upon gymnastics form a mere olla podrida, a mixture of this system and of that, with modifications introduced by the author and such emendations as obscure all means of classification.

I have myself witnessed a " display " advertised as a demonstration of the

Swedish system of gymnastics, in which musical drill, the use of bar-bells and dumb-bells, were the main features, and in which none of the familiar characteristics of the Swedish system were notable.

As a matter of fact, the terms "Swedish system," "Swedish gymnastics," and "Ling's method" are used in so indiscriminate a manner, that the expressions have in the mouths of many come to be synonymous with any form of free movements or any species of gymnastic training which is not violent or which does not involve fixed apparatus.

One soon has to conclude that no system is *per se* complete and all-sufficient, that no one can lay claim to international adoption, that evil may result from a blind adhesion to one particular method, and that considerable allowance has to be made for nationality, physical condition, and physical tastes.

While this is true, it must also be allowed that if a certain system be advocated and professed it should be maintained in its entirety so long as its distinctive title is adhered to and employed.

So far as the present purpose of this article is concerned, it may be said that there are three methods of gymnastic exercise which for purposes of convenience may be here set forth. It must not for a moment be supposed that such a classification is in any way complete, nor is it historically precise, nor perhaps even just. The systems alluded to are—1, the English ; 2, the German ; and 3, the Swedish.

1. By the *English system* is understood a method of physical training by means of athletic exercises and outdoor sports. This system is considered to include marching, running, both **long distance** running and sprint running, leaping, swimming, etc., trials of strength and endurance, and the usual outdoor sports, such as cricket, football, and rowing.

This is the sense in which most foreign writers describe **the** English system. The definition is not very liberal, but it is very convenient. It is true of physical training in England many years ago, but **of** course does not profess to represent such training as is at present carried out.

It is needless to criticize what is termed the English system. The value of athletic sports and outdoor games is recognized and is appreciated in no country so keenly as in England.

As a method of training, **it is** obviously crude, unscientific, incomplete, and of restricted application. It is a pleasant training for lusty boys and vigorous men, but it is perfectly clear that it can lay no claim to be considered as a precise and orthodox system.

2. The *German system* may be spoken of as being assimilative. The German writers and teachers have adopted and embodied whatever they found good in the practices of other peoples in the matter of physical education. No system is more liberal, more extensive, more catholic. As Mr. Metzner well says in his account of the German system of gymnastics (Physical Training Conference, Boston, 1889), "the German system does not claim to have any special exercise of its own, or to be the sole proprietor of any that no other system may also produce." The system has been slowly built up during nearly a century, and has shown as a main characteristic the power of intelligent assimilation and the ready appreciation and development of what has appeared good in physical training.

The German system embraces all the different branches of gymnastics, free movements, mass exercises in every form, with wands, dumb-bells, flags, bar-bells, etc., figure marching, trot marching, the use of a most varied and extensive series of fixed apparatus, the use of clubs and all forms of hand apparatus, and the encouragement of such exercises as come under the heading of outdoor sports.

It aims at general physical culture and does not encourage the development of especial powers or especial abilities ; it encourages exercises in classes (mass exercises) and endeavours to infuse interest and amusement in its instructions ; it aims at being complete and at being capable of adaptation by individuals of all ages and of very varied physical ability ; it encourages a gradual and progressive form of instruction, the pupil commencing with the simplest exercises and proceeding with the more difficult and arduous only when the more rudimentary have been fully mastered.

A description of the exercises carried out under the German system would require a treatise of considerable length.

(*a*) The *free exercises* imply various movements of the limbs and trunk carried out without apparatus. They include manifold movements of the arms and legs, bending and rotating of the body in various directions, and the assuming of a number of attitudes and postures.

By these free movements it is considered that every muscle is exercised ; the exercises are simple, gentle, and are especially adapted for children, although they should form the preliminary course in any scheme of physical training. They are repeated a great number of times, and are effected symmetrically so that each side of the body may be equally developed. They are so arranged as to be progressive, and every attempt should be made to render them complete. These exercises are obviously best conducted in classes, and many are very conveniently carried out to music, as the German system allows. They are popular and interesting. They tend not only to develop the muscles but also to quicken attention, to encourage rapid, precise, and well co-ordinated movements, and to bring about the mental alertness and the physical smartness which are elicited by any well-conducted drill. They tend to give grace and ease and freedom to the movements and to favor a good carriage.

No system of physical education is complete which is not founded upon a sound grounding in free exercises.

It is only fair to state that some of the best of the free movements carried out in the German system have been derived from the Swedish schools. The exercises are perhaps, on the whole, more interesting and more picturesque than those adopted by the Swedish system. They are, however, less precise and less complete, and less elaborately systematized as a part of a progressive system of education. Not a few of these German free exercises have little educational purpose, and appear to be adopted more for effect and to meet the requirements of a public display. Some recent modifications and additions have little claim to serious attention, and do not elicit the best possible employment of the pupil's time. Compared with the Swedish exercises, however, they are, on the whole, more popular with children, and are certainly more picturesque.

(*b*) Another series of exercises involve the use of very light *hand apparatus*, such as bar-bells, wooden dumb-bells, flags, hoops, etc. These exercises, although they concern to a great extent the upper part of the trunk and the upper limbs, involve also the development of the other muscles of the body. The weight of the apparatus used is but a slight element in the exercises, which are nearly of the same character as those just described. The apparatus gives precision to the movements, makes the exercises more interesting and more easily carried out, and renders the instructor's work somewhat less difficult. These exercises are adapted for older children, and form a peculiarly valuable element in education. They represent an advancement upon the free movements, and in a systematic and progressive plan of instruction would naturally follow upon those exercises. These exercises with apparatus may also be carried out to music.

(*c*) Although *drilling* does not form a very conspicuous element in the German system, the subject may be conveniently introduced here, especially

7

as the modern gymnastic drill is largely a German production. A certain amount of drilling is of value, and forms an efficient means of cultivating a good carriage and an easy and free mode of walking and marching. Military drill is a little tedious and formal, and to a considerable extent purposeless, so far as a full physical education is concerned. It tends to sharpen the wits of dull lads and to encourage precise and active movements. It is, however, uninteresting to the pupil, and does not afford in any way a complete or satisfactory method of employing the muscles. In the physical training of children it may well be replaced by more valuable exercises.

The musical drill of more modern times is very different from the drill-sergeant's work. Musical drill appears to have been introduced from America, and it now forms a conspicuous feature in most training schools. It consists of marching or running in a such a manner as to describe a variety of figures, and always to music.

Under this heading come the many forms of the musical running or marching maze, which include marching in two or four circles, or in reverse circles, or in parallel lines, or in what is known as the serpentine course. This drill is only possible with a comparatively large class. It is very popular with children and with lads and elder girls. It forms an excellent relaxation from the more formal exercises, and represents running with a purpose. Many admirable books have appeared on the subject. The three forms of exercise just described are especially well adapted for children and for instruction in schools. They serve to form the basis of a very sound and perfect physical drill.

If the work of a school could be interrupted for thirty minutes in the middle of the morning in order that the children might go through some few dumb-bell or bar-bell exercises in fresher air, and then finish up with the running maze to music, something would be done towards securing a reasonable development of the body. All that is required is a competent teacher, plenty of floor or ground space, some very simple apparatus, and equally simple music.

(d) The use of *gymnastic apparatus* is considered in a subsequent section. In the employment of apparatus and in the invention and elaboration of gymnastic appliances of various kinds the German schools have been very active. Indeed, the use of apparatus is so prominent in the system that it has been often improperly considered to represent its principal feature.

3. The *Swedish system*, or the system introduced by Ling, has attracted

very considerable attention, and has certainly been the means of effecting not only a remarkable improvement in physical education, but a change which may be spoken of as little less than a revolution. It may be that the whole method is not original, and that some of its features have been anticipated, but as a system it has been enthusiastically accepted, and certainly met a want which had been felt in physical education.

There was a time in this country when in the matter of physical education there was little between somewhat violent outdoor sports and certain acrobatic feats in the gymnasium on the one hand, and the dreary instruction of the drill-sergeant on the other. The young girls of that period had also, it must be allowed, the services of the so-called professor of deportment, but of the value of his instruction it is difficult to speak. Physical training in those days was for the strong. It encouraged specialization; it did not concern itself with a systematic and progressive development of the human body.

The Swedish system of physical training includes a very extensive series of free movements, a series of exercises involving marching, leaping, running and climbing, and certain carefully graduated exercises on the boom, rib-stool, and window ladder. The free movements are admirable, and for them these advantages can be claimed: They have been carefully worked out: each series of movements are definite and precise, and are intended to develop a special series of muscles; the exercises are systematic and progressive, and form in their entirety a complete and simple system of physical training.

The movements are not designed with a view to effect or display, but simply to carry out the scheme of muscular training. They are designed with care, and each accomplishes a specific object. The exercises begin with the very simplest and gradually become stronger and more complicated.

The use of hand apparatus is only sanctioned after a complete mastery of the free movements has been attained, and then only to add some intensity to those movements.

The fixed apparatus mostly employed by teachers of the Swedish system are the boom, the rib-stool, and the window ladder. The latter forms an excellent exercise for children and affords them no little amusement. The method prepares the way for so-called æsthetical gymnastics, for fencing, military drill, and other forms of applied gymnastics.

All the movements of the drill are applied to words of command, and the pupil gains all those advantages, mental and otherwise, which attend the teaching of exercises by the drill method, *i. e.*, by word of command rather than by imitation or by committing the movements to memory.

The Swedish system disapproves utterly of the use of music, and it is contended that the exercises cannot be adapted to one set rhythm.

Against the Swedish method it may be urged that the exercises are a little uninteresting to the pupils, that many of them appear ungainly and purposeless, and that the great advantage of a musical accompaniment is lost.

The chief movements may be classed under the following divisions :

(*a*) *Fundamental positions.*—These are intended to secure general attention and muscular control, and to establish the equilibrium and base of support before more difficult exercises are undertaken.

(*b*) *Arch flexions* comprise various forms of backward flexions of the trunk, and are intended to develop the dorsal muscles and those of the abdomen, and to expand the lower part of the chest.

(*c*) *Heaving movements.*—These comprise forms of self-suspension by means of the arms on a horizontal bar or other apparatus, and serve to expand the chest and to strengthen the muscles of the upper limb.

(*d*) *Balance movements.*—The positions are taken from a smaller area than that included within the feet in standing ; the difficulty is increased by diminution of the area of support. The exercises develop the equipoise of the body and give grace to the carriage.

(*e*) *Shoulder-blade movements* are concerned mainly with the scapular muscles.

(*f*) *Abdominal movements* call into special action the muscles of the abdomen.

(*g*) *Lateral trunk movements.*—These include various forms of lateral flexion of the body, and of rotary movements, and concern generally the muscles of the trunk.

(*h*) *Slow leg movements.*—They are to specially develop the individual muscles of the leg.

(*i*) *Jumping and vaulting*, and (*j*) respiratory exercises call for no explanation.

In the article on " Physical Development," in Keating's " Cyclopædia of the Diseases of Children " (vol. iv., p. 303), will be found a brief but lucid exposition of the actual details of the Swedish drill, illustrated by numerous figures of the various positions.

An excellent "Manual of Swedish Drill" has been produced by George Melio (London, 1889). The reader may also consult a "Manual of Free-standing Movements," by Captain Haasum, of the Royal Gymnastic Institute, Stockholm (London, 1885). Both books are admirable. Mr. Melio's various contributions to our knowledge of Swedish gymnastics have been very valuable, inasmuch as his early training was not carried out under the Swedish method.

The Swedish system of physical training originated with Ling, and has been considerably developed and extended by his pupils and followers.

Petter Henrik Ling was born at Ljunga, in Smaland, in 1766. His early life appears to have been absorbed by a struggle against poverty, and he passed through many vicissitudes. He seems to have been engaged in many pursuits and to have traveled in many countries. In 1800 he was studying gymnastics at Copenhagen, and in 1804 he was engaged as a fencing master at Lund. His system of physical training was elaborated after this date. The Royal Gymnastic Institute was founded at Stockholm in 1815 at his instigation, and remained under his supervision until his death in 1839.

Ling figured as a poet and a dramatist; he dabbled with the flimsier forms of metaphysics and held some crude conceptions of physiology. His education was scarcely such as to fit him for the position he ultimately held.

Ling held that life consisted of the blending together of three elements—the dynamic, the chemical, and the mechanical—and upon this belief his "system" was founded. Many of his exercises were only suited to invalids, and he professed to have discovered the means of curing most diseases by physical movements. His exercises were indeed divided into scholastic, military, medical, and æsthetic gymnastics. He considered that every muscular movement had a special effect upon the general health, and held that passive movements had a definite value in promoting the development of the body.

It must be confessed that his system (excellent as some features of it undoubtedly are) was founded upon not a few extravagant theories and upon bases which were not always scientific or accurate.

The medical side of the system has been the means of fostering a form of quackery, and has led to the introduction of the "remedial exercises" and "movement cures," which have done so much to bring Swedish gymnastics into discredit in this country. Out of the complex, heterogeneous, and visionary material which makes up Ling's system, much that is really good and valuable has been extracted. This is represented by the excellent system of free movements already described, and by many of the methods of treating disease by exercise which have been heartily accepted and developed by the medical men of this and other countries. In Anna Arnin's " Health Maps " (London, 1887), and in Schrieber's " Manual of Treatment by Massage " (Edinburgh, 1887), will be found good accounts of the application of movements to the treatment of abnormal and diseased conditions.

In proposing a course of " Swedish gymnastics " or in advocating " Ling's system," it is desirable that a clear knowledge should be possessed of what is implied by these terms, and that encouragement be not offered to the " remedial measures," the " movement cures," and the quackery with which this otherwise excellent system is attended. Any instructor who describes himself as a " medical gymnast " will probably not be sought for as a teacher.

Ling's system *in its entirety* could hardly be accepted at the present day. Such portion of the Swedish system as deals with the practical part of physical education pure and simple must, however, be accepted as of considerable worth.

GYMNASTIC APPARATUS.

Under this title will be considered the use of such apparatus as will be found in a well-equipped gymnasium. A good gymnasium should have ample space, good light, very free ventilation, the best possible apparatus, and a fully qualified instructor.

The fresher the air and (within limits) the cooler the room the better. A properly ventilated gymnasium has an unlimited supply of fresh air without draughts. If there be a time when plenty of oxygen is required, it is when young persons are taking violent exercise. Many gymnasia are ill-lit, cramped, and a very badly ventilated.

The majority of the exercises involved in the use of gymnastic apparatus involve considerable strength and much practice.

It is madness for a man out of training and unaccustomed to exercise to commence in a gymnasium the use of such apparatus as the horizontal bar or the vaulting horse. Many children, especially girls, have been seriously damaged by the violent exertions undertaken in improperly conducted gymnasia.

Such gymnasia have done a very great deal to bring physical training into discredit. A boy of about ten has joined a " gymnastic class ;" his physical condition has never been examined and his physical capacities never inquired into. He enters the gymnasium, and without any preliminary training attempts the feats he sees other pupils performing, without perhaps having received any definite instruction. The boy goes home dead-beat, feeble, and sick at heart at his ill-success, and aching with his unwonted exertions. Next day he presents all the phenomena of extreme fatigue, and perhaps the symptoms of muscular strain. I have known more than one instance in which a hernia made its appearance after a first attendance at a gymnasium.

The very greatest care should be exercised in the management of all children and young people sent to a gymnasium. Parents who take infinite pains to supervise the mental education of their children, often take not the least trouble to ascertain the conditions under which their bodies are being trained. A lad comes home with a headache and with all the symptoms of exhaustion from the hour's drill, and is not allowed to attend again on the grounds that he is not "strong enough for rough exercise." A visit to the gymnasium may have shown that the headache was due to an ill-ventilated and over-heated room, and the exhaustion to totally unsuitable exercises.

It must be remembered that physical training requires discretion ; that a great mass of pupils, even when of the same age and sex, cannot be all dealt with *en masse* by fixed rules. The exercises selected and the apparatus to be used must be determined, not by rule of thumb, but by the precise needs of each individual case. This observation will not apply to drilling and to simple mass exercises, but it applies in a very emphatic manner to apparatus.

A gymnasium is worse than useless without an efficient and careful instructor. Gymnastics cannot be self-taught. The process of training must be gradual, and so graduated as to meet the pupil's particular needs and particular state of development.

So-called exercise in a gymnasium without a teacher usually means purposeless romping. It may safely be said that the great majority of the accidents which occur in gymnasia occur during forbidden hours, or when the pupil is attempting exercises by himself of which he has no precise knowledge.

Put an active boy in a gymnasium and pay no attention to his training, and he will assuredly begin to "play the fool," to "skylark," to develop uncouth modes of exercising his limbs, and in the end very probably do himself more or less material damage.

The pupil in a gymnasium must be content to begin at the beginning, must learn to be patient and to overcome failures, must be ready to believe that there many exercises he can never perform, and that he is endeavoring to acquire health and strength, and not to qualify himself for the profession of an acrobat. Above all things, work in a gymnasium must be gradual, regular and systematic.

A very lamentable spectacle is that afforded by a middle-aged man who feels he is becoming stout and who thinks he will "take to gymnastics." He attempts at once the exercises he sees his younger colleagues perform with such complete ease. If such a man escapes with no greater injury than is represented by being rendered breathless, by having several muscles sprained, and by being laughed at, he may consider himself fortunate.

In general terms it may be said that the gymnasium is not well suited for children, is best suited for lads and young men between the ages of seventeen and twenty-five, and is but indifferently adapted for men over thirty, unless they have kept up the physical acquirements of their youth by constant practice.

It is important also to bear in mind that gymnastic exercises with apparatus all tend to develop the upper limbs and the upper half of the trunk.

The gymnasium cannot provide the means for a complete physical education, and work in it should never so far absorb the time devoted to physical training as to exclude recreation in the open air and outdoor games and exercises. Exercises with apparatus come at the end, and not at the beginning, of a course of physical training.

A very brief description of the commoner apparatus will now be given.

Dumb-bells.—These should be light and should be made of sycamore wood. The weight for boys should be 1 lb. each bell, 2 lb. for lads, and 3 lb. for adults. Heavy dumb-bells are to be condemned. The chief feature of proper dumb-bell exercises is the great frequency with which they are repeated and the length of time the movements are kept up. The weight of the bell is not a factor of any moment in the exercise, but the apparatus serves to give interest and precision to the movements carried out. Heavy dumb-bells involve considerable effort compressed into an inconsiderable time. Such bells are only of use to athletes who wish to specially develop their arms.

Dumb-bell exercises are admirable. They can be adapted for individuals of all ages and of all conditions of physical strength ; they are well suited for class exercises ; and a musical drill with light dumb-bells forms a pleasant feature in the training of boys and girls. Both bells should be used at the same time.

The exercises encourage a good carriage, rapid and precise movements, and the equal, symmetrical, and simultaneous use of the muscles upon both sides of the body.

These exercises tend to develop the chest and to exercise the muscles of the abdomen and back.

It is true the arms are conspicuously employed in dumb-bell movements, but if the drilling is efficient nearly all the muscles of the body are well, although not equally exercised, and especial employment can be given to the muscles of the back.

Bar-bells.—These are of ash. The shaft is five feet long (for adults) and three-quarters of an inch in diameter. The knob at each end is three inches in diameter.

The exercises carried out with bar-bells resemble those performed with dumb-bells. They have especial value in developing the muscles of the chest and of the abdomen. The muscles of the upper limbs are somewhat unduly exercised, and considerable work can be thrown upon the muscles of the back. This apparatus is excellent for the narrow-chested. It encourages symmetrical movements, a graceful carriage, and general lissomeness of the body. Bar-bells are extensively used in the training of young girls.

By the use of double bar-bells a still more extensive use of the general muscular system is involved. In these exercises two bar-bells are held at either end by two pupils; in all movements the two pupils must act in concert. The exercises concern the whole of the muscles and afford excellent training in symmetrical, rapid, and precise movements.

Indian Clubs are made of pine wood, and are about 24 in. in length and some 3½ in. in diameter at the thick end. The exercises are only suited for adults and for muscular persons. They encourage a firm and upright attitude, and develop principally the upper part of the trunk and the upper limbs.

Many of the movements are very elaborate and require great nicety of execution.

Parallel Bars should be about 9 ft. long, 20 in. apart, and about 4 ft. from the ground. Every instructor in gymnastics recognises that the parallel bars form one of the most useful apparatus in the gymnasium. "The exercises," writes Maclaren, "are not only numerous but varied, interesting, and in themselves pleasurable, capable of much artistic effect, and requiring equally muscular power and dexterity of action in the upper limb."

The usual exercises are progressive, and none are violent. The apparatus is suited for properly trained pupils of any age after twelve or fourteen, and within limits for both sexes, provided that the muscular development of the learner is efficient. The exercises improve the grasp, develop the muscles of the upper limb, and especially the muscles passing between the upper limb and the trunk. They are well adapted for individuals with slight arms, with narrow and sloping shoulders, and with contracted chests. Excessive use of the bars tends, however, to develop to excess the posterior scapular muscles. The muscles of the abdomen are employed, but comparatively little use is made of the lower extremities.

The Horizontal Bar is about six feet long, has a diameter of 1⅝ in., and is raised from three to seven feet from the ground. This valuable apparatus is adapted for pupils of almost any age above ten or twelve. The exercises are varied and progressive, and can be made to suit various degress of muscular development.

The simpler exercises develop the muscles of the upper limbs and of the upper part of the trunk ; the more advanced call into play the muscles of the back and of the abdomen, and to a less extent the muscles of the lower limbs. The apparatus if used to too great an extent tends to develop the upper limb muscles to a disproportionate extent.

The simpler exercises are adapted under careful restriction for girls with weak spines, and for those with small scapular muscles and slender shoulders.

The more elaborate exercises require considerable strength and agility, and are only suited for the athletic and very muscular.

In certain of the primary exercises the abdominal muscles are especially employed.

The Trapeze is made of hickory or ash, is about 20 in. in length and some ¾ in. in diameter. The height at which it is suspended from the ground, and the length of the ropes, must depend upon the capacity and age of the learner.

The exercises are very similar to those of the horizontal bar, but as the pupil can swing at the time of practising, this apparatus is very popular.

It mainly brings into play the muscles of the upper limb and those passing between the trunk and that member. It is of service in cases of feeble back and commencing lateral curvature, and can be made admirable use of in developing especially the muscles of the abdomen.

A mattress must always be placed beneath the low trapeze, and a net beneath the higher apparatus. Great care must be taken in carrying out the movements, and this apparatus has been the cause of not a few accidents.

The more elaborate movements are only adapted for the practised athlete, and some of the finest displays of gymnastic skill are made with the trapeze.

The Hand Rings have a diameter of from 5 to 9 in., are placed about 18 in. apart when used by adults, and at the distance of 3 to 6 ft. from the floor. This apparatus is also very popular. The exercises closely resemble those carried out upon the trapeze. The same sets of muscles are concerned. The apparatus, if properly employed, is excellent for cases of lateral curvature; the lateral muscles of the trunk can be very fully and efficiently exercised, and one side can be especially developed if required.

The more elaborate exercises concern the muscles of the back and abdomen and indeed the whole muscular system, with the exception that the lower limbs are but little involved.

Unless care be exercised it is easy for young pupils to produce an unsymmetrical development of the back muscles by an improper use of this appliance.

The Vaulting Horse is a valuable apparatus. The body should be from 5 to 6 ft. in length, and should be capable of being adjusted at any height. Mattresses must be placed around it, and a sloping board is generally placed in front of it for leaping exercises.

The vaulting horse is well suited for children and the young and for athletic adults. It is scarcely the apparatus for the middle-aged. It may be used by girls under puberty, but its use in older females is open to some question (see page 85).

The exercises are varied, are pleasurable, and are popular with young people. It is well suited for class instruction. The simpler exercises consist of vaulting over the horse in different ways. The exercises develop all the muscles of the body, the lower limbs as well as the upper, the spine as well as the abdomen. Its use brings about a good grasp, a certain amount of agility and precision of movement, and cultivates a good swing of the body. It forms an excellent means of cultivating the respiratory apparatus, and brings out the muscles about the pelvis.

One of the most popular lessons in a gymnasium is represented by a class of pupils who form in line and vault over the horse one after the other, keeping up a continued round and run.

The more advanced exercises are only suited for athletes, and are elaborate and difficult. No gymnasium can be considered to be complete without some form of vaulting horse.

The Inclined Ladder as usually employed exercises mainly the muscles of the upper limb and upper part of the trunk. The exercises, like all other suspension exercises, are excellent for cases of weak back with tendency to curvature of the spine, provided that they are carefully planned and supervised.

The apparatus affords good practice in balancing the body in the exercise of mounting the ladder with the feet only, and is useful for developing the abdominal muscles. It is suited for pupils of various ages and of both sexes, with certain limits.

The Ladder Plank is another useful and popular apparatus. The machine is made in many different ways. For adults the plank is about 18 in. wide, and from either side of it project spars which are 6 in. in length and 9 in. apart.

The exercises on this machine can be adapted to individuals of all ages, of both sexes, and of all degrees of muscular development.

The muscles of the entire body are exercised, although those of the upper limbs and of the upper part of the trunk receive most employment. Maclaren thinks that no machine in the gymnasium so rapidly and powerfully aids in the expansion and development of the upper part of the trunk as does the ladder plank.

This is a good form of apparatus for cases of lateral curvature of the spine ; especially good are the exercises which involve the descending of the plank backwards, *i. e.* with the back to the plank. These exercises also throw the chest out to its utmost, and the apparatus is useful for the narrow-chested or pigeon-breasted. It is a valuable apparatus for growing girls, and is safe.

The Horizontal Ladder gives opportunity for a good series of suspension exercises, which concern mainly the muscles of the upper limb, but which also develop, to a lesser degree, the muscles of the back and of the abdomen. This is an another apparatus of service in cases of weak or distorted back.

Apparatus for Climbing.—Climbing affords excellent exercise, is very popular among children, is suited for pupils of both sexes and for individuals of almost any age. It is not suited for those who have not had special muscular training, nor for the corpulent, nor for those who are past middle life. All climbing exercises may be considered as advanced exercises.

Climbing may be effected in different ways, and children are very apt to acquire tricks in climbing which tend to distort the body and to develop it unequally. The movements of climbing must be carried out very precisely and methodically, and must be carefully superintended by the instructor. Girls and young women often make excellent climbers. The exercise concerns all the muscles, but especially those of the upper limbs. It also tends to develop the muscles of the thighs, back, and abdomen. It is not a good exercise for the subjects of spinal curvature.

The apparatus used comprises (1) the vertical pole, a smooth pole of any height, and with a diameter varying from two to three inches; (2) the slanting pole, which involves a combination of exercises represented by the vertical pole and the slanting ladder. This apparatus is of value in developing the muscles of the abdomen as well as those of the upper limb. (3) The turning pole is hardly suited for any but active youths and trained athletes. The exercises are difficult, involve much muscular power, and, above all, great dexterity, precision, and accuracy of movement. The apparatus consists of a slanting pole so adjusted as to revolve on its longitudinal axis. The great difficulty of the exercises consists in the maintenance of the balance on a pole which is not fixed. (4) The pair of vertical poles (two parallel poles placed eighteen inches apart) is an apparatus only suited for advanced gymnasts. The exercises are very arduous, and demand great strength and much practice. They concern mainly the upper part of the trunk and upper limbs. (5) The vertical rope varies in length and has a diameter of from 1½ to 2 inches. The exercises resemble those of the vertical pole, but are a little more varied and make more use of the lower limbs. (6) The Rosary consists of a vertical rope suspended from the ceiling, but not fixed at the foot, upon which are strung at intervals of from ten to eighteen inches elm beads, four inches in diameter and flat on the top. This affords good exercise in climbing for children—boys and girls—and for beginners. It employs all the muscles—those of the abdomen and back as well as those of the limbs —it concerns most particularly the muscles of the upper limbs. It gives exercise to the muscles about the hips and loins, especially if it be understood that the rope must always be kept in the vertical line. (7) The mast (which has a diameter of ten to twelve inches) is only suited for accomplished athletes.

The Giant's Stride.—This apparatus is more often found in the playground than in a gymnasium, and is seldom among the machines contained in the room. It affords good exercise for the muscles of the body, for the arms, the legs, the abdomen, and the back. The exercise interests children and the apparatus is always popular. It is useless, however, if the exercise

be not regulated, and if children be not individually instructed in the simple
but necessary movements. The children, moreover, should be about of the
same size and if possible of the same state of physical development.

It is common to see children on the giant's stride whose movements are
aimless and useless, who swing loosely about, and who either hamper the
movements of the children behind them or are hampered by the struggles of
the performer immediately in front of them. An undisciplined crowd of
children who without instruction, selection or arrangement try to gain enjoyment and strength from the giant's stride, had better devote their energies to
simpler pursuits.

Home Gymnasia.

The so-called home gymnasium is usually more or less of a delusion and
a snare. It is, as a rule, too elaborate to be of practical value, and too complicated for children's use. It often pretends more than it can accomplish.
A swing, parallel bars, a knotted rope, and an inclined ladder, form excellent
elements in a home gymnasium, provided the children have been already well
trained by means of simpler exercises.

A good machine for home use is an American invention, the so-called
"Excelsior" gymnasium. Here the power of the performer is exercised
against weights attached to ropes passed through pulleys. The apparatus is
capable of exercising all the muscles of the body, admits of almost endless
combinations, and can be graduated to meet the needs of a child or an
athlete. The rowing exercises on a sliding seat and the contrivance for
developing the muscles of the back are in every way admirable. The
machine is, moreover, strong, simple, and portable, and occupies but little
space in a room.

The appliances which owe their main features to the elastic bands are of
limited use, are restricted chiefly to the development of the upper extremities,
and involve a very monotonous form of exercise. A home gymnasium is a
useful apparatus in a bathroom or bedroom, where it can be used every
morning before or after the morning bath.

In concluding this part of the subject, attention must once more be
directed to the circumstance that *a proper and complete physical education
cannot be carried out by means of apparatus.* Apparatus come last in a
progressive system of physical training, and must always be used with great
care and very sparingly. A large proportion of the exercises are totally
unsuited for young subjects, and are only open to athletes or professed gym-

nasts. The tendency of the usual apparatus is to produce an unequal development of the body, to develop the muscles of the arms and shoulders and pectoral regions, and to neglect the muscles of the lower part of the trunk and of the lower limbs. In a subsequent section attention is drawn to the deformity produced by an excessive or exclusive use of the usual gymnastic appliances.

OUTDOOR GAMES.

It is quite impossible to attempt to give any account of the particular value each of the many outdoor games may possess in relation to physical education.

In general terms it may be said that when played in moderation and under suitable conditions they are most excellent. They involve movement in the open air, very varied muscular exercise, a considerable amount of healthy interest and excitement, and the cultivation of a certain degree of skill and special adroitness. The parts that the great games of cricket and football have played in the development of the English people can scarcely be overrated.

These games not only involve healthy exercise and demand skill, but they require readiness of action, determination, foresight, sound judgment, and good temper. They tend to develop personal courage, self-reliance, the spirit of honor, and the impulses of loyalty. They cultivate all those qualities which make a man manly and wholesome in mind. If one wants to seek for the sneaks and cowards in a school, for the poor-hearted and unwholesome-minded, search must be made, not among the cricket and football teams, but among the loafers.

Cricket can be played at almost any age, and is as well adapted for young women as for young men. It is necessary only that the players should be as nearly equal in strength as is possible.

With regard to the game of football, I cannot do better than give two quotations from Mr. Shearman's admirable article in the Badminton Library volume. Before doing so it is needless to say that football as now played is a game which involves great skill and considerable intelligence. The heavy man who played "forward" in days gone by, and who could stand a good hacking, and could hack in turn, is now no longer of any use in a football team. Other things being equal, the more intelligent the man, the better the player. In my opinion there is no outdoor game for lads and young men equal to football, whether it be the Rugby Union or the Association game.

Thus writes Mr. Shearman: "For at least six centuries the people have loved the work and struggle of the rude and manly game, and kings with their edicts, divines with their sermons, scholars with their cultured scorn, and wits with their ridicule, have failed to keep the people away from the pastime they enjoyed. Cricket may at times have excited greater interest amongst the leisured classes; boat races may have drawn larger crowds of spectators from distant places; but football, which flourished for centuries before the arts of boating and cricketing were known, may fairly claim to be, not only the oldest and the most characteristic, but the most essentially popular sport of England.

"Football may be rough, may be at times dangerous; so is riding across country; so is boxing; so is wrestling. The very function and final cause of rough sports is to work off the superfluous animal energy for which there is little vent in the piping times of peace. Since football became popular with all classes, there have been less wrenching off of knockers and 'boxing of the watch,' and fewer 'free fights' in the streets. Football has its national uses quite apart from the cheap enjoyment it has given to thousands. It may be rough, but it is not brutal.

"Next as to the danger. Doubtless there are accidents, and doubtless men have been killed upon the football field. But during a quarter of a century how many thousands of men have played, and have a score of these many thousands lost their lives? Fewer than those who have been drowned on the river, not a tithe of those who have fallen in the hunting field, are the victims of football. If the outcry against football because of its danger could be justified, not a single outdoor sport could survive.

"For every one who may have been harmed by football a thousand have benefited by it. Health, endurance, courage, judgment, and, above all, a sense of fair play, are gained upon the football field. A footballer must learn, and does learn, to play fairly in the thick and heat of a struggle. Such qualities are those which make a nation brave and great. The game is manly and fit for Englishmen: 'it puts a courage into their hearts to meet an enemy in the face.'"

THE ELEMENTS OF PHYSICAL EDUCATION.

1. *The exercises should be adapted to meet the needs of each individual case.*

It is to be borne in mind that the object of a proper physical education is to develop health and not strength, to bring the body to its highest degree of perfection, and not to convert children and youths into gymnasts and acrobats, and that its main object is to best fit the individual for the duties and work of life, and not to elicit proficiency in mere feats of skill and adroitness.

It must not be forgotten, moreover, that individuals vary greatly in the quality of their physical powers and in their capacity for muscular exercise. It is just as impossible to form a great mass of children into one gymnastic class as it is to place those children in one school standard under one teacher. Neither age, height, size, nor sex affords sure means of classifying children, so far as the needs of a proper physical education are concerned. Each individual must be considered upon his or her own especial merits, and there is no method of physical training which is universal or all-sufficing and adapted for all sorts and conditions of human beings.

The sending of a child to a gymnasium, or the placing of it under the care of a drill-sergeant, is as crude a procedure as the conducting of a child within the walls of the first school met with, and leaving it there with the impression that it will somehow be educated. Physical education requires as much care as does mental education, and if there be ten "forms," or "standards," or "classes" in a school which is concerned in mental training, there would probably be at least as many forms and standards in any institution which deals with the training of the body.

Instructors in gymnastics and so-called calisthenics are for the most part somewhat irresponsible beings; their training has often been narrow and incomplete, and their methods are fixed and inelastic. They regard their pupils in the aggregate, and not as individuals. There are of course numerous striking exceptions.

It is to be hoped that a time will come when those who profess to train the body will be required to produce as definite evidences of fitness as are demanded of those who aim at training the mind.

One society in England—the National Health Society—has prepared a scheme for the examination of instructors in gymnastics and for the granting of diplomas and certificates to such as attain to the prescribed standard.

S

Such a scheme has been carried out in America, and serves not only to do justice to competent teachers on the one hand, but to protect the public on the other. The National Health Society requires, among other things, that the candidate shall possess a certain knowledge of elementary anatomy, of the physiology of bodily exercise, of the various methods of physical training, and of the details of the various exercises and the uses of all gymnastic apparatus and appliances. The candidate is required, moreover, to produce evidence of physical fitness and of a proper training in some recognised gymnasium or training school.

The casual, perfunctory, and unmethodical manner in which physical training in many schools is carried out at the present day is very lamentable.

The need of a proper training is especially felt in girls' schools, in schools which are patronised by the lower middle class, and in the elementary schools controlled by the Education Act.

In the great public schools, and at the two great English universities, physical education is in a very flourishing and exuberant condition, and only in need perhaps of a little more method, a little more science, and a little more regard for the individual and the development of the feeble as well as of the strong.

The first necessity in physical education is a knowledge of the condition, the wants, and the possibilities of the individuals to be educated. This can only be obtained by an individual inspection. It would be well if in the elementary schools a plan such as the following could be carried out. Each child on entering the school should have a book in which the following details should be entered :—

1. Name; 2. Age; 3. Height; 4. Weight; 5. General aspect and physique (the entries under this heading could be greatly extended and be made of much service if a competent medical man made the inspection) ; 6. Chest girth; 7. Breathing capacity; 8. Span of arms; 9. Girth of arms; 10. Drawing or pulling power as tested ; 11. Girth of legs; 12. The existence of any evident deformity, defect, or disease. (This section could only be properly developed by a medical man. The conditions dealt with would be such as the following: spinal curvature, hernia, rickets, deformed thorax, stiff joints, infantile paralysis, enlarged tonsils, glandular disease, lung disease, condition of abdominal viscera, evidence of convulsions, etc.)

In this last section much could be done by a properly trained teacher, but a medical inspector would render the evidence in every way of greater value.

The child's physical condition should be inquired into with as much care as is exercised in examining an adult for life insurance. The urine should be tested if possible, and if the parents can be seen the child's family history should be inquired into.

Still, apart from an examination by a medical man, the twelve points prescribed would form the basis of a valuable record, and place the physical education of the child upon a rational footing. Such a record should be kept also of all individuals attending gymnasia and undergoing any form of physical training. Upon the evidence afforded the precise exercises which were desirable and the precise methods of training to be carried out could be determined.

The record may well be extended, and could with great advantage record a test of the child's vision, and add evidence on the questions of astigmatism and colour-blindness. This record, kept in the form of a book, should be filled up every three months. If properly kept, the value of such a book would be enormous. To the individual it would possess more than mere interest. It would show the history of his early life, the record of his development, and would afford an admirable guide to any medical man, should the individual in the future become the subject of disease.

Mental training is exceedingly important without doubt, but it may be that the time will come when the Government of this country will recognise the importance of physical training, and will realise that among the children in elementary schools a strong body is almost as important as, and often more useful than, a well-stored mind. Many of these children are turned out into the world pale, sickly, ill-developed, and feeble. That at present many unremediable causes may conspire to prudence this is evident enough, but the state of things is susceptible of improvement. The health and strength and physique of the poorer classes may be placed upon a better basis, and a number of sturdy and strong men and women produced in the place of the multitude of poor creatures who after a more or less doleful and useless life become prematurely a burden upon the rates.

The systematic examination of the individual and the conducting of a physical education upon precise and scientific grounds have already been carried out in some cities in America.

An excellent account of some of these institutions will be found in the record of the Physical Training Conference held at Boston in 1889.

2. *The exercises should be carefully devised, systematically arranged, and suitably graduated.*

The course of education should be planned upon a definite system and the classes formed, and when occasion demands remodelled, according to the physical status of the individual members.

The exercises must be graduated, and no attempt made to pass from one series until the more elementary stages have been mastered.

It is of especial importance that none of the more complicated, difficult, and arduous exercises should be forced upon those who are physically unfit. They must be always—from the learner's standpoint—moderate and progressive.

It is desirable also that the lessons should be as varied and as interesting as possible, and that reasonable opportunity be given for competition and the encouragement of those who are specially fitted to excel.

The exercises should aim at the equal employment of all the muscles, and not at the development of a few. The work in an ordinary gymnasium tends to throw strain mainly upon the upper extremities, while most of the outdoor games tend to develop the lower limbs. No great good can be obtained from tedious drilling and purposeless marching, and the time devoted to physical training should never be so fully absorbed as to allow no leisure for games and other pleasant forms of recreation.

In any instance violent intermittent exercises should be forbidden, and the performance of feats of strength should never come within the scope of the educational scheme.

3. *The exercises should be carried out under proper guidance, and with suitable and efficient apparatus.*

The teacher should be capable of instructing a large class—a qualification which is not commonly possessed.

4. *The time for the exercises should be carefully selected.*

Violent exercise after a full meal is obviously bad, and a course of physical instruction should not be carried out in the case of children who are tired from a long day's attendance in school, or who are feeble for want of food.

In the matter of schools it is well that the period for physical training should be interpolated among the hours devoted to ordinary school work. If between the hours of nine and twelve or nine and one the children could be allowed to take systematic exercise for thirty minutes, either in the open air or in some suitable building other than the schoolroom, they would be found to be actually refreshed by the change of occupation, to enjoy a period of mental rest, and to return to their work with vigour.

Another half-hour could be introduced during the progress of the afternoon lessons. The Rev. E. Warre, one of the masters at Eton, advises that a schoolboy's day should be disposed of as follows : Rest ten hours, work seven hours, meals and play seven hours.

So far as adults are concerned, the taking of violent exercise in the evening after a long and arduous day's work is often injurious in its result.

There is no time better than the early morning, before the labours of the day are commenced.

Adults who have been accustomed to exercises of strength and endurance should return but cautiously to such pursuits if they have passed through a long period of rest from exercise and are out of condition. A man may ride fifty miles a day on a bicycle very easily in the autumn, but he would be very unwise to attempt such a distance in the following spring, provided that he had taken no exercise during the winter.

5. *Exercises, so far as is possible, should be taken in the open air or in a large and very well-ventilated room.*

6. *Those who are taking systematic exercise should be properly clad.*

The garments should be light, loose, and made of wool. It is desirable that care be taken not to catch cold by standing about in clothes which are damp with perspiration.

This question of clothing is more fully dealt with in another section of this work.

FORMS OF EXERCISE.

So far as any classification can be made—and it must of necessity be rough—exercises may be divided into the following classes :

1. Exercises of Strength.

These involve actual and considerable muscular power, and are illustrated by advanced exercises in the gymnasium, with apparatus such as the horizontal bar, the trapeze, the rings. In a special category may be placed what may be termed feats of strength, such as lifting great weights, putting the shot, throwing the hammer, and the like.

These exercises involve "effort," *i. e.* the muscular position in which the man takes a deep breath, and then, when his chest is full, closes his glottis, so that he may make the thorax a fixed base from which the upper limbs can act. During the performance of the movement he does not breathe, his face becomes engorged, and the veins which stand out upon his forehead demonstrate the distended condition of the right side of the heart. It is during "effort" that some sudden and fatal accidents have occurred, such as rupture of the heart and the giving way of blood-vessels.

2. Exercises of Speed or of Rapid Movement.

These include running in all its forms and such exercises as involve very rapid and continued movements. The individual muscular contractions are not extreme, but they are very quickly repeated. The amount of work performed is distributed over a considerable period, and is not, as in exercises of strength, concentrated into a few moments.

These exercises are susceptible of considerable modification, and range from the extreme effort of the sprint runner to the easier movements of the paper-chaser or of the devotee of the skipping-rope.

Certain forms of gymnastic exercise rank in this class. The movements tend to develop the respiratory capacity, and are the exercises which soon bring about the state of breathlessness.

3. Exercises of Endurance.

In these the muscular effort is inconsiderable at any given moment, and is distributed over a still longer period of time.

Neither breathlessness nor rapid muscular exhaustion arrests the subject of the exercise. The continuance of his movements becomes a matter merely of endurance. Walking is a type of this variety. And in the same class must be placed many outdoor games, skating, rowing and cycling, drilling, and such exercises as are generally included under the term Swedish gymnastics.

In the training of the body the exercises of endurance must occupy the first, the most prominent, and the most important place.

4. Exercises of Skill

Are illustrated by the more complex gymnastic exercises, such as those which involve balancing, etc., by fencing and any other movements which imply, not necessarily severe or continued muscular exertion, but great activity of the brain and spinal cord.

The fencer in his earlier days becomes weary in his body, but as he becomes more experienced he "feels" the exercise, not in his muscles, but in his nervous system.

5. EXERCISES WHICH DEVELOP THE CHEST

May on account of their importance be especially classified. The exercises which come under this class are such as tend to develop the muscles of the chest—namely, the pectorals, the serratus magnus, the latissimus dorsi, the anterior abdominal muscles, and some others of lesser importance.

This, however, is not all. As Dr. Lagrange has pointed out, the size of the thoracic cavity can only be increased by increasing the volume of its contents, the lungs. "It is from within outwards," writes that author, "that the force capable of expanding the chest acts, and it is in reality to the lungs, and not to the muscles, that the chief share in the changes in form and size of the chest belongs. The most powerful inspiratory muscles cannot raise the ribs, unless the lungs participate in the movement of expansion, and on the other hand the lungs can raise the ribs without the aid of the muscles, for the chests of emphysematous patients remain vaulted in spite of their efforts to lower the ribs and complete the respiratory movement. . . . Mountaineers all have large chests, and the Indians who live on the high plateaux of the Cordillera in the Andes have been noted for the extraordinary size of their chests. . . . Singers with no exercise but singing acquire great respiratory power and a remarkable increase in the dimensions of their chests."

The exercises needed, therefore, should not only be such as develop the muscles of the upper part of the trunk, but such also as increase the volume of the respiratory movements. Among the latter would be placed, so far as children are especially concerned, running, skipping, rapid limb movements, and active exercises in the open air.

Many children are born with deformed and narrow chests which they inherit from their parents; in others the thorax has been distorted by rickets, by lung affections, or by spinal disease. One potent factor in the production of a narrow chest, outside these causes, is the hypertrophied tonsil.

It is anomalous to press a child to take exercises requiring vigorous respiratory movements when enlarged tonsils so block up the opening into the air-passages as to prevent the free entrance of air.

THE SELECTION OF EXERCISES ACCORDING TO INDIVIDUAL NEEDS.

CHILDREN.

The physical training of children should be commenced early, should be made as interesting as possible, and be represented in the main by what may be termed scientific romping.

The exercises should be given whenever possible in classes. To set a child to execute formal movements with dumb-bell or bar-bell when alone, and to march with no one for company, is a little dismal.

The set exercises should not be too formal, and never be too long, and in no instance should they be allowed to take the place of the ordinary outdoor games of children.

Games which involve shouting should be encouraged, and a very prominent position given to running, skipping, games with balls, and jumping. The most rudimentary of all games, "touch," is one of the most excellent. The upper limbs may be encouraged by such amusements as battledore and shuttlecock, and the lower by such a game as hop-scotch.

The set exercises should take the form of what are known as Swedish gymnastics, the vocal march, musical drill, and the class exercises with dumb-bell and bar-bell.

Children should avoid exercises of strength, and in the main, exercises of speed. They are best suited for exercises which involve moderate endurance, and such as require no great mental effort to follow.

In the matter of gymnastic appliances there is little need of especial work. The subject is considered in the description of gymnastic apparatus. The principal of these, from the children's standpoint, are the climbing rope, the inclined ladder, the vaulting horse, the parallel bars.

GIRLS AND WOMEN.

The physical condition of a large proportion of the girls and women in this country is quite deplorable, especially among the middle and upper classes. A well-developed, perfectly proportioned girl who is possessed of normal muscular strength, who can walk naturally, and can carry herself with grace, attracts attention. The wretched physical state of a large proportion of modern girls—especially of those who inhabit the large towns—is apt to be ascribed, not to a totally neglected education, but to the belief that growing girls are always awkward, uncouth, and weedy. This belief is not well founded.

The unfortunate girl is encouraged to be dull, to be prim, to be subdued, to suppress the outbursts of pure animal spirits. She is more or less under the curse of that detestable adjective "lady-like." She spends hours in an ill-ventilated schoolroom and upon a piano-stool, and the rest of her time is occupied in eating and sleeping, in preparing lessons, in stooping over needle-work, and in taking formal walks with the governess. Her clothes are probably a collection of hygienic errors.

It is not to be wondered that a girl so fostered is often a melancholy specimen of her species. She may be highly educated and the mistress of many accomplishments, she may be cultured and "refined" according to the boarding-school standard, but she will at the same time be probably more or less unfitted for the struggle of life and the mere circumstances which attend living.

There is something about the "higher education" of the modern girl which is comparable to the manufacture of the finest Sevres china. The result is beautiful from the designer's standpoint, but the cup is delicate : it cannot be used in daily life, and it must be kept in a cabinet.

A good digestion and an active liver are more useful in the battle of life than a knowledge of advanced mathematics, and sturdy limbs and strong hands are of more value to the mother of children than even decimal fractions and a familiarity with irregular verbs.

The lady-like girl is encouraged to keep her hands "fine," to have them compressed by gloves and protected from light, and to use them as little as possible in order that she might produce the wan, feeble appendage which constitutes the lady-like hand, and which is put to little more use than to set off a few rings. The face must be protected from the sun by sunshades and veils, the pink and white complexion of the invalid must be imitated. It would appear that the lady-like are always delicate, and a certain unobstrusive feebleness and flabbiness are signs of refinement. For use and influence in the world, for a capacity to enjoy the purest pleasures of life, and as an example of all the finest qualities of womanhood, no one among the "higher educated" can compare with such an one as the "Nut Brown Maid." The ballad of the "Nut Brown Maid" might well be engraved upon the wall of every "finishing" school for young ladies.

A neglected physical education produces a sorry object—a pale child with a poking head, a narrow chest, an unshapely back, a shuffling or mincing gait, and an ungainly carriage. She is without grace and without the capacity for vigorous physical enjoyment. Her ankles and wrists are clumsy, her complexion is dull, and if her circulation be bad—as is not unusual—her sodden-looking purplish arms are covered with a fine down. When she grows up to womanhood she finds herself unfitted for the duties and responsibilities of a wife and mother. She has little strength to withstand the hardships of life, and less capacity to enjoy its pleasures. She is nervous, querulous, frail, and in more respects than one a poor creature. Walking makes her tired, the sea makes her sick, the sun makes her head ache, the wind makes her chilly, effort of any unusual kind reduces her to a general wreck. The number of women who can travel without fussing and knocking up, and who can climb a ship's side and make their way across a heavy moor, and can, indeed, become companions to their husbands and brothers in the milder of these outdoor sports, is not considerable.

Younger girls may pursue the exercises named in dealing with the education of children. Those who are a little older have an infinite variety of healthy pursuits at their service—running, skipping, outdoor games of all kinds, riding, skating, swimming, cricket, games with balls, archery, tennis, climbing (in a moderate form), and certain exercises in the gymnasium. They should practice also such movements as develop the abdominal muscles, and should never neglect rowing.

Fencing in moderation is admirable ; a tendency to flat feet and weak ankles may be met with by such simple games as hop-scotch, by dancing (in the open air), by learning Scotch dances and the hornpipe. Cycling may, I think, be avoided, and I am under the impression that jumping may well be dispensed with in girls who have passed the period of puberty.

For women such exercises as have been just detailed are open, with the obvious modifications which their age and dispositions suggest.

Rowing is an admirable exercise for women up to almost any age.

The matter of clothing need only be briefly alluded to. It is of little use to expect great good from walking exercises if tight boots are worn, with high ankles and high heels. Corsets are an abomination, and rowing in corsets forms a means of developing a pendulous abdomen and the conditions which lead to hernia.

Lads

Between fourteen and eighteen have almost every form of exercise and physical recreation open to them. They should avoid exercises of strength and feats of strength, and exercises of extreme speed such as sprint running.

Adults

Between eighteen and twenty-five have the whole of the joys of the athletic world open to them, and if a man keep in training and in practice his period of athletic life may be extended to thirty.

The Middle-aged and Elderly

Must anticipate a progressive curtailment of their more active pursuits. There remain, however, walking and all the milder forms of outdoor exercise —riding, skating, cycling, and the use of the simpler gymnastic apparatus. After thirty very few individuals, indeed, are capable of undertaking exercises of speed without actual risk.

FEBRUARY, 1892.

CATALOGUE

OF

MEDICAL, DENTAL,

PHARMACEUTICAL AND SCIENTIFIC PUBLICATIONS,

WITH A SUBJECT INDEX,

PUBLISHED BY

P. BLAKISTON, SON & CO.,

(SUCCESSORS TO LINDSAY & BLAKISTON)

PUBLISHERS, IMPORTERS AND BOOKSELLERS,

1012 WALNUT ST., PHILADELPHIA.

THE FOLLOWING CATALOGUES WILL BE SENT FREE TO ANY ADDRESS, UPON APPLICATION.

This Catalogue, No. 1, including all of our own publications.

A Catalogue of Books for Dental Students and Practitioners.

A Catalogue of **Books on Chemistry, Technology,** Pharmacy, Microscopy, Hygiene, Sanitary Science, etc.

Students' Catalogue, including the "**Quiz-Compends**" and the most prominent Text-books and Manuals for medical students.

A Complete Classified Catalogue (68 pages) of all Books on Medicine, Dentistry, Pharmacy and Collateral Branches. English and American.

A Monthly Bulletin containing lists of all **new** Medical Books issued by various publishers.

P. Blakiston, Son & Co.'s publications may be had through Booksellers in all the principal cities of the United States and Canada, or any book will be sent by them, postpaid, upon receipt of the price. They will forward parcels by express, C. O. D., upon receiving a remittance of 25 per cent. of the amount ordered, to cover express charges. Money should **be remitted by** Express, money order, registered letter, or bank draft.

All new books received as soon as published. Special facilities for importing books from England, Germany and France.

Gould's New Medical Dictionary now ready. See page 4.

CLASSIFIED LIST, WITH PRICES,

OF ALL BOOKS PUBLISHED BY
P. BLAKISTON, SON & CO., PHILADELPHIA.

When the price is not given below, the book is out of print or about to be published.
Cloth binding, unless otherwise specified. For full descriptions, see following Catalogue.

ANÆSTHETICS.

Buxton. Anæsthetics. -	$——
Sansom. Chloroform. -	1.25
Turnbull. 3d Ed. -	3.00

ANATOMY.

Ballou. Veterinary Anat.	1.00
Heath. Practical. 7th Ed.	5.00
Holden. Dissector, Oil-cloth,	4.50
—— Osteology. -	6.00
—— Landmarks. 4th Ed.	1.25
Macalister's Text-Book.	
816 Illus. Clo. 7.50; Sh.	8.50
Potter. Compend of, 5th	
Ed. 133 Illustrations. -	1.00
Sutton. Ligaments. -	1.25

ATLASES AND DIAGRAMS.

Flower. Of Nerves. -	3.50
Marshall's Phys. and Anat.	
Diagrams. $40.00 and 60.00	

BRAIN AND INSANITY.

Blackburn. Autopsies. -	1.25
Bucknill and Tuke. Psycho-	
logical Medicine. -	8.00
Gowers. Diagnosis of Dis-	
eases of the Brain. New Ed.	2.00
Lewis, (Bevan). Mental	
Diseases. -	6.00
Mann's Psychological Med.	5.00
Wood. Brain and Overwork.	.50

CHEMISTRY.

See *Technological Books.*

Allen. Commercial Organic	
Analysis. 2d Ed. Volume I.	——
—— Volume II. -	——
—— Volume III. Part I.	4.50
Bartley. Medical. 2d Ed.	2.50
Bloxam's Text-Book. 7th Ed.	4.50
Bowman's Practical. -	2.00
Groves and Thorp. Chemi-	
cal Technology Vol. I. Fuels	7.50
Holland's Urine, Poisons and	
Milk. 4th Ed. -	1.00
Leffmann's New Compend.	1.00
——, Progressive Exercises.	1.00
Müter. Pract. and Anal.	2.00
Ramsay. Inorganic. Illus.	4.50
Richter's Inorganic. 3d Ed.	2.00
—— Organic. 2d Ed.	4.50
Smith. Electro-Chem. Anal.	1.00
Smith and Keller. Experi-	
ments. 2d Ed. Illus. Net,	.60
Stammer. Problems. -	.75
Sutton. Volumetric Anal.	5.00
Symonds. Manual of. -	2.00
Trimble. Analytical. -	1.50
Watts. (Fowne's) Inorg.	2.25
—— (Fowne's) Organ.	2.25
Wolff. Applied Medical.	1.00
Woody. Essentials of. 3d Ed.	1.25

CHILDREN.

Goodhart and Starr. 3.00; Sh.	3.50
Hale. Care of. -	.75
Hatfield. Compend of.	1.00
Meigs. Infant Feeding and	
Milk Analysis. -	1.00
Meigs and Pepper's Treatise.	5.00
Money. Treatment of. -	3.00
Muskett. Treatment of.	1.75
Osler. Cerebral Palsies of.	2.00
Smith. Wasting Diseases of.	3.00
Starr. Digestive Organs of.	2.25
—— Hygiene of the Nursery.	1.00

CLINICAL CHARTS.

Davis. Obstetrical. Pads, $	.50
Griffiths. Graphic. -	.50
Temperature Charts. "	.50

COMPENDS
And The Quiz-Compends.

Ballou. Veterinary Anat.	1.00
Brubaker's Physiol. 6th Ed.	1.00
Fox and Gould. The Eye.	1.00
Hatfield. Children. -	1.00
Horwitz. Surgery. 4th Ed.	1.00
Hughes. Practice. 2 Pts. Ea.	1.00
Landis. Obstetrics. 4th Ed.	1.00
Leffmann's Chemistry. 3d Ed.	1.00
Mason. Electricity. -	1.00
Morris. Gynæcology. -	1.00
Potter's Anatomy. 5th Ed.	1.00
—— Materia Medica. 5th Ed.	1.00
Stewart. Pharmacy. 3d Ed.	1.00
Warren. Dentistry. -	1.00

DEFORMITIES.

Reeves. Bodily Deformities	
and their Treatment. Illus.	2.25

DENTISTRY.

Barrett. Dental Surg. -	1.25
Blodgett. Dental Pathology.	1.75
Flagg. Plastic Filling. -	4.00
Fillebrown. Op. Dent. Illus.	2.50
Gorgas. Dental Medicine.	3.50
Harris. Principles and Prac.	7.00
—— Dictionary of. 5th Ed.	5.00
Heath. Dis. of Jaws. -	4.50
—— Lectures on Jaws. Bds.	1.00
Leber and Rottenstein.	
Caries. Paper	75
Richardson. Mech. Dent.	4.50
Sewell. Dental Surg. -	3.00
Stocken. Materia Medica.	2.50
Taft. Operative Dentistry.	4.25
—— Index of Dental Lit.	2.00
Talbot. Irregularity of Teeth.	3.00
Tomes. Dental Surgery.	5.00
—— Dental Anatomy.	4.00
Warren's Compend of. -	1.00
White. Mouth and Teeth.	.50

DICTIONARIES.

Cleveland's Pocket Medical.	.75
Gould's New Medical Diction-	
ary. ½ Lea, 3.25; ½ Mor.	
Thumb Index. -	4.25
Harris' Dental. Clo. 5.00; Ship,	6.00
Longley's Pronouncing -	1.00
Maxwell. Terminologia Med-	
ica Polyglotta. -	4.00
Treves. German English.	3.75

DIRECTORY.

Medical, of Philadelphia,	2.50

EAR.

Burnett. Hearing, etc.	.50
Pritchard. Diseases of.	1.50

ELECTRICITY.

Bigelow. Plain Talks on Medi-	
cal Electricity. 43 Illus.	1.00
Mason's Compend of Electric-	
ity and its Medical and Sur-	
gical Uses. -	1.00

EYE.

Arlt. Diseases of. -	2.50
Fox and Gould. Compend.	1.00
Gower's Ophthalmoscopy.	5.50
Harlan. Eyesight. -	.50
Hartridge. Refraction. 5th Ed.	1.75
—— Ophthalmoscope. -	1.50

HEADACHES.

Day. Their Treatment, etc.	1.25

HEALTH AND DOMESTIC MEDICINE.

Bulkley. The Skin. -	.50
Burnett. Hearing. -	.50
Cohen. Throat and Voice.	.50
Dulles. Emergencies. 3d Ed.	.75
Harlan. Eyesight. -	.50
Hartshorne. Our Homes.	.50
Hufeland. Long Life. -	1.00
Lincoln. Hygiene. -	.50
Osgood. Dangers of Winter.	.50
Packard. Sea Air, etc.	.50
Richardson's Long Life.	.50
Tanner. On Poisons. 6th Ed.	75
White. Mouth and Teeth.	.50
Wilson. Summer and its Dis.	.50
Wood. Brain Work. -	.50

HISTOLOGY.

See *Microscope and Pathology.*

HYGIENE.

See *Water.*

Fox. Water, Air, Food.	4.00
Lincoln. School Hygiene.	.50
Parke's (E.) Hygiene. 8th Ed.	5.00
—— (L. C.), Manual.	2.50
Starr. Hygiene of the Nursery.	1.00
Wilson's Handbook of. -	

JOURNALS, Etc.

Archives of Surgery. 4 Nos.	3.00
Jl. of Dermatology. -	3.00
Ophthalmic Review. " "	3.00
New Sydenham Society's	
Publications -	8.00

KIDNEY DISEASES.

Beale. Renal and Urin.	1.75
Ralfe. Dis. of Kidney, etc.	2.75
Thornton. Surg. of Kidney.	1.75
Tyson. Bright's Disease	
and Diabetes, Illus. -	3.50

LUNGS AND CHEST.

See *Phy. Diagnosis and Throat.*

Hare. Mediastinal Disease.	2.00

MASSAGE.

Murrell. Massage. 5th Ed.	1.50
Ostrom. Massage. 87 Illus.	1.00

MATERIA MEDICA.

Biddle. 11th Ed. Clo.	4.25
Gorgas. Dental. 4th Ed	3.50
Merrell's Digest. -	4.00
Potter's Compend of. 5th Ed.	1.00

HIGGINS, etc. (right column top)

Higgins. Practical Manual.	$1.75
Liebreich. Atlas of Ophth.	15.00
Macnamara. Diseases of.	4.00
Meyer and Fergus. Com-	
plete Text-Book, with Colored	
Plates. 270 Illus. Clo. 4.50; Sh.	5.50
Morton. Refraction. 4th Ed.	1.00
Ophthalmic Review.	
Monthly. -	3.00
Swanzy's Handbook. 3d Ed.	3.00

FEVERS.

Collie. On Fevers. -	2.50

⁎⁎ FOR SELF EXAMINATION, "3000 Questions on Medical Subjects."
Just Ready. Price, 10 cents *net.*

Potter's Handbook of. Third
  Ed. Clo. 4.00; Sheep, - $5.00

MEDICAL JURISPRUDENCE.

Reese Medical Jurisprudence
  & Toxicology, 3d Ed 3.00; Sh 3.50

MICROSCOPE.

Beale. How to Work with. 7.50
—— In Medicine. - 7.50
Carpenter. The Microscope.
  7th Ed 782 Illus. Cl. 6.50 Lea. 7.50
Lee Vade Mecum of. 2d Ed. 4.00
MacDonald. Examination of
  Water by. - - - 2 75

MISCELLANEOUS.

Beale. Slight Ailments. 1.25
Black. Microorganisms. 1.50
Burnet. Food and Dietaries. 1.75
Davis. Text book of Biology. 4.00
Duckworth. On Gout. - 7.00
Garrod. Rheumatism, etc. 6.00
Gross. Life of J. Hunter. Pa. .75
Haddon. Embryology. - 6.00
Haig. Uric Acid. - -
Henry. Anæmia. - - .75

NERVOUS DISEASES, Etc.

Flower. Atlas of Nerves. 3.50
Bowlby. Injuries of. - 4.50
Gowers. Manual of. 2d Ed.
  350 Illustrations. Vol. 1. 3 50
  Vol. 2 Nearly Ready.
—— Dis. of Spinal Cord
—— Diseases of Brain. 2.00
—— Syphilis and the Ner-
  vous System.
Obersteiner. Central Nervous
  System. - - - 6.00
Ormerod. Manual of. -
Osler. Cerebral Palsies. 2.00
Page. Injuries of Spine.
—— Railway Injuries. - 2 25
Thorburn. Surgery of the
  Spinal Cord. - 4.50
Watson. Concussions. 1.00

NURSING

Cullingworth. Manual of. .75
—— Monthly Nursing. .50
Domville's Manual. 7th Ed. .75
Fullerton. Obst. Nursing. 1.25
—— Nursing in Abdominal
  Surg. and Dis. of Women.
Humphrey. Manual of 1.25
Luckes. Hospital Sisters. 1.00
Parvin. Obstetric Nursing. .75
Starr. Hygiene of the Nursery 1.00
Temperature Charts. - .50

OBSTETRICS

Bar. Antiseptic Obstet. 1.75
Cazeaux and Tarnier. Stu-
  dents Ed. Colored Plates. 5.00
Davis. Obstetrical Chart. .50
Davis. Obstetrics. Illus 2.00
Galabin's Manual of. 3.00
Landis. Compend. 4 h Ed 1.00
Rigby. Obstetric Mem. .50
Schultze. Obstet. Diagrams 2.50
Strahan. Extra Uterine Preg. 1.00
Winckel's Text-book. 6.00

PATHOLOGY & HISTOLOGY

Blackburn. Autopsies. 1.00
Blodgett. Dental Pathology 1.25
Bowlby. Surgical Path. 2.00
Gibbes. Practical. 1.75
Gilliam. Essentials of. - 2.00
Stirling's Practical. 2.00
Virchow. Post-mortems. 1.00
—— Cellular Pathology 4.00
Wynter & Wethered. Path. 2.00

PHARMACY.

Beasley's Druggists' Rec'ts. 2.25
—— Formulary. - 2.25
Flückiger. Cinchona Barks 1.00
Mackenzie. Phar. of Throat 1.25

Merrell's Digest. - $4.00
Proctor. Practical Pharm. 4.50
Robinson. Latin Grammar of 2.00
Stewart's Compend. 3d Ed. 1.00
Tuson. Veterinary Pharm. 2.50

PHYSICAL DIAGNOSIS.

Fenwick's Student's Guide. 2 25
Tyson's Manual. - 1.25

PHYSIOLOGY.

Brubaker's Compend. Illus-
  trated. 6th Ed. - 1.00
Kirkes' 12th Ed. (Author's
  Ed.) Cloth, 4.00; Sheep, 5.00
Landois' Text-book. 845 Illus-
  trations. 4th Ed. Cl. 7.00; Sh. 8.00
Sanderson's Laboratory B'k. 5.00
Sterling. Practical Phys. 2.25
Tyson's Cell Doctrine. - 2.00
Yeo's Manual. 321 Illustrations
  5th Ed Cloth, 3.00; Sheep, 3.50

POISONS.

Aitken. The Ptomaines, etc. 1.25
Black. Formation of. - 1.50
Reese. Toxicology. 3d Ed. 3.00
Tanner. Memoranda of. .75

PRACTICE.

Beale. Slight Ailments. 1.25
Charteris. Guide to. - 3.00
Fagge's Practice. 2 Vols. 8.00
Fowler's Dictionary of. - 5.00
Hughes. Compend. of. 2 Pts. 2.00
—— Physicians' Edition.
  1 Vol. Morocco, Gilt edge. 2.50
Roberts. Text-book. 6th Ed. 5.50
Taylor's Manual of. - 4.00

PRESCRIPTION BOOKS.

Beasley's 3000 Prescriptions. 2.25
—— Receipt Book. - 2.25
—— Formulary. - 2.25
Pereira's Pocket-book. - 1.00
Wythe's Dose and Symptom
  Book. 17th Ed. - - 1.00

SKIN AND HAIR.

Anderson's Text-Book. - 4.50
Bulkley. The Skin. - .50
Crocker. Dis. of Skin. Illus.
Van Harlingen. Diagnosis
  and Treat. of Skin Dis.
  Col. Plates & Engravings. 2.50

STIMULANTS & NARCOTICS.

Lizars. On Tobacco. - .50
Miller. On Alcohol. .50
Parrish. Inebriety. - 1.25

SURGERY AND SURGICAL DISEASES.

Caird and Cathcart. Surgi-
  cal Handbook. Leather 2.50
Dulles. Emergencies. - .75
Heath's Minor. 9th Ed. 2.00
—— Diseases of Jaws 4.50
—— Lectures on Jaws. 2.50
Horwitz. Compend. 4th Ed 1.00
Jacobson. Operations of - 5.00
Moullin. Complete Text-
  book, 497 Illus.
  Subscription only, Colored
  Plates. Net. Cl. 7.00, Sh. 8.00
  ½ Rus. - - 9.00
Porter's Surgeon's Pocket-
  book. - - Leather 2.25
Smith. Abdominal Surg. 7.00
Swain. Surg. Emergencies. 1.50
Walsham. Practical Surg. 3.00
Watson's Amputations. 5.50

TECHNOLOGICAL BOOKS

Studies Chemistry
Cameron. Oils & Varnishes 2.50
—— Soap and Candles. 2.25
Gardner. Brewing, etc. 1.75
Gardner. Acetic Acid, etc. 1.75
—— Bleaching & Dyeing. 1.75
Groves and Thorp. Chemi-
  cal Technology. Vol. 1
  Midsof Fuels. Cl. 5.00 ½M. 9.00
Overman. Mineralogy. - 1.00

THERAPEUTICS.

Allen, Harlan, Harte, Van
  Harlingen. Local Thera ——
Biddle. 11th Ed. Cl 4 25; Sh $5.00
Burnet. Food and Dietaries. 1.75
Field. Cathartics and Emetics 1.75
Headland. Action of Med. 3.00
Jaworski. Carlsbad Salts. 1.00
Mays. Therap. Forces. 1.25
—— Theine - .50
Napheys' Medical. - -
—— Surgical. -
Ott. Action of Medicines. 2.00
Potter's Compend. 5th Ed. 1.00
—— Handbook of. 4.00; Sh 5.00
Waring's Practical. 4th Ed. 3.00

THROAT AND NOSE.

Cohen. Throat and Voice. .50
Greenhow. Bronchitis 1.25
Hutchinson. Nose & Throat 1.25
McBride. Clinical Manual,
  Colored Plates, - 7.00
Mackenzie. Throat and Nose.
  2 vols.
—— Pharmacopœia. - 1.25
Murrell. Bronchitis. 1.50
Potter. Stammering, etc. 1.00
Woakes. Post-Nasal Catarrh 1.50
—— Deafness, Giddiness, etc.

TRANSACTIONS AND REPORTS.

Penna. Hospital Reports. 1.25
Power and Holmes' Reports. 1.25
Trans. College of Physicians. 3.50
—— Amer. Surg. Assoc. 3.50
—— Assoc. Amer. Phys. 3.50

URINE & URINARY ORGANS.

Acton. Repro. Organs. 2.00
Beale. Urin. & Renal Dis. 1 75
—— Urin. Deposits. Plates 2.00
Holland. The Urine, Milk and
  Common Poisons. 4th Ed. 1.00
Legg. On Urine. - .75
Marshall and Smith. Urine 1.00
Ralfe. Kidney and Uri. Org. 2.75
Schnée. Diabetes. - 2.00
Thompson. Urinary Organs. 3.50
—— Surg. of Urin. Organs 1.25
—— Calculous Dis. 3d. Ed. 1.00
—— Lithotomy. - 3.50
—— Prostate. 6th Ed. 3.00
Thornton. Surg. of Kidney. 1.75
Tyson. Exam. of Urine. 1.50
Van Nuys. Urine Analysis. 2.00

VENEREAL DISEASES.

Hill and Cooper's Manual. 1.00

VETERINARY

Armatage. Vet. Rem. 3.00
Ballou. Anat. and Phys. 1.00
Tuson. Vet. Pharm 2.50

VISITING LISTS

Lindsay and Blakiston's
  Regular Edition. *Send for
  Circular.* - 1.00 to 2.00
—— Perpetual Ed. 1.25 to 1.50
—— Monthly Ed.
  Plain, 1.25; Tucks, 1.50

WATER.

Blair. Potable Waters. 2.00
Fox. Water, Air, Food. 2.00
Frankland. Analysis of. 1.00
Leffmann & Beam. Exam of 1.25
MacDonald. Examination of 2.75

WOMEN, DISEASES OF.

Byford's Text-book. 4th Ed. 5.00
—— Uterus. - 1.25
Edis. Sterility. - 2.00
Lewers. Dis. of Women. 2.50
Morris. Compend. 3d Ed. 1.00
Tilt. Change of Life. - 1.25
Winckel, by Parvin. Manual
  of. Illus. Cl. 3.00; Sh 3.50

A NEW MEDICAL DICTIONARY.

A compact, concise Vocabulary, including all the Words and Phrases used in medicine, with their proper Pronunciation and Definitions.

BASED ON RECENT MEDICAL LITERATURE.

BY

GEORGE M. GOULD, A.B., M.D.,

Ophthalmic Surgeon to the Philadelphia Hospital, Clinical Chief Ophthalmological Dept. German Hospital, Philadelphia.

It is not a mere compilation from other dictionaries. The definitions have been made by the aid of the most recent standard text-books in the various branches of medicine. It includes

Small 8vo, Half Morocco, as above, with
Thumb Index, ... $4.25
Plain Dark Leather, without Thumb Index, 3.25

SEVERAL THOUSAND NEW WORDS NOT CONTAINED IN ANY SIMILAR WORK.

IT CONTAINS TABLES of the ABBREVIATIONS used in Medicine, of the ARTERIES, of the BACILLI, giving the Name, Habitat, Characteristics, etc.; of GANGLIA, LEUCOMAÏNES, MICROCOCCI, MUSCLES, NERVES, PLEXUSES, PTOMAÏNES, with the Name, Formula, Physiological Action, etc.; and the COMPARISON OF THERMOMETERS, of all the most used WEIGHTS AND MEASURES of the world, of the MINERAL SPRINGS OF THE U. S., VITAL STATISTICS, etc. Much of the material thus classified is not obtainable by English readers in any other work.

OPINIONS OF PROMINENT MEDICAL PAPERS.

"One pleasing feature of the book is that the reader can almost invariably find the definition under the word he looks for, without being referred from one place to another, as is too commonly the case in medical dictionaries. The tables of the bacilli, micrococci, leucomaïnes and ptomaïnes are excellent, and contain a large amount of information in a limited space. The anatomical tables are also concise and clear. . . . We should unhesitatingly recommend this dictionary to our readers, feeling sure that it will prove of much value to them."—*American Journal of Medical Science, Sept. 1890.*

"As a handy, concise and accurate, and complete medical dictionary it decidedly claims a very high place among works of this description. In fact, taking handiness and cheapness into account, we certainly think this is the general practitioner's model dictionary, and we cordially recommend it to our readers. The definitions are for the most part terse and accurate, and the derivations up to modern lights."—*British Medical Journal, London, Sept. 1890.*

May be obtained through all Booksellers. Sample pages free.

P. BLAKISTON, SON & CO.'S
Medical and Scientific Publications,
No. 1012 Walnut St., Philadelphia.

ACTON. The Functions and Disorders of the Reproductive Organs in Childhood, Youth, Adult Age and Advanced Life, considered in their Physiological, Social and Moral Relations. By WM. ACTON, M.D., M.R.C.S. 7th Edition. Cloth, $2.00

AITKEN. Animal Alkaloids, the Ptomaïnes, Leucomaïnes and Extractives in their Pathological Relations. By WILLIAM AITKEN. M.D., F.R.S., Prof. of Path. in the Army Medical School, Netley, England. 2d Ed. Enlarged. Cloth, $1.25

ALLEN, HARLAN. HARTE, VAN HARLINGEN. Local Therapeutics. A Handbook of Local Therapeutics, being a practical description of all those agents used in the local treatment of disease, such as Ointments, Plasters, Powders, Lotions, Inhalations, Suppositories, Bougies, Tampons, etc., and the proper methods of preparing and applying them. By HARRISON ALLEN, M.D., Emeritus Professor of Physiology in the University of Penna.; Laryngologist to the Rush Hospital for Consumption ; late Surgeon to the Philadelphia and St. Joseph's Hospitals. GEORGE C. HARLAN, M.D., late Professor of Diseases of the Eye in the Philadelphia Polyclinic and College for Graduates in Medicine ; Surgeon to the Wills Eye Hospital, and Eye and Ear Department of the Pennsylvania Hospital. RICHARD H. HARTE, M.D., Demonstrator of Osteology, University of Pennsylvania ; Assistant Surgeon, University Hospital, and ARTHUR VAN HARLINGEN, M.D., Professor of Diseases of the Skin in the Philadelphia Polyclinic and College for Graduates in Medicine ; late Clinical Lecturer on Dermatology in Jefferson Medical College ; Dermatologist to the Howard Hospital. In One Handsome Compact Volume. *Nearly Ready.*

ALLEN. Commercial Organic Analysis. A Treatise on the Modes of Assaying the Various Organic Chemicals and Products employed in the Arts, Manufactures, Medicine, etc., with Concise Methods for the Detection of Impurities, Adulterations, etc. Second Edition. Revised and Enlarged. By ALFRED ALLEN, F.C.S.
    Vol. I. Alcohols, Ethers, Vegetable Acids, Starch, etc. *Out of Print.*
    Vol. II. Fixed Oils and Fats, Hydrocarbons and Mineral Oils, Phenols and their Derivatives, Coloring Matters, etc. *Out of Print.*
    Vol. III.—Part I. Acid Derivatives of **Phenols, Aromatic** Acids, Tannins, Dyes, and Coloring Matters. 8vo. Cloth, $4.50

ANDERSON. A Treatise on Skin Diseases. With special reference to Diagnosis and Treatment, and including an Analysis of 11,000 consecutive cases. By T. McCALL ANDERSON, M.D., Professor of Clinical Medicine, University of Glasgow. With several Full-page Plates, two of which are Colored Lithographs, and numerous Wood Engravings. Octavo. 650 pages. Cloth, $4.50 ; Leather, $5.50

ARCHIVES OF SURGERY. Edited by JONATHAN HUTCHINSON, F.R.S. Colored Illustrations. Published Quarterly. 75 cents a number. Per Vol. $3.00

ARLT. Diseases of the Eye. Clinical Studies on Diseases of the Eye. Including the Conjunctiva, Cornea and Sclerotic, Iris and Ciliary Body. By Dr. FERD. RITTER VON ARLT, University of Vienna. Authorized Translation by LYMAN WARE, M.D., Surgeon to the Illinois Charitable Eye and Ear Infirmary, Chicago. Illustrated. 8vo. Cloth, $2.50

ARMATAGE. The Veterinarian's Pocket Remembrancer : being Concise Directions for the Treatment of Urgent or Rare Cases, embracing Semeiology, Diagnosis, Prognosis, Surgery, Therapeutics, Toxicology, Detection of Poisons by their appropriate tests, Hygiene, etc. By GEORGE ARMATAGE, M.R.C.V.S. Second Edition. 32mo. Boards, $1.25

BALLOU. Veterinary Anatomy and Physiology. By WM. R. BALLOU, M.D.,
Prof. of Equine Anatomy, New York College of Veterinary Surgeons; Physician
to Bellevue Dispensary, and Lecturer on Genito-Urinary Surgery, New York
Polyclinic, etc. With 29 Graphic Illustrations. 12mo. *No. 12 ? Quiz-Compend
Series. ?*   Cloth, $1.00. Interleaved, for the addition of Notes, $1.25

BAR. Antiseptic Midwifery. The Principles of Antiseptic Methods Applied to
Obstetric Practice. By Dr. PAUL BAR, Obstetrician to, formerly Interne in, the
Maternity Hospital, Paris. Authorized Translation by HENRY D. FRY, M.D.,
with an Appendix by the author. Octavo.   Cloth, $1.75

BARRETT. Dental Surgery for General Practitioners and Students of Medicine
and Dentistry. Extraction of Teeth, etc. By A. W. BARRETT, M.D. Second
Edition. Illustrated *Practical Series.* [*See page 19.*]   Cloth, $1.25

BARTLEY. Medical Chemistry. Second Edition. A Text-book for Medical and
Pharmaceutical Students. By E. H. BARTLEY, M.D., Professor of Chemistry and
Toxicology at the Long Island College Hospital; President of the American
Society of Public Analysts; Chief Chemist, Board of Health, of Brooklyn, N.Y.
Revised and enlarged. With 62 Illustrations. Glossary and Complete Index.
423 pages. 12mo.   Cloth, $2.50

BEALE. On Slight Ailments; their Nature and Treatment. By LIONEL S. BEALE,
M.D., F.R.S., Professor of Practice, King's Medical College, London. Second
Edition. Enlarged and Illustrated. 8vo.   Cloth, $1.25

> **Urinary and Renal Diseases** and Calculous Disorders. Hints on Diagnosis
> and Treatment. Demi-8vo. 356 pages.   Cloth, $1.75

> **The Use of the Microscope in Practical Medicine.** For Students and
> Practitioners, with full directions for examining the various secretions, etc.,
> in the Microscope. Fourth Edition. 500 Illustrations. 8vo. Cloth, $7.50

> **How to Work with the Microscope.** A Complete Manual of Microscopical
> Manipulation, containing a full description of many new processes of
> investigation, with directions for examining objects under the highest
> powers, and for taking photographs of microscopic objects. Fifth Edition.
> Containing over 400 Illustrations, many of them colored. 8vo. Cloth, $7.50

> **One Hundred Urinary Deposits,** on eight sheets, for the Hospital, Labora-
> tory, or Surgery. New Edition. 4to.   Paper, $2.00

BEASLEY'S Book of Prescriptions. Containing over 3100 Prescriptions, collected
from the Practice of the most Eminent Physicians and Surgeons—English,
French and American; a Compendious History of the Materia Medica, Lists of
the Doses of all Officinal and Established Preparations, and an Index of Diseases
and their Remedies. By HENRY BEASLEY. Seventh Edition.   Cloth, $2.25

> **Druggists' General Receipt Book.** Comprising a copious Veterinary Formu-
> lary; Recipes in Patent and Proprietary Medicines, Druggists' Nostrums,
> etc.; Perfumery and Cosmetics; Beverages, Dietetic Articles and Condi-
> ments; Trade Chemicals, Scientific Processes, and an Appendix of Useful
> Tables. Ninth Edition. Revised.   Cloth, $2.25

> **Pocket Formulary** and Synopsis of the British and Foreign Pharmacopœias.
> Comprising Standard and Approved Formulæ for the Preparations and
> Compounds Employed in Medical Practice. Eleventh Edition. Cloth, $2.25

BIDDLE'S Materia Medica and Therapeutics. Eleventh Edition. For the Use of
Students and Physicians. By Prof. JOHN B. BIDDLE, M.D., Professor of Materia
Medica in Jefferson Medical College, Philadelphia. The Eleventh Edition, thor-
oughly revised, and in many parts rewritten, by his son, CLEMENT BIDDLE, M.D.,
Assistant Surgeon, U. S. Navy, and HENRY MORRIS, M.D., Fellow of the College
of Physicians, of Philadelphia, etc.   Cloth, $4.25; Sheep, $5.00

BIGELOW. Plain Talks on Medical Electricity and Batteries, with a Therapeutic Index and a Glossary. Prepared for Practitioners and Students of Medicine. By HORATIO R. BIGELOW, M.D., Fellow of the British Gynæcological
Society; of the American Electro-Therapeutic Association; Member American
Medical Association, etc. 43 Illustrations, and a Glossary. 12mo. Cloth, $1.00

BLACK. Micro-Organisms. The Formation of Poisons. A Biological study of
the Germ Theory of Disease. By G. V. BLACK, M.D., D.D.S.   Cloth, $1.50

BLACKBURN. Autopsies. A Manual of Autopsies, Designed for the use of Hospitals for the Insane and other Public Institutions. By I. W. BLACKBURN, M.D., Pathologist to the Government Hospital for the Insane, Washington, D. C. With ten Full-page Plates and four other Illustrations. 12mo. · Cloth, $1.25

BLAIR. Potable Waters. The Organic Analysis of. By J. A. BLAIR, M. E., C. M., D. SC. Edin., etc. 12mo. Cloth, $1.00

BLODGETT'S Dental Pathology. By ALBERT N. BLODGETT, M.D., Late Prof. of Pathology and Therapeutics, Boston Dental Coll. 33 Illus. 12mo. Cloth, $1.75

BLOXAM. Chemistry, Inorganic and Organic. With Experiments. By CHARLES L. BLOXAM. Edited by J. M. THOMPSON, Professor of Chemistry in King's College, London, and A. G. BLOXAM, Dem. of Chem., Royal Agricultural College, Cirencester. Seventh Edition. Revised and Enlarged. With 281 Engravings. 8vo. Cloth, $4.50; Leather, $5.50

BOWLBY. Injuries **and Diseases of the Nerves,** and their surgical treatment. By ANTHONY A. BOWLBY, F.R.C.S., Dem. of Practical Surgery at St. Bartholomew's Hospital. Illus. by 4 Colored and 20 Full-page Plates. 8vo. Cloth, $4.50
Surgical Pathology and Morbid Anatomy. 135 Illustrations. Cloth, $2.00

BOWMAN. Practical Chemistry, including analysis, with about 100 Illustrations. By Prof. JOHN E. BOWMAN. Eighth English Edition. Revised by Prof. BLOXAM, Professor of Chemistry, King's College, London. Cloth, $2.00

BRUBAKER. Physiology. A Compend of Physiology, specially adapted for the use of Students and Physicians. By A. P. BRUBAKER, M.D., Demonstrator of Physiology at Jefferson Medical College, Prof. of Physiology, Penn'a College of Dental Surgery, Philadelphia. Sixth Edition. Revised, Enlarged and Illustrated. *No. 4. ? Quiz-Compend Series ?* 12mo. Cloth, $1.00; Interleaved, $1.25

BUCKNILL AND TUKE'S Manual of Psychological Medicine: containing the Lunacy Laws, the Nosology, Ætiology, Statistics, Description, Diagnosis, Pathology (including morbid Histology) and Treatment of Insanity. By JOHN CHARLES BUCKNILL, M.D., F.R.S., and DANIEL HACK TUKE, M.D., F.R.C.P. Fourth Edition. Numerous illustrations. 8vo. Cloth, $8.00

BULKLEY. The Skin in Health and Disease. By L. DUNCAN BULKLEY, M.D., Attending Physician at the New York Hospital. Illustrated. Cloth, .50

BUXTON. On Anæsthetics. A Manual. By DUDLEY WILMOT BUXTON, M.R.C.S., M.R.C.P., Ass't to Prof. of Med., and Administrator of Anæsthetics, University College Hospital, London. *Practical Series.* [*See page 19.*] Cloth, $1.25

BURNET. Foods and Dietaries. A Manual of Clinical Dietetics. By R. W. BURNET, M.D., M.R.C.P., Physician to the Great Northern Central Hospital. General Contents—Diet in Derangements of the Digestive, Nervous and Respiratory Organs; in Gout, Rheumatism, Anæmia, Fevers, Obesity, etc.; in Diseases of Children, Alcoholism, etc. With Appendix on Predigested Foods and Invalid Cookery. Full directions as to hours of taking nourishment, quantity, etc., are given. 12mo. Cloth, $1.75

BURNETT. Hearing, and How to Keep It. By CHAS. H. BURNETT, M.D., Prof. of Diseases of the Ear at the Philadelphia Polyclinic. Illustrated. Cloth, .50

BYFORD. Diseases of Women. The Practice of Medicine and Surgery, as applied to the Diseases and Accidents Incident to Women. By W. H. BYFORD, A.M., M.D., Professor of Gynæcology in Rush Medical College and of Obstetrics in the Woman's Medical College; Surgeon to the Woman's Hospital; Ex-President American Gynæcological Society, etc., and HENRY T. BYFORD, M.D., Surgeon to the Woman's Hospital of Chicago; Gynæcologist to St. Luke's Hospital; President Chicago Gynæcological Society, etc. Fourth Edition. Revised. Rewritten and Enlarged. With 306 Illustrations, over 100 of which are original. Octavo. 832 pages. Cloth, $5.00; Leather, $6.00
On the Uterus. Chronic Inflammation and Displacement. Cloth, $1.25

CAIRD and CATHCART. Surgical Handbook for the use of Practitioners and Students. By F. MITCHELL CAIRD, M.B., F.R.C.S., and C. WALKER CATHCART, M.B., F.R.C.S., Ass't Surgeons Royal Infirmary. With over 200 Illustrations. 32mo. 400 pages. Pocket size. Leather covers, $2.50

CAMERON. Oils and Varnishes. A Practical Handbook, by JAMES CAMERON, F.I.C. With Illustrations, Formulæ, Tables, etc. 12mo. Cloth, $2.50
Soap and Candles. A New Handbook for Manufacturers, Chemists, Analysts, etc. Compiled from all reliable and recent sources. 54 Illustrations. 12mo. Cloth, $2.25

CARPENTER. The Microscope and Its Revelations. By W. B. CARPENTER, M.D., F.R.S. Seventh Edition. By Rev. DR. DOLLINGER, F. R. S. Revised and Enlarged, with 800 Illustrations and many Lithographs. Octavo. 1100 Pages. Cloth, $6.50; Sheep, $7.50

CAZEAUX and TARNIER'S Midwifery. With Appendix, by Mundé. Eighth Revised and Enlarged Edition. With Colored Plates and numerous other Illustrations. The Theory and Practice of Obstetrics, including the Diseases of Pregnancy and Parturition, Obstetrical Operations, etc. By P. CAZEAUX, Member of the Imperial Academy of Medicine, Adjunct Professor in the Faculty of Medicine in Paris. Remodeled and rearranged, with revisions and additions, by S. TARNIER, M.D., Professor of Obstetrics and Diseases of Women and Children in the Faculty of Medicine of Paris. Eighth American, from the Eighth French and First Italian Edition. Edited and Enlarged by ROBERT J. HESS, M.D., Physician to the Northern Dispensary, Phila., etc., with an Appendix by PAUL F. MUNDÉ, M.D., Professor of Gynæcology at the New York Polyclinic, and at Dartmouth College ; Vice-President American Gynæcological Society, etc. Illustrated by Chromo-Lithographs, Lithographs, and other Full-page Plates, seven of which are beautifully colored, and numerous Wood Engravings. *Students' Edition.* One Vol., 8vo. Cloth, $5.00 ; Full Leather, $6.00

CHARTERIS. Practice of Medicine. The Student's Guide. By M. CHARTERIS, M.D., Professor of Therapeutics and Materia Medica, Glasgow University, etc. Sixth Edition, with Therapeutical Index and many Illustrations. Cloth, $3.00

CLEVELAND'S Pocket Dictionary. A Pronouncing Medical Lexicon, containing correct Pronunciation and Definition of terms used in medicine and the collateral sciences, abbreviations used in prescriptions, list of poisons, their antidotes, etc. By C. H. CLEVELAND, M.D. Thirty-third Edition. Very small pocket size. Cloth, .75 ; Tucks with Pocket, $1.00

COHEN. The Throat and Voice. By J. SOLIS-COHEN, M.D. Illus. 12mo. Cloth, .50

COLLIE, On Fevers. A Practical Treatise on Fevers, Their History, Etiology, Diagnosis, Prognosis and Treatment. By ALEXANDER COLLIE, M.D., M.R.C.P., Lond. With Colored Plates. *Practical Series. See Page 19.* Cloth, $2.50

CROCKER. Diseases of the Skin. Their Description, Pathology, Diagnosis and Treatment. By H. RADCLIFFE CROCKER, M.D., Physician to the Dept. of Skin Dis. University College Hospital, London. With Illustrations. Second Edition. Enlarged. *In Press.*

CULLINGWORTH. A Manual of Nursing, Medical and Surgical. By CHARLES J. CULLINGWORTH, M.D., Physician to St. Thomas' Hospital, London. Third Revised Edition. With 18 Illustrations. 12mo. Cloth, .75
A Manual for Monthly Nurses. Third Edition. 32mo. Cloth, .50

DAVIS. Biology. An Elementary Treatise. By J. R. AINSWORTH DAVIS, of University College, Aberystwyth, Wales. Thoroughly Illustrated. 12mo. $4.00

DAVIS. A Manual of Obstetrics. Being a complete manual for Physicians and Students. By EDWARD P. DAVIS, M.D., Demonstrator of Obstetrics, Jefferson Medical College ; Physician to the Philadelphia Hospital ; Editor American Journal Medical Sciences ; etc. With 11 Colored and other Lithograph Plates and 128 other Illustrations. 12mo. Cloth, $2.00
Clinical Obstetrical Chart. Designed by ED. P. DAVIS, M.D., and J. P. CROZER GRIFFITH, M.D. Sample copies free. Put up in loose packages of 50, .50
Price to Hospitals, 500 copies, $4.00; 1000 copies, $7.50. With name of Hospital printed on, 50 cents extra.

DAY. On Headaches. The Nature, Causes and Treatment of Headaches. By WM. H. DAY, M.D. Fourth Edition. Illustrated. 8vo. Paper, .75 ; Cloth, $1.25

DERMATOLOGY, Journal of. Edited by MALCOLM MORRIS, M.R.C.S. London, and D. G. BROOKE, M.R.C.S. Manchester, Eng. Monthly. Per Annum, $3.00

DOMVILLE. **Manual for Nurses** and others engaged in attending to the sick. By Ed. J. Domville, M.D. 7th Edition. Revised. With Recipes for Sick-room Cookery, etc. 12mo. Cloth, .75

DUCKWORTH. **On Gout.** **Illustrated.** A treatise on Gout. By Sir Dyce Duckworth, M.D. (Edin.), F.R.C.P., Physician to, and Lecturer on Clinical Medicine at, St. Bartholomew's Hospital, London. With Chromo-lithographs and Engravings. Octavo. Cloth, $7.00

DULLES. **What to Do First,** In Accidents and Poisoning. By C. W. Dulles, M.D. Third Edition, Enlarged, with new Illustrations. Cloth, .75

EDIS. **Sterility in Women.** By A. W. Edis, M.D., F.R.C.P., late President British Gynæcological Society; Senior Physician, Chelsea Hospital for Women; Physician to British Lying-in Hospital, etc. Illustrated. 8vo. Cloth, $1.75

FAGGE. **The Principles and Practice of Medicine.** By C. Hilton Fagge, M.D., F.R.C.P., F.R.M.C.S., Examiner in Medicine, University of London; Physician to, and Lecturer on Pathology in, Guy's Hospital; Senior Physician to Evelina Hospital for Sick Children, etc. Arranged for the press by Philip H. Pye-Smith, M.D., Lect. on Medicine in Guy's Hospital. Including a section on Cutaneous Affections, by the Editor; Chapter on Cardiac Diseases, by Samuel Wilkes, M.D., F.R.S., and Complete Indexes by Robert Edmund Carrington. 2 vols. Royal 8vo. Cloth, $8.00; Leather, $10.00; Half Russia, $12.00.

FENWICK. **Student's Guide to Physical Diagnosis.** By Saml. Fenwick, M.D., M.R.C.P., Physician to the London Hospital. Seventh Edition. 117 Illustrations. 12mo. Cloth, $2.25

FIELD. **Evacuant Medication**—Cathartics and Emetics. By Henry M. Field, M.D., Professor of Therapeutics, Dartmouth Medical College, Corporate Member Gynæcological Society of Boston, etc. 12mo. 288 pp. Cloth, $1.75

FILLEBROWN. **A Text-Book of Operative** Dentistry. Written by invitation of the National Association of Dental Faculties. By Thomas Fillebrown, M.D., D.M.D., Professor of Operative Dentistry in the Dental School of Harvard University; Member of the American Dental Assoc., etc. Illus. 8vo. Clo., $2.50

FLAGG. Plastics and Plastic Fillings, as pertaining to the filling of all Cavities of Decay in Teeth below medium in structure, and to difficult and inaccessible cavities in teeth of all grades of structure. By J. Foster Flagg, D.D.S., Professor of Dental Pathology in Philadelphia Dental College. Fourth Revised Edition. With many Illustrations. 8vo. Cloth, $4.00

FLOWER'S Diagrams of **the Nerves** of the Human Body. Exhibiting their Origin, Divisions and Connections, with their Distribution to the various Regions of the Cutaneous Surface and to all the Muscles. By William H. Flower, F.R.C.S., F.R.S., Hunterian Professor of Comparative Anatomy, and Conservator of the Museum of the Royal College of Surgeons. Third Edition, thoroughly revised. With six Large Folio Maps or Diagrams. 4to. Cloth, $3.50

FLÜCKIGER. The Cinchona Barks Pharmacognostically Considered. By Professor Friedrich Flückiger, of Strasburg. Translated by Frederick B. Power, ph.d. With 8 Lithographic Plates. Royal octavo. Cloth, $1.50

FOWLER'S Dictionary of Practical Medicine. By Various Writers. An Encyclopedia of Medicine. Edited by James Kingston Fowler, M.A., M.D., F.R.C.P., Senior Asst. Physician to, and Lecturer on Pathological Anatomy at, the Middlesex Hospital and the Hospital for Consumption and Diseases of the Chest, Brompton, London. 8vo. Cloth, $5.00; Half Morocco, $6.00

FOX. Water, Air and Food. Sanitary Examinations of Water, Air and Food. By Cornelius B. Fox, M.D. 110 Engravings. 2d Ed. Revised. Cloth, $4.00

FOX AND GOULD. Compend on Diseases of the Eye and Refraction, including Treatment and Surgery. By L. WEBSTER FOX, M.D., Chief Clinical Assistant, Ophthalmological Department, Jefferson Medical College Hospital; Ophthalmic Surgeon, Germantown Hospital, Philadelphia; late Clinical Assistant at Moorfields, London, England, etc., and GEO. M. GOULD, M.D. Second Edition. Enlarged. 71 Illustrations and 39 Formulæ. *Being No. 8, ? Quiz-Compend ? Series.* Cloth, $1.00. Interleaved for the addition of notes, $1.25

FRANKLAND'S Water Analysis. For Sanitary Purposes, with Hints for the Interpretation of Results. By E. FRANKLAND, M.D., F.R.S. Illustrated. 12mo. Cloth, $1.00

FULLERTON. Obstetrical Nursing. A Handbook for Nurses, Students and Mothers. By ANNA M. FULLERTON, M.D., Demonstrator of Obstetrics in the Woman's Medical College; Physician in charge of, and Obstetrician and Gynæcologist to, the Woman's Hospital, Philadelphia, etc. 34 Illustrations. Second Edition. Revised and Enlarged. 12mo. Cloth, $1.25
　　Nursing in Abdominal Surgery and Diseases of Women. Comprising the Regular Course of Instruction at the Training School of the Woman's Hospital, Philadelphia. 70 Illustrations. 12mo. Cloth, $1.50

GALABIN'S Midwifery. A Manual for Students and Practitioners. By A. LEWIS GALABIN, M.D., F.R.C.P., Professor of Midwifery at, and Obstetric Physician to, Guy's Hospital, London. 227 Illustrations. Cloth, $3.00; Leather, $3.50

GARDNER. The Brewer, Distiller and Wine Manufacturer. A Handbook for all Interested in the Manufacture and Trade of Alcohol and Its Compounds. Edited by JOHN GARDNER, F.C.S. Illustrated. Cloth, $1.75
　　Bleaching, Dyeing, and Calico Printing. With Formulæ. Illustrated. $1.75
　　Acetic Acid, Vinegar, Ammonia and Alum. Illustrated. Cloth, $1.75

GARROD. On Rheumatism. A Treatise on Rheumatism and Rheumatic Arthritis. By ARCHIBALD EDWARD GARROD, M.A. Oxon., M.D., M.R.C.S. Eng., Asst. Physician, West London Hospital. Illustrated. Octavo. Cloth, $6.00

GIBBES'S Practical Histology and Pathology. By HENEAGE GIBBES, M.B. 12mo. Third Edition. Cloth, $1.75

GILLIAM'S Pathology. The Essentials of Pathology; a Handbook for Students. By D. TOD GILLIAM, M.D., Professor of Physiology, Starling Medical College, Columbus, O. With 47 Illustrations. 12mo. Cloth, $2.00

GOODHART and STARR'S Diseases of Children. The Student's Guide to the Diseases of Children. By J. F. GOODHART, M.D., F.R.C.P., Physician to Evelina Hospital for Children; Demonstrator of Morbid Anatomy at Guy's Hospital. Second American from the Third English Edition. Rearranged and Edited, with notes and additions, by LOUIS STARR, M.D., Clinical Professor of Diseases of Children in the University of Pennsylvania; Physician to the Children's Hospital. With many new prescriptions. Cloth, $3.00; Leather, $3.50

GORGAS'S Dental Medicine. A Manual of Materia Medica and Therapeutics. By FERDINAND J. S. GORGAS, M.D., D.D.S., Professor of the Principles of Dental Science, Dental Surgery and Dental Mechanism in the Dental Dep. of the Univ. of Maryland. 4th Edition. Revised and Enlarged. 8vo. Cloth, $3.50

GOULD'S New Medical Dictionary. Including all the Words and Phrases used in Medicine, with their proper Pronunciation and Definitions, based on Recent Medical Literature. By GEORGE M. GOULD, B.A., M.D., Ophthalmic Surgeon to the Philadelphia Hospital, etc., With Tables of the Bacilli, Micrococci, Leucomaïnes, Ptomaïnes, etc., of the Arteries, Muscles, Nerves, Ganglia and Plexuses; Mineral Springs of U. S., Vital Statistics, etc. Small octavo, 520 pages.
　　　　　　Half Dark Leather, $3.25; Half Morocco, Thumb Index, $4.25

. *Sample pages and descriptive circular of Gould's Dictionary sent free upon application.*

GOWERS, Manual of Diseases of the Nervous System. A Complete Text-book By WILLIAM R. GOWERS, M.D., Prof. Clinical Medicine, University College London. Physician to National Hospital for the Paralyzed and Epileptic. Second Edition. Revised, Enlarged and in many parts rewritten. With many new Illustrations. Two Volumes. Octavo.

> VOL. I. **Diseases of the Nerves and Spinal Cord.** 616 pages. Cloth, $3.50
>
> VOL. II. Diseases of the Brain and Cranial Nerves; General and Functional Diseases. *Nearly Ready.*

> **Diagnosis of Diseases of the Brain.** 8vo. Second Ed. Illus. Cloth, $2.00
>
> **Diagnosis of Diseases of the Spinal Cord.** 4th Edition. *Preparing.*
>
> **Medical Ophthalmoscopy.** A Manual and Atlas, with Colored Autotype and Lithographic Plates and Wood-cuts, comprising Original Illustrations of the changes of the Eye in Diseases of the Brain, Kidney, etc. Third Edition. Revised, with the assistance of R. MARCUS GUNN, F.R.C.S., Surgeon, Royal London Ophthalmic Hospital, Moorfields. Octavo. Cloth, $3.50

> Syphilis **and the Nervous System.** Being the Lettsomian Lectures for 1889. 8vo. *In Press.*

GROSS'S Biography **of John Hunter.** John Hunter and His Pupils. By Professor S. D. GROSS, M.D. With a Portrait. 8vo. Paper, .75

GREENHOW. Chronic Bronchitis, as connected with Gout, Emphysema, and Diseases of the Heart. By E. H. GREENHOW, M.D. Paper, .75 ; Cloth, $1.25

GRIFFITH'S Graphic Clinical Chart. Designed by J. P. CROZER GRIFFITH, M.D., Instructor in Clinical Medicine in the University of Pennsylvania. *Printed in three colors.* Sample copies free. Put up in loose packages of 50, .50 Price to Hospitals, 500 copies, $4.00; 1000 copies, $7.50. With name of Hospital printed on, 50 cents extra.

GROVES AND THORP. Chemical Technology. A new and Complete Work. The Application of Chemistry to the Arts and Manufactures. Edited by CHARLES E. GROVES, F.R.S., and WM. THORP, B.SC., F.I.C. In about eight volumes, with numerous illustrations. *Each volume sold separately.*

> VOL. I. FUEL. By Dr. E. J. MILLS, F.R.S., Professor of Chemistry, Anderson College, Glasgow; and Mr. F. J. ROWAN, assisted by an American expert. 607 Illustrations and 4 plates. Octavo. Cloth, 7.50 ; Half Morocco, $9.00

HADDON'S Embryology. An Introduction to the Study of Embryology. For the Use of Students. By A. C. HADDON, M.A., Prof. of Zoölogy, Royal College of Science, Dublin. 190 Illustrations. Cloth, $6.00

HAIG. Causation of Disease by Uric Acid. A Contribution to the Pathology of High Arterial Tension, Headache, Epilepsy, Gout, Rheumatism, Diabetes, Bright's Disease, etc. By ALEX. HAIG, M.A., M.D. Oxon, F.R.C.P., Physician to Metropolitan Hospital, London. Illustrated. Octavo. *In Press.*

HALE. On **the Management of** Children in Health and Disease. A Book for Mothers. By AMIE M. HALE, M.D. New Enlarged Edition. 12mo. Cloth, .75

HARE. Mediastinal Disease. The Pathology, Clinical History and Diagnosis of Affections of the Mediastinum other than those of the Heart and Aorta, with tables giving the Clinical History of 520 cases. The essay to which was awarded the Fothergillian Medal of the Medical Society of London, 1888. By H. A. HARE, M.D. (Univ. of Pa.), Professor of Materia Medica and Therapeutics in Jefferson Medical College, Phila. 8vo. Illustrated by Six Plates. Cloth, $2.00

HARLAN. Eyesight, and How to Care for It. By GEORGE C. HARLAN, M.D., Prof. of Diseases of the Eye, Philadelphia Polyclinic. Illustrated. Cloth, .50

HARRIS'S Principles and Practice of Dentistry. Including Anatomy, Physiology, Pathology, Therapeutics, Dental Surgery and Mechanism. By CHAPIN A. HARRIS, M.D., D.D.S., late President of the Baltimore Dental College, author of "Dictionary of Medical Terminology and Dental Surgery." Twelfth Edition. Revised and Edited by FERDINAND J. S. GORGAS, A.M., M.D., D.D.S., author of "Dental Medicine;" Professor of the Principles of Dental Science, Dental Surgery and Dental Mechanism in the University of Maryland. Two Full-page Plates and 1086 Illustrations. 1225 pages. 8vo.   Cloth, $7.00; Leather, $8.00

> **Dictionary of Dentistry.** Fifth Edition, Revised. Including Definitions of such Words and Phrases of the Collateral Sciences as Pertain to the Art and Practice of Dentistry. Fifth Edition. Rewritten, Revised and Enlarged. By FERDINAND J. S. GORGAS, M.D., D.D.S., Author of "Dental Medicine;" Editor of Harris's "Principles and Practice of Dentistry;" Professor of Principles of Dental Science, Dental Surgery, and Prosthetic Dentistry in the University of Maryland. Octavo.   Cloth, $5.00; Leather, $6.00

HARTRIDGE. Refraction. The Refraction of the Eye. A Manual for Students. By GUSTAVUS HARTRIDGE, F.R.C.S., Consulting Ophthalmic Surgeon to St. Bartholomew's Hospital; Ass't Surgeon to the Royal Westminster Ophthalmic Hospital, etc. 96 Illustrations and Test Types. Fifth Edition.   Cloth, $1.75

> **On The Ophthalmoscope.** A Manual for Physicians and Students. With Colored Plates and many Woodcuts. 12mo.   Cloth, $1.50

HARTSHORNE. Our Homes. Their Situation, Construction, Drainage, etc. By HENRY HARTSHORNE, M.D. Illustrated.   Cloth, .50

HATFIELD. Diseases of Children. By MARCUS P. HATFIELD, Professor of Diseases of Children, Chicago Medical College. With a Colored Plate. *Being No. 14, ? Quiz-Compend ? Series.* 12mo.   Cloth, $1.00
> Interleaved for the addition of notes, $1.25

HEADLAND'S Action of Medicines. On the Action of Medicines in the System. By F. W. HEADLAND, M.D. Ninth American Edition. 8vo.   Cloth, $3.00

HEATH'S Minor Surgery and Bandaging. By CHRISTOPHER HEATH, F.R.C.S., Holme Professor of Clinical Surgery in University College, London. Ninth Edition. Revised and Enlarged. With 142 Illustrations. 12mo. Cloth, $2.00

> **Practical Anatomy.** A Manual of Dissections. Seventh London Edition. 24 Colored Plates, and nearly 300 other Illustrations.   Cloth, $5.00

> **Injuries and Diseases of the Jaws.** Third Edition. Revised, with over 150 Illustrations. 8vo.   Cloth, $4.50

> **Lectures on Certain Diseases of the Jaws,** delivered at the Royal College of Surgeons of England, 1887. 64 Illustrations. 8vo.   Boards, $1.00

HENRY. Anæmia. A Practical Treatise. By FRED'K P. HENRY, M.D., Prof. Clinical Med. Phila. Polyclinic, Physician to Episcopal and Phila. Hospitals, to Home for Consumptives, etc. 12mo.   Half Cloth, .75

HIGGENS' Ophthalmic Practice. A Manual for Students and Practitioners. By CHARLES HIGGENS, F.R.C.S. Ophthalmic Surgeon at Guy's Hospital. *Practical Series. See Page 19.*   Cloth, $1.75

HILL AND COOPER. Venereal Diseases. The Student's Manual of Venereal Diseases, being a concise description of those Affections and their Treatment. By BERKELEY HILL, M.D., Professor of Clinical Surgery, University College, and ARTHUR COOPER, M.D., Late House Surgeon to the Lock Hospital, London. 4th Edition. 12mo.   Cloth, $1.00

HOLDEN'S **Anatomy**. A Manual of the Dissections of the Human Body. By LUTHER HOLDEN, F.R.C.S. Fifth Edition. Carefully Revised and Enlarged. Specially concerning the Anatomy of the Nervous System, Organs of Special Sense, etc. By JOHN LANGTON, F.R.C.S., Surgeon to, and Lecturer on Anatomy at, St. Bartholomew's Hospital. 208 Illustrations. 8vo.
Oilcloth Covers, for the Dissecting Room, $4.50

Human Osteology. Comprising a Description of the Bones, with Colored Delineations of the Attachments of the Muscles. The General and Microscopical Structure of Bone and its Development. Carefully Revised. By the Author and Prof. STEWART, of the Royal College of Surgeons' Museum. With Lithographic Plates and Numerous Illustrations. 7th Ed. Cloth, $6.00

Landmarks. Medical and Surgical. 4th Edition. 8vo. Cloth, $1.25

HOLLAND. **The Urine, the Common Poisons and the Milk**. Memoranda, Chemical and Microscopical, for Laboratory Use. By J. W. HOLLAND, M.D., Professor of Medical Chemistry and Toxicology in Jefferson Medical College, of Philadelphia. Fourth Edition, Revised and Enlarged. Illustrated and Interleaved. 12mo.
Cloth, $1.00

HORWITZ'S **Compend of Surgery**, including Minor Surgery, Amputations, Fractures, Dislocations, Surgical Diseases, and the Latest Antiseptic Rules, etc., with Differential Diagnosis and Treatment. By ORVILLE HORWITZ, B.S., M.D., Demonstrator of Anatomy, Jefferson Medical College ; Chief, Out-Patient Surgical Department, Jefferson Medical College Hospital. Third Edition. Very much Enlarged and Rearranged. 91 Illustrations and 77 Formulæ. 12mo. *No. 9 ? Quiz-Compend ? Series*. Cloth, $1.00. Interleaved for the addition of notes, $1.25

HUFELAND. **Long Life**. Art of Prolonging Life. By C. W. HUFELAND. Edited by ERASMUS WILSON, M.D. 12mo. Cloth, $1.00

HUGHES. **Compend of the Practice of Medicine**. Fourth Edition. Revised and Enlarged. By DANIEL E. HUGHES, M.D., Demonstrator of Clinical Medicine at Jefferson Medical College, Philadelphia. In two parts. *Being Nos. 2 and 3, ? Quiz-Compend ? Series*.

PART I.—Continued, Eruptive and Periodical Fevers, Diseases of the Stomach, Intestines, Peritoneum, Biliary Passages, Liver, Kidneys, etc., and General Diseases, etc.

PART II.—Diseases of the Respiratory System, Circulatory System and Nervous System ; Diseases of the Blood, etc.
Price of each Part, in Cloth, $1.00 ; interleaved for the addition of Notes, $1.25

Physicians' Edition.—In one volume, including the above two parts, a section on Skin Diseases, and an index. *Fourth revised, enlarged Edition*. 462 pages. Full Morocco, Gilt Edge, $2.50

HUMPHREY A Manual for Nurses. Including general Anatomy and Physiology, management of the sick-room, etc. By LAURENCE HUMPHREY, M.A., M.B., M.R.C.S., Assistant Physician to, and Lecturer at, Addenbrook's Hospital, Cambridge, England. 4th Edition. 12mo. Illustrated. Cloth, $1.25

HUTCHINSON. **The Nose and Throat**. A Manual of the Diseases of the Nose and Throat, including the Nose, Naso-Pharynx, Pharynx and Larynx. By PROCTER S. HUTCHINSON, M.R.C.S., Ass't Surgeon to the London Hospital for Diseases of the Throat. Illustrated by several Lithograph Plates and 40 other plates, many of which have been made from original drawings. 12mo. Cloth, $1.25

JACOBSON. **Operations of Surgery**. By W. H. A. JACOBSON, B.A. OXON., F.R.C.S., Eng., Ass't Surgeon, Guy's Hospital ; Surgeon at Royal Hospital for Children and Women, etc. With over 200 Illust. Cloth, $5.00 ; Leather, $6.00

JAWORSKI. **Carlsbad Sprudel Salt**. Its Action, Therapeutic Value and Use, and its relation to the Carlsbad Thermal Water. By Dr. W. JAWORSKI, Universitats-Dozenten in Krakau, with a Dietary by the Translator, A. E. A. LIMOUSIN, M.D., Ass't Demonstrator of Pharmacy, University of Pennsylvania.
Octavo. Cloth, $2.00

KIRKES' Physiology. (*Authorized Edition. 12mo. Dark Red Cloth.*) A Handbook of Physiology. Twelfth London Edition, Revised and Enlarged. By W. MORRANT BAKER, M.D., and VINCENT DORMER HARRIS, M D. 502 Illustrations. 12mo. 880 Pages.   Cloth, $4.00; Leather, $5 00

LANDIS' Compend of Obstetrics ; especially adapted to the Use of Students and Physicians. By HENRY G. LANDIS, M.D., Professor of Obstetrics and Diseases of Women, in Starling Medical College, Columbus, Ohio. Fourth Edition. Enlarged. With Many Illustrations. *No. 5 ? Quiz-Compend ? Series.*
                    Cloth, $1.00; interleaved for the addition of Notes, $1.25

LANDOIS. A Text-Book of Human Physiology ; including Histology and Microscopical Anatomy, with special reference to the requirements of Practical Medicine. By DR. L. LANDOIS, Professor of Physiology and Director of the Physiological Institute in the University of Greifswald. Fourth American, translated from the Seventh German Edition, with additions, by WM. STIRLING, M.D., D.SC., Brackenbury Professor of Physiology and Histology in Owen's College, and Professor in Victoria University, Manchester ; Examiner in Physiology in University of Oxford, England. With 845 Illustrations, many of which are printed in Colors. 8vo.   Cloth, $7.00 ; Leather, $8.00

LEBER AND ROTTENSTEIN. Dental Caries and Its Causes. An Investigation into the Influence of Fungi in the Destruction of the Teeth. By Drs. LEBER and ROTTENSTEIN. Illustrated.   Paper, .75

LEE. The Microtomist's Vade Mecum. Second Edition. A Handbook of Methods of Microscopical Anatomy. By ARTHUR BOLLES LEE, Ass't in the Russian Laboratory of Zoölogy, at Villefranche-sur-Mer (Nice). 660 Formulæ, etc. Enlarged and Revised.   Cloth, $4.00

LEFFMANN'S Compend of Chemistry, Inorganic and Organic. Including Urine Analysis. By HENRY LEFFMANN, M.D., Prof. of Chemistry and Metallurgy in the Penna. College of Dental Surgery and in the Wagner Free Institute of Science, Philadelphia. *No. 10 ? Quiz-Compend ? Series.* Third Edition. Rewritten and Adapted for Students of Medicine and Dentistry. 12mo.
                    Cloth, $1.00. Interleaved for the addition of Notes, $1.25

LEFFMANN & BEAM. Examination of Water for Sanitary and Technical Purposes. By HENRY LEFFMANN, M.D., Professor of Chemistry and Metallurgy, Penna. College of Dental Surgery, Hygienist and Food Inspector Penna. State Board of Agriculture, etc.; and WILLIAM BEAM, A.M., formerly Chief Chemist B. & O. R. R. Second Edition. Enlarged. Illustrated. 12mo.   Cloth, $1.25

Progressive Exercises in Practical Chemistry. A Laboratory Handbook. Illustrated. 12mo.   Cloth, $1.00

LEGG on the Urine. Practical Guide to the Examination of the Urine, for Practitioner and Student. By J. WICKHAM LEGG, M.D. Sixth Edition, Enlarged. Illustrated. 12mo.   Cloth, .75

LEWERS. On the Diseases of Women. Second Edition. With 146 Engravings. *Practical Series. See Page 19.* 12mo.   Cloth, $2.50

LEWIS, (BEVAN). Mental Diseases. A text-book having special reference to the Pathological aspects of Insanity. By BEVAN LEWIS, L.R.C.P., M.R.C.S., Medical Director, West Riding Asylum, Wakefield, England. 18 Lithographic Plates and other Illustrations. 8vo.   Cloth, $6.00

LIEBREICH'S Atlas of Ophthalmoscopy, composed of 12 Chromo-Lithographic Plates (containing 59 Figures), with Text. Translated by H. R. SWANZY, M.D. Third Edition. 4to.   Boards, $15.00

LINCOLN. School and Industrial Hygiene. By D. F. LINCOLN, M.D.   Cloth, .50

LIZARS. (JOHN). On Tobacco. The Use and Abuse of Tobacco.   Cloth, .50

LONGLEY'S Pocket Medical Dictionary for Students and Physicians. Giving the Correct Definition and Pronunciation of all Words and Terms in General Use in Medicine and the Collateral Sciences, with an Appendix, containing Poisons and their Antidotes, Abbreviations Used in Prescriptions, and a Metric Scale of Doses. By ELIAS LONGLEY.   Cloth, $1.00; Tucks and Pocket, $1.25

LÜCKES. Hospital Sisters and their Duties. By EVA C. E. LÜCKES, Matron to the London Hospital ; Author of " Lectures on Nursing." 12mo.   Cloth, $1.00

MACNAMARA. On the Eye. A Manual of the Diseases of the Eye. By C. MACNAMARA, M.D. Fifth Edition, Carefully Revised; with Additions and Numerous Colored Plates, Diagrams of Eye, Wood-cuts, and Test Types. Demi 8vo.   Cloth, $4.00

MACALISTER'S Human Anatomy. 800 Illustrations. A New Text-book for Students and Practitioners. Systematic and Topographical, including the Embryology, Histology and Morphology of Man. With special reference to the requirements of Practical Surgery and Medicine. By ALEX. MACALISTER, M.D., F.R.S., Professor of Anatomy in the University of Cambridge, England; Examiner in Zoology and Comparative Anatomy, University of London; formerly Professor of Anatomy and Surgery, University of Dublin. With 816 Illustrations, 400 of which are original. Octavo.   Cloth, $7.50; Leather, $8.50

MACDONALD'S Microscopical Examinations of Water and Air. A Guide to the Microscopical Examination of Drinking Water, with an Appendix on the Microscopical Examination of Air. By J. D. MACDONALD, M.D. With 25 Lithographic Plates, Reference Tables, etc. Second Ed., Revised. 8vo. Cloth, $2.75

MACKENZIE. Diseases of the Throat and Nose. By SIR MORELL MACKENZIE, M.D., Senior Physician to the Hospital for Diseases of the Chest and Throat, London. Illustrated. 2 Volumes. Octavo.

    The Pharmacopœia of the Hospital for Diseases of the Throat and Nose. Fourth Edition, Enlarged, Containing 250 Formulæ, with Directions for their Preparation and Use. 16mo.   Cloth, $1.25

MANN'S Manual of Psychological Medicine and Allied Nervous Diseases. Their Diagnosis, Pathology, Prognosis and Treatment, including their Medico-Legal Aspects; with chapter on Expert Testimony, and an abstract of the laws relating to the Insane in all the States of the Union. By EDWARD C. MANN, M.D., member of the New York County Medical Society. With Illustrations of Typical Faces of the Insane, Handwriting of the Insane, and Micro-photographic Sections of the Brain and Spinal Cord. Octavo.   Cloth, $5.00

MARSHALL'S Physiological **Diagrams, Life Size, Colored.** Eleven Life-size Diagrams (each 7 feet by 3 feet 7 inches). Designed for Demonstration before the Class. By JOHN MARSHALL, F.R.S., F.R.C.S., Professor of Anatomy to the Royal Academy; Professor of Surgery, University College, London, etc.

                    In Sheets Unmounted, *net*, $40.00
            Backed with Muslin and Mounted on Rollers, *net*, $60.00
Ditto, Spring Rollers, in Handsome Walnut Wall Map Case (Send for Special Circular), ... *Net*, $100.00
Single Plates, Sheets, *net*, $5.00; Mounted, $7.50; Explanatory Key, 50 cents.

No. 1—The Skeleton and Ligaments. No. 2—The Muscles and Joints, with Animal Mechanics. No. 3—The Viscera in Position. The Structure of the Lungs. No. 4—The Heart and Principal Blood-vessels. No. 5—The Lymphatics or Absorbents. No. 6—The Digestive Organs. No. 7—The Brain and Nerves. Nos. 8 and 9—The Organs of the Senses. Nos. 10 and 11—The Microscopic Structure of the Textures and Organs. (*Send for Special Circular*.)

MARSHALL & SMITH. On the Urine. The Chemical Analysis of the Urine. By JOHN MARSHALL, M.D., and Prof. EDGAR F. SMITH, of the Chemical Laboratories, University of Pennsylvania. Phototype Plates. 12mo.   Cloth, $1.00

MASON'S Compend of Electricity, and its Medical and Surgical **Uses.** By CHARLES F. MASON, M.D., Assistant Surgeon U. S. Army. With an Introduction by CHARLES H. MAY, M.D., Instructor in the New York Polyclinic. Numerous Illustrations. 12mo.   Cloth, $1.00

McBRIDE. Diseases of the Throat, Nose and Ear. A Clinical Manual for Students and Practitioners. By P. McBRIDE, M.D., F.R.C.P. Edin., Surgeon to the Ear and Throat Department of the Royal Infirmary, Lecturer on Diseases of Throat and Ear, Edinburgh School of Medicine, etc. With Colored Illustrations from Original Drawings. Octavo.   Handsome Cloth, Gilt Top, $7.00

MAXWELL. Terminologia Medica Polyglotta. By Dr. THEODORE MAXWELL, assisted by others in various countries. 8vo.　　　　Cloth, $4.00

The object of this work is to assist the medical men of any nationality in reading medical literature written in a language not their own. Each term is usually given in seven languages, viz.: English, French, German, Italian, Spanish, Russian and Latin.

MAYS' Therapeutic Forces; or, The Action of Medicine in the Light of the Doctrine of Conservation of Force. By THOMAS J. MAYS, M.D.　　　Cloth, $1.25

　　Theine in the Treatment of Neuralgia. Being a Contribution to the Therapeutics of Pain. 16mo.　　　　　　　½ bound, .50

MEDICAL Directory of Philadelphia and Camden, 1889. Containing lists of Physicians *of all Schools of Practice,* Dentists, Veterinarians, Druggists and Chemists, with information concerning Medical Societe , Colleges and Associations, Hospitals, Asylums, Charities, etc.　　　Morocco, Gilt edges, $2.50

MEIGS. Milk Analysis and Infant Feeding. A Practical Treatise on the Examination of Human and Cows' Milk, Cream, Condensed Milk, etc., and Directions as to the Diet of Young Infants. By ARTHUR V. MEIGS, M.D., Physician to the Pennsylvania Hospital, Philadelphia. 12mo.　　　Cloth, $1.00

MEIGS and PEPPER on Children. A Practical Treatise on the Diseases of Children. By J. FORSYTH MEIGS, M.D., Fellow of the College of Physicians of Philadelphia, etc., etc., and WILLIAM PEPPER, M.D., Professor of the Principles and Practice of Medicine in the Medical Department, University of Pennsylvania. Seventh Edition.　　　　　Cloth, $5.00; Leather, $6.00

MERRELL'S Digest of Materia Medica. Forming a Complete Pharmacopœia for the use of Physicians, Pharmacists and Students. By ALBERT MERRELL, M.D. Octavo.　　　　　　　　Half dark Calf, $4.00

MEYER. Ophthalmology. A Manual of Diseases of the Eye. By DR. EDOUARD MEYER, Prof. à l'École de la Faculté de Médecine de Paris, Chev. of the Legion of Honor, etc. Translated from the Third French Edition, with the assistance of the author, by A. FREEDLAND FERGUS, M.B., Assistant Surgeon Glasgow Eye Infirmary. With 270 Illustrations, and two Colored Plates prepared under the direction of DR. RICHARD LIEBREICH, M.R.C.S., Author of the "Atlas of Ophthalmoscopy." 8vo.　　　　　Cloth, $4.50; Leather, $5.50

MILLS. Fuel and Its Applications. By E. J. MILLS, D.Sc., F.R.S., and E. J. ROWAN, C.E. (See Groves and Thorp Technology.) 8vo. Clo., $7.50; Half Mor. $9.00

MONEY. On Children. Treatment of Disease in Children, including the Outlines of Diagnosis and the Chief Pathological Differences between Children and Adults. By ANGEL MONEY, M.D., M.R.C.P., Ass't Physician to the Hospital for Sick Children, Great Ormond St., and to the Victoria Park Chest Hospital, London. *Practical Series. See Page 19.* 12mo. 560 pages.　　　Cloth, $3.00

MORRIS. Compend of Gynæcology. By HENRY MORRIS, M.D., Demonstrator of Obstetrics, Jefferson Medical College, Phila., etc. With Forty-five illustrations. *Being ? Quiz-Compend ? No. 7.*　　Cloth, $1.00; Interleaved for Notes, $1.25

MOULLIN. Surgery. A Complete Text-book. By C. W. MANSELL MOULLIN, M.A., M.D. OXON., F.R.C.S., Surgeon and Lecturer on Physiology to the London Hospital; formerly Radcliffe Travelling Fellow and Fellow of Pembroke College, Oxford. With colored Frontispiece. 497 Illustrations, 200 of which are original, and many of which are printed in Colors. *By Subscription only.* Royal Octavo. 1190 pages. Handsomely Bound in Cloth, *Net, $7.00;* Leather, *Net, $8.00* Half Russia Crushed, Marbled edges and linings, *Net,* 9.00

MURRELL. Massotherapeutics. Massage as a Mode of Treatment. By WM. MURRELL, M.D., F.R.C.P., Lecturer on Pharmacology and Therapeutics at Westminster Hospital. 5th Edition. Revised. 12mo.　　　Cloth, $1.50

　　Chronic Bronchitis and its Treatment. (*Authorized Edition.*) A Clinical Study. 12mo. 176 pages.　　　　　　　　Cloth, $1 50

MUSKETT. Prescribing and Treatment in the Diseases of Infants and Children. By PHILIP E. MUSKETT, Late Surgeon to the Sydney Hospital, Formerly Senior Resident Medical Officer, Sydney Hospital. 32mo.　　Cloth, $1.75

MORTON on Refraction of the Eye. Its Diagnosis and the Correction of its Errors. With Chapter on Keratoscopy, and Test Types. By A. MORTON, M.B. Fourth Edition, Revised and Enlarged.　　　　　Cloth, $1.00

MUTER. **Practical and Analytical Chemistry.** By JOHN MUTER, F.R.S., F.C.S., etc. Fourth Edition. Revised, to meet the requirements of American Medical Colleges, by CLAUDE C. HAMILTON, M.D., Professor of Analytical Chemistry in University Med. Col. and Kansas City Col. of Pharmacy. 51 Illus. Cloth, $2.00

NAPHEYS' **Modern Therapeutics.** **New Revised Edition, Enlarged and Improved.** In Two Handsome Volumes. Edited by ALLEN J. SMITH, M.D., Ass't Demonstrator of Morbid Anatomy and Pathological Histology, Lecturer on Urinology, University of Pennsylvania; Physician in the Dispensary for Diseases of Children, University Hospital, etc.; and L. AUBREY DAVIS, M.D., Assistant Demonstrator of Obstetrics, University of Pennsylvania. *Nearly Ready.*

  VOL. I.—Medical Therapeutics. Therapeutics **of Diseases of Children.**

  VOL. II.—Surgical Therapeutics. Therapeutics **of Gynæcology and** Obstetrics.

NEW SYDENHAM SOCIETY Publications. Three to Six Volumes published each year. *List of Volumes upon application.* Per annum, $8.00

OBERSTEINER. The **Anatomy of the Central Nervous Organs.** A Guide to the study of their structure in Health and Disease. By Professor H. OBERSTEINER, of the University of Vienna. Translated, with annotations and additions, by Alex. Hill, M.A., M.D., Master of Downing College, Cambridge. 198 Illustrations. Sq. Octavo. Cloth, $6.00

OPHTHALMIC REVIEW. A Monthly Record of Ophthalmic Science. Published in London. *Sample Numbers, 25 cents.* Per annum, $3.00

OSGOOD. The **Winter** and Its Dangers. By HAMILTON OSGOOD, M.D. Cloth, .50

OSLER. **Cerebral Palsies of Children.** A Clinical Study from the Infirmary for Nervous Diseases, Philadelphia. By WILLIAM OSLER, M.D., F.R.C.P. London, etc. 8vo. Cloth, $2.00

OSTROM. **Massage and the Original Swedish Movements.** Their Application to Various Diseases of the Body. A Manual for Students, Nurses and Physicians. By KUREE W. OSTROM, from the Royal University of Upsala, Sweden; Instructor in Massage and Swedish Movements in the Hospital of the University of Pennsylvania, and in the Philadelphia Polyclinic and College for Graduates in Medicine, etc. Second Edition. Enlarged. Illustrated by 87 Wood Engravings, many of which were drawn especially for this purpose. 12mo. Cloth, $1.00

OVERMAN'S **Practical Mineralogy, Assaying** and Mining, with a Description of the Useful Minerals, etc. By FREDERICK OVERMAN, Mining Engineer. Eleventh Edition. 12mo. Cloth, $1.00

PACKARD'S **Sea Air and Sea Bathing.** By JOHN H. PACKARD, one of the Physicians to the Pennsylvania Hospital, Philadelphia. Cloth, .50

PAGE. **Railroad Injuries.** With Special Reference to those of the Back and Nervous System. By HERBERT PAGE, M.A., M.C., CANTAB., F.R.C.S., Eng. Surgeon to St. Mary's Hospital, and Lecturer on Surgery at its Medical School. Square Octavo. Cloth, $2.25

  Injuries of the **Spine** and Spinal Cord, without apparent Lesion and Nervous Shock. In their Surgical and Medico-Legal Aspects. Third Edition, Revised. Octavo. *Preparing.*

PARKES' Practical Hygiene. By EDWARD A. PARKES, M.D. The Eighth Revised and Enlarged Edition. Edited by J. LANE NOTTER, M.A., M.D., F.C.S., Professor of Hygiene, Army Medical School, Netley, England. With 10 Lithographic Plates, and over 100 other Illustrations. 8vo. Cloth, $5.50

PARKES. **Hygiene and Public Health.** A Practical Manual. By LOUIS C. PARKES, M.D., D.P.H. London Hospital; Assistant Professor of Hygiene and Public Health at University College, etc. 12mo. Second Edition. Cloth, $2.50

PARRISH'S **Alcoholic Inebriety.** From a Medical Standpoint, with Illustrative Cases from the Clinical Records of the Author. By JOSEPH PARRISH, M.D., President of the Amer. Assoc. for Cure of Inebriates. Paper, .75. Cloth, $1.25

OMEROD. **Diseases of Nervous System.** Student's Guide to. By J. A. ORMEROD, M.D., Oxon., F.R.C.P. (Lond.), Mem. Path., Clin., Ophth., and Neurol. Societies, Physician to National Hospital for Paralyzed and Epileptic and to City of London Hospital for Diseases of the Chest, Dem. of Morbid Anatomy, St. Bartholomew's Hospital, etc. With 75 wood engravings. *In Press.*

PARVIN'S Winckel's Diseases of Women. (See Winckel, page 25.)

PARVIN. Lectures on Obstetric Nursing. Delivered at the Training School for Nurses of the Philadelphia Hospital. By THEOPHILUS PARVIN, M.D., Professor of Obstetrics and Diseases of Women and Children at Jefferson Medical College; Obstetrician to Philadelphia Hospital. 12mo. Cloth, .75

PENNSYLVANIA Hospital Reports. Edited by a Committee of the Hospital Staff: J. M. DaCOSTA, M.D., and WILLIAM HUNT. Containing Original Articles by the Staff. With many other Illustrations. Paper, .75; Cloth, $1.25

PHYSICIAN'S VISITING LIST. Published Annually. Forty-First Year of its Publication.

REGULAR EDITION.

For 25 Patients weekly.			Tucks, pocket and pencil, Gilt Edges,							$1.00
50	"	"	"	"	"	"	"	.	.	1.25
75	"	"	"	"	"	"	"	.	.	1.50
100	"	"	"	"	"	"	"	.	.	2.00
50	"	" 2 vols.	{ Jan. to June } { July to Dec. }	"	"	"		.	.	2.50
100	"	" 2 vols.	{ Jan. to June } { July to Dec. }	"	"	"			.	3.00

INTERLEAVED EDITION.

For 25 Patients weekly, interleaved, tucks, pocket, etc.,			"	"			.	.	1.25
50	"	"	"	"	"	"	"	"	.	.	1.50
50	"	" 2 vols.	{ Jan. to June } { July to Dec. }	"	"	"	"	.	.	3.00

Perpetual Edition, without Dates and with Special Memorandum Pages.
For 25 Patients, interleaved, tucks, pocket and pencil, ... $1.25
50 " " " " " " 1.50

Monthly Edition, without Dates. Can be commenced at any time and used until full. Requires only one writing of patient's name for the whole month.
Plain binding, without Flap or Pencil, .75
Leather cover, Pocket and Pencil, $1.00

EXTRA Pencils will be sent, postpaid, for 25 cents per half dozen.

☞ This List combines the several essential qualities of strength, compactness, durability and convenience. It is made in all sizes and styles to meet the wants of all physicians. It is not an elaborate, complicated system of keeping accounts, but a plain, simple record, that may be kept with the least expenditure of time and trouble— hence its popularity. A special circular, descriptive of contents and improvements, will be sent upon application.

PEREIRA'S Prescription Book. Containing Lists of Terms, Phrases, Contractions and Abbreviations used in Prescriptions, Explanatory Notes, Grammatical Construction of Prescriptions, Rules for the Pronunciation of Pharmaceutical Terms. By JONATHAN PEREIRA, M.D. Sixteenth Edition. Cloth, $1.00; Tucks $1.25

PORTER'S Surgeon's Pocket-Book. By SURGEON-MAJOR J. H. PORTER, late Professor of Military Surgery in the Army Medical School, Netley, England. Revised, and partly Rewritten. Third Edition. Small 12mo. Leather Covers, $2.25

POWER, HOLMES, ANSTIE and BARNES (Drs.). Reports on the Progress of Medicine, Surgery, Physiology, Midwifery, Diseases of Women and Children, Materia Medica, Medical Jurisprudence, Ophthalmology, etc. Reported for the New Sydenham Society. 8vo. Paper, .75; Cloth, $1.25

POTTER. A Handbook of Materia Medica, Pharmacy and Therapeutics, including the Action of Medicines, Special Therapeutics, Pharmacology, etc. Including over 600 Prescriptions and Formulæ. By SAMUEL O. L. POTTER, M.A., M.D., M.R.C.P. (Lond.), Professor of the Practice of Medicine, Cooper Medical College, San Francisco; late A. A. Surgeon U. S. Army. Third Edition, Revised and Enlarged. 8vo. *With Thumb Index in each copy.* Cloth, $4.00; Leather, $5.00

THE PRACTICAL SERIES.

THREE NEW VOLUMES.

PARKES. Hygiene and Public Health. A Practical Manual. By Louis C. PARKES, M.D., D.P.H., London Hospital; Fellow of the Sanitary Institute; Assistant Professor of Hygiene and Public Health at University College, etc. 12mo. Second Edition. Cloth, $2.50

LEWERS. On the Diseases of Women. A Practical Treatise. By Dr. A. H. N. LEWERS, Assistant Obstetric Physician to the London Hospital; and Physician to Out-patients, Queen Charlotte's Lying-in Hospital; Examiner in Midwifery and Diseases of Women to the Society of Apothecaries of London. With 146 Engravings. Second Edition, Revised. Cloth, $2.50

BUXTON. On Anæsthetics. A Manual of their Uses and Administration. By DUDLEY WILMOT BUXTON, M.D., B.S., Ass't to Prof. of Med., and Administrator of Anæsthetics, University College Hospital, London. Illustrated.
Second Edition in Press.

MONEY. On Children. Treatment of Disease in Children, including the Outlines of Diagnosis and the Chief Pathological Differences between Children and Adults. By ANGEL MONEY, M.D., M.R.C P., Ass't Physician to the Hospital for Sick Children, Great Ormond St., and to the Victoria Park Chest Hospital, London. 12mo. 560 pages. Cloth, $3.00

PRITCHARD. On the Ear. Handbook of Diseases of the Ear. By URBAN PRITCHARD, M.D., F.R.C.S., Professor of Aural Surgery, King's College, London, Aural Surgeon to King's College Hospital, Senior Surgeon to the Royal Ear Hospital, etc. 12mo. 2d Edition. Illustrated. Cloth, $1.50

BARRETT. Dental Surgery for General Practitioners and Students of Medicine and Dentistry. Extraction of Teeth, etc. By A. W. BARRETT, M.D. 2d Edition, Revised and Enlarged. 80 Illustrations. Cloth, $1.25

COLLIE On Fevers. A Practical Treatise on Fevers, Their History, Etiology, Diagnosis, Prognosis and Treatment. By ALEXANDER COLLIE, M.D., M.R. C.P., Lond. Medical Officer of the Homerton, and of the London Fever Hospitals. Colored Plates. Cloth, $2.50

RALFE. Diseases of the Kidney and Urinary Derangements. By C. H. RALFE, M.D., F.R.C.P., Ass't Physician to the London Hospital. Illustrated. 12mo. Cloth, $2.75

REEVES. Bodily Deformities and their Treatment. A Handbook of Practical Orthopædics. By H. A. REEVES, M.D., Senior Ass't Surgeon to the London Hospital, Surgeon to the Royal Orthopædic Hospital. 228 Illus. Cloth, $2.25

HIGGENS. Ophthalmic Practice. A Manual for Students and Practitioners. By CHARLES HIGGENS, F.R.C.P., Ophthalmic Surgeon to Guy's Hospital. Illustrated. 274 pages. Cloth, $1.75

** The volumes of this series, written by well-known physicians and surgeons of large private and hospital experience, embrace the various branches of medicine and surgery. They are of a thoroughly practical character, calculated to meet the requirements of the practitioner, and present the most recent methods and information in a compact shape and at a low price.

Bound Uniformly, **in a Handsome and** Distinctive Cloth Binding, **and** mailed to **any** address, **on** receipt of the price.

POTTER. Compend of Anatomy, including **Visceral Anatomy.** *Based upon Gray.* Fifth Edition. Revised, and greatly Enlarged. With 16 Lithographed Plates and 117 other Illustrations. *Being No. 1 ? Quiz-Compend ? Series.*
Cloth, $1.00; Interleaved for taking Notes, $1.25

    Compend of Materia Medica, Therapeutics and Prescription Writing. with special reference to the Physiological Action of Drugs. Fifth Revised and Improved Edition, with Index. *Being No. 6 ? Quiz-Compend ? Series.*
Cloth, $1.00. Interleaved for taking Notes, $1.25

    Speech and Its Defects. Considered Physiologically, Pathologically and Remedially; being the Lea Prize Thesis of Jefferson Medical College, 1882. Revised and Corrected. 12mo. Cloth, $1.00

PRITCHARD on the Ear. Handbook of Diseases of the Ear. By URBAN PRITCHARD, M.D., F.R.C.S.,Professor of Aural Surgery, King's College, London, Aural Surgeon to King's College Hospital, Senior Surgeon to the Royal Ear Hospital, etc. Second Edition. Many Illustrations and Formulæ. 12mo. *Practical Series. See Page 19.* Cloth, $1.50

PROCTER'S Practical Pharmacy. Lectures on Practical Pharmacy. With 43 Engravings and 32 Lithographic Fac-simile Prescriptions. By BARNARD S. PROCTER. Second Edition. Cloth, $4.50

RALFE. Diseases of the Kidney and Urinary Derangements. By C. H. RALFE. Illustrated. 12mo. *Practical Series. See Page 19.* Cloth, $2.75

RAMSAY. A System of Inorganic Chemistry. By WILLIAM RAMSAY, PH.D., F.R.S., Professor of Chemistry in University College, London. Illustrated. 8vo. Cloth, $4.50

REESE'S Medical Jurisprudence and Toxicology. A Text-book for Medical and Legal Practitioners and Students. By JOHN J. REESE, M.D., Editor of Taylor's Jurisprudence, Professor of the Principles and Practice of Medical Jurisprudence, including Toxicology, in the University of Pennsylvania Medical Department. Third Edition. Enlarged. Crown Octavo. 666 pages. Cloth, $3.00; Leather, $3.50

REEVES. Bodily Deformities and their Treatment. A Handbook of Practical Orthopædics. By H. A. REEVES, M.D. *Practical Series. See Page 19.* Cl., $2.25

RICHARDSON. Long Life, and How to Reach It. By J. G. RICHARDSON, Prof. of Hygiene, University of Penna. Cloth, .50

RICHARDSON'S Mechanical Dentistry. A Practical Treatise on Mechanical Dentistry. By JOSEPH RICHARDSON, D.D.S. Fifth Edition. Thoroughly Revised. With 569 Illustrations. 8vo. Cloth, $4.50; Leather, $5.50

RIGBY'S Obstetric Memoranda. 4th Ed. By MEADOWS. 32mo. Cloth, .50

RICHTER'S Inorganic Chemistry. A Text-book for Students. By Prof. VICTOR VON RICHTER, University of Breslau. Third American, from Fifth German Edition. Authorized Translation by EDGAR F. SMITH, M.A., PH.D., Prof. of Chemistry, University of Pennsylvania, Member of the Chemical Societies of Berlin and Paris. 89 Illustrations and a Colored Plate. 12mo. Cloth, $2.00

    Organic Chemistry. The Chemistry of the Carbon Compounds. Second American Edition, translated from the Sixth German by EDGAR F. SMITH, M. A., PH. D., Professor of Chemistry, University of Pennsylvania. Illustrated. 1040 pages. 12mo. Cloth, $4.50

ROBERTS. Practice of Medicine. The Theory and Practice of Medicine. By FREDERICK ROBERTS, M.D., Professor of Therapeutics at University College, London. Eighth Edition, with Illustrations. 8vo. Cloth, $5.50; Leather, $6.50

ROBINSON. Latin Grammar of Pharmacy and Medicine. By D. H. ROBINSON, PH.D., Professor of Latin Language and Literature, University of Kansas, Lawrence. With an Introduction by L. E. SAYRE, PH.G., Professor of Pharmacy in, and Dean of the Dept. of Pharmacy, University of Kansas. 12mo. Cloth, $2.00

SANDERSON'S **Physiological Laboratory.** A Handbook of the Physiological Laboratory. Being Practical Exercises for Students in Physiology and Histology. By J. BURDON SANDERSON, M.D., E. KLEIN, M.D., MICHAEL FOSTER, M.D., F.R.S., and T. LAUDER BRUNTON, M.D. With over 350 Illustrations and Appropriate Letter-press Explanations and References. One Volume. Cloth, $5.00

SANSOM. **On Chloroform.** Its Action and Administration. By ARTHUR ERNEST SANSOM, M.D. Illustrated. 12mo. Paper, .75; Cloth, $1.25

SCHNÉE. **Diabetes,** its Cause and Permanent Cure. From the standpoint of experience and Scientific Investigation. By EMIL SCHNÉE, Consulting Physician at Carlsbad. Translated from the German by R. L. TAFEL, A.M., PH.D. Revised and Enlarged by the author. Octavo. Cloth, $2.00

SCHULTZE. **Obstetrical Diagrams.** Being a Series of 20 Colored Lithograph Charts, imperial map size, of Pregnancy and Midwifery, with accompanying explanatory (German) text, illustrated by wood-cuts. By DR. B. S. SCHULTZE, Professor of Obstetrics, University of Jena. Second Revised Edition.
Price, in Sheets, $26.00; Mounted on Rollers, Muslin Backs, $36.00

SELF-EXAMINATION, **being 3000 Questions** on Medical Subjects, Anatomy, Physiology, Materia Medica, Therapeutics, Chemistry, Surgery, Practice, Obstetrics, Gynaecology, Diseases of Children, etc. 64mo. Cloth, *Net*, 10 cents.

SEWELL. **Dental Surgery,** including Special Anatomy and Surgery. By HENRY SEWELL, M.R.C.S., L.D.S., President Odontological Society of Great Britain. 3d Edition, greatly enlarged, with about 200 Illustrations. Cloth, $3.00

SMITH'S **Wasting Diseases of Infants and** Children. By EUSTACE SMITH, M.D., F.R.C.P., Physician to the East London Children's Hospital. Fifth London Edition, Enlarged. 8vo. Cloth, $3.00

SMITH. **Abdominal Surgery.** Being a Systematic Description of all the Principal Operations. By J. GREIG SMITH, M.A., F.R.S.E., Surg. to British Royal Infirmary; Lecturer on Surgery, Bristol Medical School; Late Examiner in Surgery, University of Aberdeen, etc. Over 80 Illustrations. Fourth Edition. *In Press*

SMITH. **Electro-Chemical Analysis.** By EDGAR F. SMITH, Professor of Chemistry, University of Penna. 26 Illustrations. 12mo. Cloth, $1.00

SMITH AND KELLER. **Experiments.** Arranged for Students in General Chemistry. By EDGAR F. SMITH, Professor of Chemistry, University of Penn'a. and DR. H. F. KELLER, Professor of Chemistry, Michigan School of Mines, Houghton, Michigan. Second Edition. 12mo. Illustrated. Cloth, *net*, .60

STAMMER. **Chemical Problems,** with Explanations and Answers. By KARL STAMMER. Translated from the 2d German Edition, by Prof. W. S. HOSKINSON, A.M., Wittenberg College, Springfield, Ohio. 12mo. Cloth, .75

STARR. **The Digestive Organs in Childhood.** Second Edition. The Diseases of the Digestive Organs in Infancy and Childhood. With Chapters on the Investigation of Disease and the Management of Children. By LOUIS STARR, M.D., Late Clinical Prof. of Diseases of Children in the Hospital of the University of Penn'a; Physician to the Children's Hospital, Phila. Second Edition. Revised and Enlarged. Illustrated by two Colored Lithograph Plates and numerous wood engravings. Crown Octavo. Cloth, $2.25

The **Hygiene of** the Nursery, including the General Regimen and Feeding of Infants and Children, and the Domestic Management of the Ordinary Emergencies of Early Life. Massage, etc. Third Edition. Enlarged. 25 Illustrations. 12mo. 280 pages. Cloth, $1.00

See also Goodhart and Starr. *Page 10.*

STEWART'S Compend of Pharmacy. Based upon "Remington's Text-Book of Pharmacy." By F. E. STEWART, M.D., PH.G., Quiz Master in Chem. and Theoretical Pharmacy, Phila. College of Pharmacy; Demonstrator and Lect. in Pharmacology, Medico-Chirurgical College, and in Woman's Medical College. 3d. Ed. With complete tables of Metric and English Systems of Weights and Measures and an elaborate Index. *? Quiz-Compend ? Series.* Cloth, $1.00
Interleaved for the addition of notes, $1.25

STIRLING. Outlines of Practical Physiology. Including Chemical and Experimental Physiology, with Special Reference to Practical Medicine. By W. STIRLING, M.D., SC.D., Prof. of Phys., Owens College, Victoria University, Manchester. Examiner in Honors School of Science, Oxford, England. 142 Illustrations. 309 pages. Cloth, $2.25

Outlines of Practical Histology. A Manual for Students. With 344 Illustrations. 12mo. Cloth, $4.00

STOCKEN'S Dental Materia Medica. Dental Materia Medica and Therapeutics, with Pharmacopœia. By JAMES STOCKEN, D.D.S. Third Edition. Cloth, $2.50

STRAHAN. Extra-Uterine Pregnancy. The Diagnosis and Treatment of Extra-Uterine Pregnancy. Being the Jenks Prize Essay of the College of Physicians of Philadelphia. By JOHN STRAHAN, M.D. (Univ. of Ireland), late Res. Surgeon Belfast Union Infirmary and Fever Hospital. Octavo. Cloth, $1.50

SUTTON'S Volumetric Analysis. A Systematic Handbook for the Quantitative Estimation of Chemical Substances by Measure, Applied to Liquids, Solids and Gases. By FRANCIS SUTTON, F.C.S. Sixth Edition, Revised and Enlarged, with Illustrations. 8vo. Cloth, $5.00

SUTTON. Ligaments. Their Nature and Morphology. By JOHN BLAND SUTTON, F.R.C.S., Lecturer on Pathology, Royal College of Surgeons; Ass't Surg. and Dem. of Anatomy, Middlesex Hospital, London. Illustrated. 12mo. Cloth, $1.25

SWAIN. Surgical Emergencies, together with the Emergencies Attendant on Parturition and the Treatment of Poisoning. A Manual for the Use of General Practitioners. By W. F. SWAIN, F.R.C.S. Fourth Edition. Illustrated. $1.50

SWANZY. Diseases of the Eye and their Treatment. A Handbook for Physicians and Students. By HENRY R. SWANZY, A.M., M.B., F.R.C.S.I., Surgeon to the National Eye and Ear Infirmary; Ophthalmic Surgeon to the Adelaide Hospital, Dublin; Examiner in Ophthalmic Surgery in the Royal University of Ireland. Third Edition. Thoroughly Revised. 158 Illustrations. 508 pages. 12mo. Cloth, $3.00

SYMONDS. Manual of Chemistry, for the special use of Medical Students. By BRANDRETH SYMONDS, A.M., M.D., Ass't Physician Roosevelt Hospital, Out-Patient Department; Attending Physician Northwestern Dispensary, New York. 12mo. Cloth, $2.00

TAFT'S Operative Dentistry. A Practical Treatise on Operative Dentistry. By JONATHAN TAFT, D.D.S. Fourth Revised and Enlarged Edition. Over 100 Illustrations. 8vo. Cloth, $4.25 ; Leather, $5.00

Index of Dental Periodical Literature. 8vo. Cloth, $2.00

TALBOT. Irregularities of the Teeth, and Their Treatment. By EUGENE S. TALBOT, M.D., Professor of Dental Surgery Woman's Medical College, and Lecturer on Dental Pathology in Rush Medical College, Chicago. Second Edition, Revised and Enlarged by about 100 pages. Octavo. 234 Illustrations (169 of which are original). 261 pages. Cloth, $3.00

TANNER'S Memoranda of Poisons and their Antidotes and Tests. By THOS. HAWKES TANNER, M.D., F.R.C.P. Sixth American, from the Last London Edition. Revised by HENRY LEFFMANN, M.D., Professor of Chemistry in Pennsylvania College of Dental Surgery and in the Philadelphia Polyclinic. 12mo. Cloth, .75

TAYLOR. Practice of Medicine. A Manual. By FREDERICK TAYLOR, M.D., Physician to, and Lecturer on Medicine at, Guy's Hospital, London; Physician to Evelina Hospital for Sick Children, and Examiner in Materia Medica and Pharmaceutical Chemistry, University of London. Cloth, $4.00 ; Sheep, $5.00

TEMPERATURE **Charts** for Recording Temperature, Respiration, Pulse, Day of Disease, Date, Age, Sex, Occupation, Name, etc. Put up in pads ; each .50

HOMPSON. **Lithotomy and Lithotrity.** Practical Lithotomy and Lithotrity ; or an Inquiry into the best Modes of Removing Stone from the Bladder. By Sir HENRY THOMPSON, F.R.C.S., Emeritus Professor of Clinical Surgery in University College. Third Edition. With 87 Engravings, 8vo. Cloth, $3.50

Urinary **Organs.** Diseases of the Urinary Organs. Containing 32 Lectures. Eighth London Ed. Octavo. 470 pages. Cloth, $3.50

On the Prostate. Diseases of the Prostate. Their Pathology and Treatment. Sixth London Edition. 8vo. Illustrated. Cloth, $2.00

Calculous Diseases. The Preventive Treatment of Calculous Disease, and the Use of Solvent Remedies. Third Edition. 16mo. Cloth, $1.00

Surgery **of the Urinary Organs.** Some Important Points connected with the Surgery of the Urinary Organs. Illus. Paper, .75 ; Cloth, $1.25

THORBURN. **Surgery of the Spinal Cord.** A Contribution to the study of. By WILLIAM THORBURN, B.S., B.Sc., M.D., Lond., F.R.C.S., Eng. With Illustrations. Octavo. Cloth, $4.50

THORNTON. **The Surgery of the Kidney.** By JOHN KNOWSLEY THORNTON, M.B. Edin. With 19 Illustrations. Cloth, $1.75

TILT'S Change of Life in Women, in Health and Disease. A Practical Treatise on the Diseases incidental to Women at the Decline of Life. By EDWARD JOHN TILT, M.D. Fourth London Edition. 8vo. Cloth, $1.25

TOMES' Dental **Anatomy.** A Manual of Dental Anatomy, Human and Comparative. By C. S. TOMES, D.D.S. 212 Illustrations. 3d Ed. 12mo. Cloth, $4.00

Dental Surgery. A System of Dental Surgery. By JOHN TOMES, F.R.S. Third Edition, Revised and Enlarged. By C. S. TOMES, D.D.S. With 292 Illustrations. 12mo. 772 pages. Cloth, $5.00

TRANSACTIONS of the College of Physicians of Philadelphia. Third Series. Vols. I, II, III, IV, V, Cloth, each, $2.50. VI, VII, Cloth, each, $3.50. Vol. VIII, 1886, Cloth, $3.75. Vol. IX, Cloth, $2.50.

TRANSACTIONS American Surgical Association. Illustrated. Royal 8vo. Price of Vol. I, II, III, IV, V, each, Cloth, $3.00. **Vol. VI, Cloth, $4.50.** Vol. VII, VIII, each, Cloth, $3.00.

TRANSACTIONS of the Association of American Physicians. Vols. I and II, Cloth, $2.50 each. Vol. III, Cloth, $3.50. Vol. IV, Cloth, $3.00. Vol. V, Cloth, $2.50. Vol. VI, **$3.00.**

TREVES. German-English Medical Dictionary. By FREDERICK TREVES, F.R.C.S., assisted by DR. HUGO LANG, B.A. (Munich). 12mo. ½ Russia, $3.75

TRIMBLE. Practical and Analytical Chemistry. Being a complete course in Chemical Analysis. By HENRY TRIMBLE, PH.M., Professor of Analytical Chemistry in the Philadelphia College of Pharmacy. Fourth Edition. Enlarged. Illustrated. **8vo.** Cloth, $1.50

TURNBULL'S Artificial Anæsthesia. The Advantages and Accidents of Artificial Anæsthesia ; Its Employment in the Treatment of Disease ; Modes of Administration ; Considering their Relative Risks ; Tests of Purity ; Treatment of Asphyxia ; Spasms of the Glottis ; Syncope, etc. By LAURENCE TURNBULL, M.D., PH. G., Aural Surgeon to Jefferson College Hospital, etc. Third Edition, Revised and Enlarged. 40 Illustrations. 12mo. Cloth, $3.00

TUSON. Veterinary Pharmacopœia. Including the Outlines of Materia Medica and Therapeutics. For the Use of Students and Practitioners of Veterinary Medicine. By RICHARD V. TUSON, F.C.S. Third Edition. 12mo. Cloth, $2.50

TYSON. Bright's Disease and Diabetes. With Especial Reference to Pathology and Therapeutics. By JAMES TYSON, M.D., Professor of Clinical Medicine in the University of Pennsylvania. Including a Section on Retinitis in Bright's Disease. By WM. F. NORRIS, M.D., Clin. Prof. of Ophthalmology in Univ. of Penna. With Colored Plates and many Wood Engravings. 8vo. Cloth, $3.50

> **Guide to the Examination of Urine. Seventh Edition.** For the Use of Physicians and Students. With Colored Plates and Numerous Illustrations Engraved on Wood. Seventh Edition. Revised. 12mo. 255 pages. Cloth, $1.50

> **Cell Doctrine.** Its History and Present State. With a Copious Bibliography of the subject. Illustrated. Second Edition. 8vo. Cloth, $2.00

> **Handbook of Physical Diagnosis.** Illustrated. 12mo. Cloth, $1.25

VAN HARLINGEN on Skin Diseases. A Practical Manual of Diagnosis and Treatment. By ARTHUR VAN HARLINGEN, M.D., Professor of Diseases of the Skin in the Philadelphia Polyclinic; Clinical Lecturer on Dermatology at Jefferson Medical College. Second Edition. Revised and Enlarged. With Formulæ. Eight Colored and other full-page plates, and New Illustrations. Cloth, $2.50

VAN NÜYS on The Urine. Chemical Analysis of Healthy and Diseased Urine, Qualitative and Quantitative. By T. C. VAN NÜYS, Professor of Chemistry Indiana University. 39 Illustrations. Octavo. Cloth, $2.00

VIRCHOW'S Post-mortem Examinations. A Description and Explanation of the Method of Performing them in the Dead House of the Berlin Charité Hospital, with especial reference to Medico-legal Practice. By Prof. VIRCHOW. Translated by Dr. T. P. SMITH. Third Edition, with Additions. Cloth, $1.00

> **Cellular Pathology,** as based upon Physiological and Pathological Histology. 20 Lectures delivered at the Pathological Institute of Berlin. Translated from the 2d Ed. by F. CHANCE, M.D. 134 Illus. 8th Am. Ed. Cloth, $4.00

WALSHAM. Manual of Practical Surgery. For Students and Physicians. By WM. J. WALSHAM, M.D., F.R.C.S., Ass't Surg. to, and Dem. of Practical Surg. in, St. Bartholomew's Hospital, Surg. to Metropolitan Free Hospital, London. Third Edition, Revised and Enlarged. With 318 Engravings. *New Series of Manuals.* Cloth, $3.00; Leather, $3.50

WARING. Practical Therapeutics. A Manual for Physicians and Students. By Edward J. Waring, M.D. Fourth Edition. Revised, Rewritten and Rearranged by DUDLEY W. BUXTON, M.D., Assistant to the Professor of Medicine, University College, London. Crown Octavo. Cloth, $3.00; Leather, $3.50

WARREN. Compend Dental Pathology and Dental Medicine. Containing all the most noteworthy points of interest to the Dental student. By GEO. W. WARREN, D.D.S., Clinical Chief, Penn'a College of Dental Surgery, Phila. Illus. *Being No. 13 ? Quiz-Compend ? Series.* 12mo. Cloth, $1.00
Interleaved for the addition of Notes, $1.25

WATSON on Amputations of the Extremities and Their Complications. By B. A. WATSON, A.M., M.D., Surgeon to the Jersey City Charity Hospital and to Christ's Hospital, Jersey City, N. J.; Member of the American Surgical Association. 250 Wood Engravings and two Full-page Colored Plates. Cloth, $5.50

> **Concussions.** An Experimental Study of Lesions arising from Severe Concussions. 8vo. Paper cover, $1.00

WATTS' Inorganic Chemistry. A Manual of Chemistry, Physical and Inorganic. (Being the 14th Edition of FOWNE'S PHYSICAL AND INORGANIC CHEMISTRY.) By HENRY WATTS, B.A., F.R.S., Editor of the Journal of the Chemical Society; Author of "A Dictionary of Chemistry," etc. With Colored Plate of Spectra and other Illustrations. 12mo. 595 pages. Cloth, $2.25

> **Organic Chemistry.** Second Edition. By WM. A. TILDEN, D.SC., F.R.S. (Being the 13th Edition of FOWNE'S ORGANIC CHEMISTRY.) Illustrated. 12mo. Cloth, $2.25

WHITE. **The Mouth and Teeth.** By J. W. WHITE, M.D., D.D.S. Editor of the Dental Cosmos. Illustrated. Cloth, .50

WILSON. **Handbook of Hygiene** and Sanitary Science. With Illustrations. Seventh Edition, Revised and Enlarged. 8vo. *In Press.*

WILSON. **The Summer** and its Diseases. By JAMES C. WILSON, M.D., Professor of the Practice of Medicine and Clinical Medicine, Jefferson Medical College, Philadelphia. Cloth, .50

WINCKEL. **Diseases of Women.** Second Edition. Including the Diseases of the Bladder and Urethra. By Dr. F. WINCKEL, Professor of Gynæcology, and Director of the Royal University Clinic for Women, in Munich. Translated by special authority of Author and Publisher, under the supervision of, and with an Introduction by, THEOPHILUS PARVIN, M.D., Professor of Obstetrics and Diseases of Women and Children in Jefferson Medical College, Philadelphia. With 150 Engravings on Wood, most of which are original. 2d Edition, Revised and Enlarged. Cloth, $3.00; Leather, $3.50

Text-Book **of Obstetrics;** Including the Pathology and Therapeutics of the Puerperal State. Authorized Translation by J CLIFTON EDGAR, A.M., M.D., Adjunct Professor to the Chair of Obstetrics, Medical Department, University, City of New York. With nearly 200 Handsome Illus., the majority of which are original with this work. Octavo. Cloth, $6.00; Leather, $7.00

WOAKES. **Post-Nasal Catarrh** and Diseases of the Nose, causing Deafness. By EDWARD WOAKES, M.D., Senior Aural Surgeon to the London Hospital for Diseases of the Throat and Chest. 26 Illustrations. Cloth, $1.50

WOLFF. **Manual of Applied Medical Chemistry** for Students and Practitioners of Medicine. By LAWRENCE WOLFF, M.D., Demonstrator of Chemistry in Jefferson Medical College, Philadelphia. Cloth, $1.00

WOOD. **Brain Work** and Overwork. By Prof. H. C. WOOD, Clinical Professor of Nervous Diseases, University of Pennsylvania. 12mo. Cloth, .50

WOODY. **Essentials of Chemistry and Urinalysis.** By SAM E. WOODY, A.M., M.D., Professor of Chemistry and Public Hygiene, and Clinical Lecturer on Diseases of Children, in the Kentucky School of Medicine. Third Edition. Illustrated. 12mo. Cloth, $1.25

WYNTER and WETHERED. **Clinical and Practical Pathology.** A Manual of Clinical and Practical Pathology. By W. ESSEX WYNTER, M.D., Medical Registrar and late Dem. of Anat. and Chem. at the Middlesex Hospital, and FRANK J. WETHERED, M.D., Ass't Phys. to the City of London Hospital for Dis. of the Chest. 4 Colored Plates and 67 other Illustrations. 8vo. Cloth, $4.00

WYTHE. **Dose and Symptom Book.** The Physician's Pocket Dose and Symptom Book. Containing the Doses and Uses of all the Principal Articles of the Materia Medica, and Officinal Preparations. By JOSEPH H. WYTHE, A.M., M.D. 17th Edition, Revised and Rewritten. Cloth, $1.00; Leather, with Tucks and Pocket, $1.25

YEO'S **Manual of Physiology.** Fifth Edition. A Text-book for Students of Medicine. By GERALD F. YEO, M.D., F.R.C.S., Professor of Physiology in King's College, London. Fifth Edition; revised and enlarged by the author. With 321 Wood Engravings and a Glossary. Crown Octavo. *Being No. 4, New Series of Manuals.* Cloth, $3.00; Leather, $3.50.

THERAPEUTICS AND MATERIA MEDICA.

Allen, Harlan, Penrose, Van Harlingen.   Local Therapeutics.   1892.

A HANDBOOK OF LOCAL THERAPEUTICS, being a practical description of all those agents used in the local treatment of disease, such as Ointments, Plasters, Powders, Lotions, Inhalations, Suppositories, Bougies, Tampons, etc., and the proper methods of preparing and applying them.   By HARRISON ALLEN, M.D., Emeritus Professor of Physiology in the University of Penna.; Laryngologist to the Rush Hospital for Consumption; late Surgeon to the Philadelphia and St. Joseph's Hospitals.   GEORGE C. HARLAN, M.D., late Professor of Diseases of the Eye in the Philadelphia Polyclinic and College for Graduates in Medicine; Surgeon to the Wills Eye Hospital, and Eye and Ear Department of the Pennsylvania Hospital.   CHARLES B. PENROSE, M.D., Surgeon to the German Hospital; Instructor in Clinical Surgery, University of Pennsylvania, and ARTHUR VAN HARLINGEN, M.D., Professor of Diseases of the Skin in the Philadelphia Polyclinic and College for Graduates in Medicine; late Clinical Lecturer on Dermatology in Jefferson Medical College; Dermatologist to the Howard Hospital.

In One Handsome Compact Volume, about 400 pages.   *Nearly Ready.*

ANNOUNCEMENT.—The importance of the local application of simple remedies in slight ailments of special organs, is not always realized by the general practitioner, and the average text-book omits altogether any mention of many agents that in the hands of the specialist become valuable aids to cure.   The diseases which chiefly require local treatment are those of the Respiratory Passages, Ear, Eye, Skin, together with certain general Surgical affections, including the Diseases of Women.   In order, therefore, that the various uses of each remedy should be thoroughly set forth, it was necessary to have a combination of authors who have had a large practical experience in these various branches of Medicine and Surgery.

Each remedy will be taken up in alphabetical order, and after a succinct description of their pharmaceutical properties, by Dr. GEORGE I. McKELWAY, will be considered with reference to the local treatment of the affections above outlined.   The publishers believe that the information contained in this work will not be found elsewhere, as much of it is the results obtained in private and hospital practice, by eminent professors and specialists.   The activity in the various lines of special medicine is one of the most striking phases of the times, and has materially changed many of the older methods of treating disease by local means.   The greater part of the literature which has appeared is not accessible to most physicians.   The HANDBOOK, it is believed, will be of value to general practitioners as well as to those who, like the authors, are especially interested in subdivisions of the clinical field.

The work will form a compact volume of about 400 pages, arranged in a manner to facilitate reference and containing, besides the usual index, a complete index of diseases, that will greatly enhance its usefulness.

This book is being pushed forward as fast as possible.   Advance orders may be sent in at once, and copies will be promptly delivered upon publication.

Biddle's Materia Medica and Therapeutics.   Eleventh Edition.   1889.

WITH MANY ADDITIONS AND NEW ILLUSTRATIONS.   For the Use of Students and Physicians.   By Prof. JOHN B. BIDDLE, M.D., Late Professor of Materia Medica in Jefferson Medical College, Philadelphia.   11th Edition.   Revised by his son, CLEMENT BIDDLE, M.D., Assistant Surgeon, U. S. N., and HENRY MORRIS, M.D., Fellow of the College of Physicians of Philadelphia, etc.   Cloth, $4.25; Leather, $5.00

THERAPEUTICS AND MATERIA MEDICA.

Potter's Materia Medica, Pharmacy and Therapeutics.
Third Edition.   Revised and Enlarged.   1891.

A HANDBOOK OF MATERIA MEDICA, PHARMACY AND THERAPEUTICS—including the Physiological Action of Drugs, Special Therapeutics of Diseases, Official and Extemporaneous Pharmacy, etc.   By SAM'L O. L. POTTER, M.A., M.D., Professor of the Practice of Medicine in Cooper Medical College, San Francisco; Late A. A. Surgeon, U. S. Army; Author of "Speech and its Defects," and the "Quiz-Compends" of Anatomy and Materia Medica, etc.   Revised, Enlarged and Improved.   Octavo. *With Thumb Index.*   Leather, $5.00

"The author has aimed to embrace in a single volume the essentials of practical materia medica and therapeutics, and has produced a book small enough for easy carriage and easy reference, large enough to contain a carefully digested, but full, clear and well-arranged mass of information. He has not adhered to any pharmacopœia, as is the case of certain recent manuals, thereby limiting his work, and in this day of new remedies causing constant disappointment, but has brought it up to date in the most satisfactory way. No new remedy of any acknowledged value is omitted from this list. Under each section on physiological action and therapeutics has been written with care. . . . In the enumeration of drugs suited to different disorders a very successful effort at discrimination has been made, both in the stage of disease and in the cases peculiarly suited to the remedy. It is no mere list of diseases followed by a catalogue of drugs, but is a digest of modern therapeutics, and as such will prove of immense use to its possessor."—*The Therapeutic Gazette.*

A UNIQUE BOOK.—The plan of this work is new and original with Dr. Potter, and its contents have been combined and arranged in such a way that it offers a compact statement of the subjects in hand, containing more correct information in a practical, concise form than any other publication of the kind.

The work commences with a section on the classification of medicines, as follows:— AGENTS acting on the Nervous System, Organs of Sense, Respiration, Circulation, Digestive System, on Metabolism (including Restoratives, Alteratives, Astringents, Antipyretics, Antiphlogistics and Antiperiodics, etc.) Agents acting upon Excretion, the Generative System, the Cutaneous Surfaces, Microbes and Ferments, and upon each other.

PART I.—MATERIA MEDICA and THERAPEUTICS (351 pages), the drugs being arranged in alphabetical order, with the synonym of each first; then the description of the plant, its preparations, physiological action, and lastly its *Therapeutics*.

PART II.—PHARMACY AND PRESCRIPTION WRITING (56 pages). This is written for the use of physicians who desire or of necessity must put up their own prescriptions, and includes—Weights and Measures, English and the Metric Systems; Specific Gravity and Volume; Prescriptions, their principles and combinations; proper methods of writing them; Abbreviations; Stock solutions and preparations, and Incompatibility, etc.

PART III.—SPECIAL THERAPEUTICS (211 pages) is an alphabetical List of Diseases— a real INDEX OF DISEASES—giving the drugs that have been found serviceable in each disease, and the authority recommending the use of each, a very important feature, as it gives an authoritative character to the book that is unusual in works on Therapeutics, and displays an immense amount of research on the part of the author. 600 Prescriptions are given in this part, many being over the names of eminent men.

THE APPENDIX (36 pages) contains lists of Latin words, phrases and abbreviations, with their English equivalents, Genitive Case Endings, etc.   36 formulæ for Hypodermic Injections; 10 of Chlorodyne; Formulæ of prominent patent medicines; Poisons and their Antidotes; Differential Diagnosis; Temperature Notes; Obstetrical Memoranda; Clinical Examination of Urine; Table of Specific Gravities and Volumes; Table showing the number of drops in a fluidrachm of various liquids, the weight of one fluidrachm in grains, and a table for converting apothecaries' weights and measures into grains, etc., etc.

THE INDEX covers thirty-five pages, and will be found very elaborate.

THE WHOLE WORK is a statement of known facts in terse language; it is, in fact, the essentials of Practical Materia Medica and Therapeutics. Although it is to a great extent a compilation, as any such book must be, from the works of prominent writers and teachers, yet it will be found to contain much original matter and many useful suggestions not included in any other book.

PRACTICE OF MEDICINE.

Roberts' Practice of Medicine. Eighth Edition. Revised, Enlarged and Illustrated. 1890.

A HANDBOOK OF THE THEORY AND PRACTICE OF MEDICINE. By FREDERICK T. ROBERTS, M.D., B.Sc., F.R.C.P., Professor of Materia Medica and Therapeutics, and of Clinical Medicine, at University College Hospital, London; Physician to Brompton Hospital for Consumption and Diseases of the Chest, etc. Eighth Edition. Revised and Enlarged. 51 Illustrations. 1059 pages. Octavo.

Handsome Cloth, $5.50 ; Full Sheep, Raised Bands, $6.50

"The various subjects have been treated in a complete and masterly manner. . . . We heartily commend this handbook, not only to gentlemen preparing for the medical profession, but to those who may have finished their professional education; as this work contains, in a brief and concise shape, all that the busy general practitioner needs to know to enable him to carry on his practice with comfort to himself and with advantage to his patients."—*British Medical Journal.*

"It is unsurpassed by any work that has fallen into our hands as a compendium for students."—*The Clinic.*

"We particularly recommend it to students about to enter upon the practice of their profession."—*St. Louis Medical and Surgical Journal.*

"If there is a book in the whole of medical literature in which so much is said in so few words, it has never come within our reach."—*Chicago Medical Journal.*

"The regularity with which fresh editions of this admirable text-book make their appearance, serves to show that it continues to maintain its favored position with the student, who finds it a safe and reliable guide. Apart from the clearness of style and its thoroughly practical character, a great feature of Dr. Roberts' work is the systematic method with which each subject is treated. The value of this kind of instruction is high, as it enables the student to marshal his ideas in an orderly manner, and to assign to each part its special importance. The author has not been unmindful of the necessity of keeping his book 'up to date,' and he has evidently bestowed much pains on its revision. It is enough to say that it fully merits its popularity."—*The Lancet*, London, February 7th, 1891.

"The arrangement of the subject is admirable, each disease is very fully considered in elegant phraseology without any undue verbosity, and the matter is presented in a manner which is easily grasped and retained in the memory. It is quite unnecessary to refer further to the pages of this valuable and reliable text-book. It will be found a trustworthy guide both by students and practitioners, and the latter will find much more information as to treatment, than is usually recorded in such works."—*Liverpool Medico-Chir. Journal*, Jan., 1891.

Hughes' Compend of the Practice of Medicine. 4th Enlarged Edition. 1890.

A COMPEND OF THE PRACTICE OF MEDICINE. By DANIEL E. HUGHES, M.D., late Demonstrator of Clinical Medicine at Jefferson Medical College, Philadelphia; now Physician-in-Chief, Philadelphia Hospital In two parts.

PART I.—Continued, Eruptive and Periodical Fevers, Diseases of the Stomach, Intestines, Peritoneum, Biliary Passages, Liver, Kidneys, etc., and General Diseases, etc.

PART II.—Diseases of the Respiratory System, Circulatory System and Nervous System; Diseases of the Blood, etc. Price of each Part, strongly bound in cloth, $1.00
Interleaved for the addition of notes, 1.25

*** These books are a complete set of notes upon the practice of medicine. The synonyms, definition, causes, symptoms, pathology, prognosis, diagnosis, treatment, etc., of each disease being given. The treatment is especially full and a number of valuable prescriptions have been incorporated. Reference has been made to the latest writings and teachings of Drs. Flint, Roberts, Loomis, Bartholow, DaCosta, etc. Dr. Hughes' long experience as demonstrator of clinical medicine under the last named famous professors gave him unrivaled opportunities for the preparation of a book of this character.

Physicians' Edition. Fourth Edition. Same as above, but in one volume, and including a section on Skin Diseases and a very complete index.
Full Morocco, Gilt Edges, $2.50

"The best condensation of the essentials of Practice I have yet seen. . . . It will be an admirable review book for students after a solid course of study, and it will be scarcely less useful to the busy practitioner as a ready means of refreshing his memory."—*C. A. Lindsley, M.D., Professor of Theory and Practice of Medicine, Yale College, New Haven.*

? QUIZ-COMPENDS. ?

A SERIES OF PRACTICAL MANUALS FOR THE PHYSICIAN AND STUDENT.

Compiled in accordance with the latest teachings of prominent lecturers
and the most popular Text-books.

Bound in Cloth, each $1.00. Interleaved, for the Addition of Notes, $1.25.

They form a most complete, practical and exhaustive set of manuals, containing information nowhere else collected in such a practical shape. Thoroughly up to the times in every respect, containing many new prescriptions and formulæ, and over 300 illustrations, many of which have been drawn and engraved specially for this series. The authors have had large experience as quiz-masters and attachés of colleges, with exceptional opportunities for noting the most recent advances and methods. The arrangement of the subjects, illustrations, types, etc., are all of the most approved form. They are constantly being revised, so as to include the latest and best teachings, and can be used by students of any college of medicine, dentistry and pharmacy.

No. 1. **Human Anatomy.** Fifth Edition (1891), including Visceral Anatomy, formerly published **separately.** 16 Lithograph Plates, Tables, and 117 Illustrations. By SAMUEL O. L. POTTER, M.A., M.D., late A. A. Surgeon, U. S. Army. Professor of Practice, Cooper Med. College, San Francisco.

Nos. 2 and 3. **Practice of Medicine.** Fourth Edition, Enlarged (1890). By DANIEL E. HUGHES, M.D., late Demonstrator of Clinical Medicine in Jefferson Med. College, Phila.; Physician-in-Chief, Philadelphia Hospital. **In two parts.**

PART I.—Continued, Eruptive and Periodical Fevers, Diseases of the Stomach, Intestines, Peritoneum, Biliary Passages, Liver, Kidneys, etc. (including Tests for Urine), General Diseases, etc.
PART II.— Diseases of the Respiratory System (including Physical Diagnosis), Circulatory System and Nervous System; Diseases of the Blood, etc.
. These little books can be regarded as a full set of notes upon the Practice of Medicine, containing the Synonyms, Definitions, Causes, Symptoms, Prognosis, Diagnosis, Treatment, etc., of each disease, and including a number of prescriptions hitherto unpublished.

No. 4. **Physiology, including Embryology.** Sixth Edition (1891). By ALBERT P. BRUBAKER, M.D., Prof. of Physiology, Penn'a College of Dental Surgery; Demonstrator of Physiology in Jefferson Med. College, Phila. Revised, Enlarged and Illustrated. *In Press.*

No. 5. **Obstetrics.** Illustrated. Fourth Edition (1889). For Physicians and Students. By HENRY G. LANDIS, M.D., Prof. of Obstetrics and Diseases of Women, in Starling Medical College, Columbus. Revised Edition. New Illustrations.

No. 6. **Materia Medica, Therapeutics and Prescription Writing.** Fifth Revised Edition (1891). With especial Reference to the Physiological Action of Drugs, and a complete article on Prescription Writing. Based on the Last Revision (Sixth) of the U. S. Pharmacopœia, and including many unofficinal remedies. By SAMUEL O. L. POTTER, M.A., M.D., late A. A. Surg. U. S. Army; Prof. of Practice, Cooper Med. College, San Francisco. 5th Edition. Improved and Enlarged.

No. 7. **Gynæcology.** (1891.) A Compend of Diseases of Women. By HENRY MORRIS, M.D., Demonstrator of Obstetrics, Jefferson Medical College, Philadelphia. Many Illustrations.

No. 8. **Diseases of the Eye and Refraction.** Second Edition (1888). Including Treatment and Surgery. By L. WEBSTER FOX, M.D., Chief Clinical Assistant Opthalmological Dept., Jefferson Medical College, etc., and GEO M. GOULD, M.D. 71 Illustrations, 39 Formulæ.

No. 9. **Surgery, Minor Surgery and Bandaging.** Illustrated. Fourth Edition (1890). Including Fractures, Wounds, Dislocations, Sprains, Amputations and other operations; Inflammation, Suppuration, Ulcers, Syphilis, Tumors, Shock, etc. Diseases of the Spine, Ear, Bladder, Testicles, Anus, and other Surgical Diseases. By ORVILLE HORWITZ, A.M., M.D., Demonstrator of Surgery, Jefferson Medical College. 84 Formulæ and 136 Illustrations.

No. 10. **Medical Chemistry.** Third Edition (1890). Inorganic and Organic, including Urine Analysis For Medical and Dental Students. By HENRY LEFFMANN, M.D., Prof. of Chemistry in Penn'a College of Dental Surgery, Phila. Third Edition. Revised and Enlarged.

No. 11. **Pharmacy.** Third Edition (1890). Based upon "Remington's Text-Book of Pharmacy." By F. E. STEWART, M.D., PH.D., Professor of Pharmacy, Powers College of Pharmacy; late Quiz-Master at Philadelphia College of Pharmacy. Third Edition. Revised.

No. 12. **Veterinary Anatomy and Physiology.** Illustrated. (1890.) By WM. R. BALLOU, M.D., Prof. of Equine Anatomy, New York College of Veterinary Surgeons, etc. 29 Illustrations.

No. 13. **Dental Pathology and Dental Medicine.** (1890.) Containing all the most noteworthy points of interest to the Dental Student. By GEO. W. WARREN, D.D.S., Clinical Chief, Penn'a College of Dental Surgery, Philadelphia. Illus.

No. 14. **Diseases of Children.** (1890.) By MARCUS P. HATFIELD, Professor of Diseases of Children, Chicago Medical College. With Colored Plate.

☞ *These books are constantly revised to keep up with the latest teachings and discoveries.*

FROM THE SOUTHERN CLINIC.—*"We know of no series of books issued by any house that so fully meets our approval as these ? Quiz-Compends ? They are well arranged, full and concise, and are really the best line of text-books that could be found for either student or practitioner."*

Potter. A Compend of Anatomy. Fifth Edition. 16 Lithograph Plates. 117 other Illus. 1891.

INCLUDING THE VISCERA. (*Based on Gray.*) By SAML. O. L. POTTER, M.A., M.D., late A. A. Surg. U. S. Army; Professor of the Practice of Medicine, Cooper Medical College, San Francisco. Revised and Enlarged. 12mo. *Being No. 1 ? Quiz-Compend ? Series. See page 29.* Strongly bound in cloth, $1.00
Interleaved, for the addition of notes, 1.25

*** An Appendix has been added to this edition, containing 16 Lithographic Plates of the Arterial and Nervous Systems, with explanatory tables that will be found exceedingly useful and practical. We would call special attention to these tables, as being entirely original in design and arrangement, giving graphic views of the most difficult part of Human Anatomy, and including anastomoses (the arteries) and distribution (the arteries and nerves); a thing never before shown completely in tabular form. The different types are so arranged as to grade the branches according to relative importance, and by the systematic and ingenious use of brackets with various types, the tables are veritable pictures themselves of their objects.

Dr. Potter's power of condensation and arrangement, have never been displayed to such advantage as in these tables, which must take their proper place as the best of all attempts of the kind, even in the restricted space of pages the size of which was previously determined, and to which the tables had to conform.

The plates are equally original, having been made from new drawings by Dr. Potter's own hand; they are graphic delineations, and being diagrammatic, do not represent the exact forms or proportions of the parts thus shown. If colored by hand, by the student, as may be done with very little trouble, their value will be greatly increased.

" In the particular line to which it belongs, and as one of the pioneers, this work of the indefatigable Dr. Potter stands in the list of the very best. This is particularly conspicuous in view of the many failures to render the subject of anatomy attractive when presented in compends."—*American Practitioner and News,* January, 1891.

" This is ? Quiz-Compend No. 1, based on Gray principally, and is a book that to a student is almost a necessity, and to the practicing physician a great aid as a ready reference work, enabling him, at almost a glance, to keep in mind a great many valuable points in anatomy that otherwise he would forget."—*The Cincinnati Medical Journal, February 15th, 1891.*

" Of all the studies in a medical course, anatomy is the most important. To wade through a 'Gray,' for review, is very irksome, and by having an Anatomy in an epitomized form and thoroughly reliable, both time and labor will be saved. Dr. Potter has thus conferred a boon on both the student and practitioner alike, by publishing his Compend of Anatomy. The tables and plates of the nerves and arteries are excellent; these constitute the Appendix, and by their aid one can review this important part of the work in a short space of time."—*Canada Lancet, Toronto, February, 1891.*

Robinson. The Latin Grammar of Pharmacy and Medicine. 1890.

By H. D. ROBINSON, PH.D., Professor of Latin Language and Literature, University of Kansas, Lawrence. With an Introduction by L. E. SAYRE, PH.G., Professor of Pharmacy, and Dean of the Dept. of Pharmacy, in the University of Kansas. 12mo. 275 Pages. Cloth, $2.00

" It is a work that meets with my hearty approval. There is great need of just such a book in our American schools of pharmacy and medicine."—*E. S. Bastin, Professor of Botany, Dept. of Pharmacy, Northwestern University, Chicago.*

" The object of this useful book is a very laudable one, namely, to improve, if possible, the Latin used by both physicians and druggists, chiefly in the prescribing of drugs. While it is true that many of the profession find it unnecessary to remember the genitive endings of words used in medicine, because of the customary abbreviations in prescribing-writing, there are others who frequently desire to write their directions to the druggist in Latin, in order that the patient may not learn of facts about which it is often necessary for him to remain in ignorance. We hope that the book will prove a success, and by its general employment in both pharmaceutical and medical schools, improve the knowledge of Latin in both professions."—*The Medical News,* Philadelphia, January 10th, 1891.

" The plan of the book is excellent, the field new, as it fills a long-felt want. All medical students should have it, both the collegian, as it will give a practical turn to his knowledge of Latin, and the non-graduate, as it will give him a direct and useful acquaintance with that language. The country doctor who has not had the advantages of the younger men will find it a great help in overcoming this defect, and may speedily acquire a familiarity with this language that will surprise his classical *confrere.*"—*Southern Cal. Practitioner,* December, 1890.

NURSING, MASSAGE, ETC.

Ostrom. Massage and the Original Swedish Movements. Illustrated. Second Edition. 1891.

AND THEIR APPLICATION TO VARIOUS DISEASES OF THE BODY. A Manual for Students, Nurses, and Physicians. By KURRE W. OSTROM, from the Royal University of Upsala, Sweden; Instructor in Massage and Swedish Movements in the Hospital of the University of Pennsylvania and in the Philadelphia Polyclinic and College for Graduates in Medicine, etc. Illustrated by 87 explanatory Wood Engravings, drawn specially for this purpose. 12mo. Second Edition. Cloth, $1.00

"This book, which is well written and carefully illustrated, will be of service both to physicians and nurses as well as to manipulators. Mr. Ostrom, who came to this country from Sweden, has proven himself a capable teacher as well as a good *masseur*, his instructions being careful, accurate, and complete."— *University Medical Magazine, Philadelphia, March, 1890.*

Parvin. Obstetric Nursing. 1889.

LECTURES DELIVERED AT THE TRAINING SCHOOL FOR NURSES OF THE PHILADELPHIA HOSPITAL. By THEOPHILUS PARVIN, M.D., Professor of Obstetrics and Diseases of Women and Children in the Jefferson Medical College; Obstetrician to the Philadelphia Hospital. Revised and Enlarged. 12mo. Cloth, $ .75

Humphrey. A Manual for Nurses. 4th Edition 1891.

INCLUDING GENERAL ANATOMY AND PHYSIOLOGY, Management of the Sick-Room, etc. By LAURENCE HUMPHREY, M.D., M.R.C.S., Ass't Physician to, and Lecturer at, Addenbrook's Hospital, Cambridge, England. 12mo. 79 Illustrations. Cloth, $1.25

"That a work of such a character should be addressed to nurses at all is in itself a significant indication of the high standard to which the art of nursing has risen in recent years, and also a good proof of the estimation in which really good nursing is held alike by the public and by medical men. To the intelligent and often well educated women who now take up nursing either as an occupation or as a profession, some theoretical training in the elements of anatomy and physiology is very generally recognized as necessary by all hospital authorities. . . ."—*The Practitioner, London, April, 1890.*

Fullerton. Obstetrical Nursing. Illustrated. 1891.

A HANDBOOK FOR NURSES, STUDENTS, AND MOTHERS. By ANNA M. FULLERTON, M.D., Demonstrator of Obstetrics in the Women's Medical College; Physician in charge of, and Obstetrician and Gynæcologist to, the Woman's Hospital, Philadelphia, etc. 34 Illustrations, several of which are original. Second Edition, Revised and Enlarged. 12mo. 222 pages. Cloth, $1.25

BY THE SAME AUTHOR.

Nursing in Abdominal Surgery and Diseases of Women. 1891.

COMPRISING THE REGULAR COURSE OF INSTRUCTION AT THE TRAINING SCHOOL OF THE WOMAN'S HOSPITAL, PHILADELPHIA. 70 Illustrations. 12mo. 284 pages. Cloth, $1.50

OBSTETRICS—GYNÆCOLOGY.

Winckel's Text-Book of Obstetrics. With many Original Illustrations.

INCLUDING THE PATHOLOGY AND THERAPEUTICS OF THE PUERPERAL STATE. By Dr. F. Winckel, Professor of Gynæcology and Director of the Royal Hospital for Women in Munich. Authorized Translation, by J. Clifton Edgar, M.D., Adjunct Prof. of Obstetrics, Medical Depart., University of the City of New York. 192 handsome illustrations, the majority of which are original with this work. 927 pages. 8vo.

Cloth, $6.00; Sheep, $7.00

" His practical experience and laborious researches in the literature of the subject have qualified him to place before the profession a book which is certainly of great value, and we desire to compliment Dr. Edgar upon his foresight and admirable work in the preparation of the American translation. One of the useful things about the work is that bibliographies accompany the articles upon each special subject, while the illustrations seem to us to be almost entirely original, which is but natural when we consider the enormous amount of material from which the author may obtain figures. The work of the American publisher has been well carried out, as it is usual under the circumstances, and we venture to say the translation is put before the profession of this country in much better form than the German publishers placed the original before the physicians of the Fatherland."—*Medical News, Philadelphia.*

" These additions make the perusal of the work a labor of pleasure, besides adding greatly to its value. One lays down the book with a heightened admiration for the author's learning, as well as a deep respect for his careful and conservative teaching."—*American Journal of Obstetrics, New York.*

" In this hasty manner we have only sought to call attention to the salient points of this admirable work, which, though intended and especially adapted to the student, nevertheless will well repay a careful perusal by all who aspire to practice obstetrics according to the most improved modern methods. We would like to see this text-book used in this country, for the reason that it is clear and concise, that it gives special prominence to pathology, and that every page bears evidence of that thoroughness and sound conservatism which makes its distinguished author unequaled as a teacher of obstetrics."—*Medical Record.*

Winckel. Diseases of Women. By Parvin. Second Edition, Enlarged.

INCLUDING DISEASES OF THE BLADDER AND URETHRA. By Dr. F. Winckel, Professor of Gynæcology and Director of the Royal University Clinic for Women in Munich. Authorized Translation. Edited by Theophilus Parvin, M.D., Professor of Obstetrics and Diseases of Women and Children in Jefferson Medical College, Philadelphia. Second Edition, Revised and Enlarged. 152 Engravings on Wood. 12mo. No. 2, *New Series of Manuals.* 766 pages.

Cloth, $3.00; Leather, $3.50

" The popularity of the work is shown by the rapidity with which the first edition was exhausted. There is, perhaps, no more scholarly or influential authority on gynæcological subjects among our German *confreres* than Winckel, and this fact, added to the respect and esteem in which his American editor is universally held, may serve to explain the early demand for a second edition in advance of a second German edition. . . . A novel feature is furnished by the chapters on diseases of the mammary gland. They are not generally discussed in works of this character, but we have always been of the opinion that their consideration was quite as appropriate as that of any other portion of the genital apparatus, of which they form an essential element." —*The American Journal of the Medical Sciences, Philadelphia.*

" It is nearly three years since we had the pleasure of reviewing the English translation of Professor Winckel's 'Diseases of Women.' The favorable comments we then made we now but to endorse in connection with the second edition of this excellent, lucidly written gynæcological work. Dr. Theophilus Parvin has most thoroughly revised the former issue, so that the reader meets with only the latest and most matured opinions on the various debatable topics. We should like again to direct the attention of those interested in gynæcological literature to the subjects on pelvic neoplasms and diseases of the female urethra and bladder. The work is profusely illustrated, and we feel confident that those of our readers who accord it careful study will derive much pleasure and instruction from its pages."—*The Practitioner, London.*